Sara Snow's
Fresh  Living

Sara Snow's
Fresh Living

The Essential Room-by-Room Guide
to a Greener, Healthier Family and Home

Bantam Books

SARA SNOW'S FRESH LIVING
A Bantam Book / April 2009

Published by Bantam Dell
A Division of Random House, Inc.
New York, New York

Interior illustrations by Jill Weber
Cover photo by © Drew Endicott Photography

Book design by Virginia Norey

Library of Congress Cataloging-in-Publication Data
Snow, Sara.
[Fresh living]
Sara Snow's fresh living : the essential room-by-room guide to a greener,
healthier family and home / Sara Snow.
p. cm.
Includes bibliographical references and index.
ISBN 978-0-553-38596-0 (trade pbk.)—ISBN 978-0-553-90625-7 (ebook)
1. House cleaning—United States—Environmental aspects.
2. Sustainable living—United States. 3. Organic living—United States.
I. Title. II. Title: Fresh living.
TX324.S593 2009
648—dc22   2008047807

Printed in the United States of America
Published simultaneously in Canada
Printed on recycled paper

www.bantamdell.com

RRDN 10 9 8 7 6 5 4 3 2 1

I dedicate this book to my parents for showing the way,
to Nate, Joe, and Elizabeth for discovering it with me,
and to Ryan for being my rock and walking with me ever since.

Contents

Acknowledgments   ix

My Story   1

In the Kitchen   23

In the Bathroom   61

In the Bedroom   87

In the Nursery   107

In the Living Room   137

In the Laundry Room   155

In the Office   175

Outdoors   193

Now It's Your Turn   227

Bibliography   253

Index   265

Acknowledgments

The process of writing this book brought me more pleasure than I ever dreamed it would. My heartfelt thanks goes out to my editor at Bantam Dell, Philip Rappaport, for his tireless support and willingness to explore things like recycled papers with me. And to so many others at Bantam: Nita Taublib, Paolo Pepe, Virginia Norey, Jill Weber, Glen Edelstein, Barb Burg, Theresa Zoro, Melissa Lord, Betsy Hulsebosch, and Loren Noveck, thank you for helping to design and distribute a book that meets my goals of being accessible as well as informative. I offer huge words of thanks to my book agent, Kim Witherspoon at Inkwell Management, who allowed me to dream that I could write this book; to my publicists and good friends, Denise Arrigali and Reenie Kuhlman, whose day-to-day support means more than they know; to Robin Albin and Susan Hunter at Brash Creative for their encouragement and creative contribution; to Alan, Tera, Lisa, and Amie at CAA for their help in so many other arenas, and to my colleagues and comrades at the Organic Center, the Organic Trade Association, the Environmental Working Group, and so many other organizations for working so hard toward a greater goal every day.

This book is not the result of a year's worth of research and writing, it is the result of a lifetime spent among people who have lived their lives with a dedication to the creation of healthy foods, continued research, or simply a more healthy and sustainable planet. Of these people, some have passed but most are still with us, and I am filled with knowledge, passion, and encouragement from their careers, their lives, and their generous spirits: Mark and Terry Retzloff, Drake Sadler, Denny Deschaine, Jonathan and Katrina Frey, Mark Blumenthal, Morris Shriftman, Steve Terre, Walter Robb, Peter Roy, Marci Zaroff, Robyn

O'Brien, Dr. Lev Linkner, Bill Bolduc, Peter and Betsey Murray, Vic and Martha Leabu, and Jim and Marylee Fuchs.

Of course, I would be a different person today were it not for the nearness of my family every day of my life. I thank Tom and Nancy for their love and their willingness to voyage with me. To the Prentices and the Krueger/Bolduc clans, I pray that as our families grow we find a way to give them the fresh air and wide-open spaces we enjoyed as kids. I give thanks for and to my grandparents: to Grandma and Grandpa R for teaching me how to enjoy life and for passing on this entrepreneurial spirit; and to Grandma and Grandpa S, whose love for the natural world has served as a constant reminder to me that "green" is not about headlines and certificates, it's about living as if what you take can't be replaced. Thank you for your lessons and your encouragement.

I owe an enormous amount to my parents, who gave up so much so that we could live the life we were blessed with. Your dedication and exploration empowered four children to go among others and live according to the practices and ideals we learned under your roof. You two have been my leaders and my best friends.

To my siblings, Nate, Joe, and Elizabeth, I say this: it has been one of my greatest pleasures growing up and growing older with each of you. As I watch you carve your ways in this world still using sustainable energies and materials, local and organic foods, and lighter living as your compass, you inspire me to do more and to live better. I know it's not easy to have your family stories splashed across all media platforms, but you've ridden this wave with me and have kept me grounded and honest.

And finally, to my husband, Ryan: every day I am astounded by your steadfast support, your ability to adapt, and your willingness to travel this road together—even when it means giving up things you once loved. Thank you for your unwavering encouragement, for letting me be who I am, and for journeying with me. I couldn't do it without you.

Sara Snow's
Fresh Living

My Story

My unusual upbringing and family story are fundamental to who I have become. These days, what fuels my passion and activism are not only the changes I see happening in the world around me, but also the way I was raised and the environmental lessons my parents taught as I was growing up. For this reason, any time I speak to an audience, whether through television or on stage, whether I'm talking about ways people can create healthier homes or how businesses can green their practices, I always start out with a primer on my upbringing. And the first line of my story is almost always "I grew up in a home that was different from most." But I started wondering one day if I was exaggerating. Maybe most people's homes *were* a little like mine, and they lived off the land the way I did growing up. When I tell the story, I'm not trying to imply that my family's lifestyle was *better* than everyone else's, just that it probably was different, and, in truth, it was likely more sustainable. And though it was also rough and tough in many senses, we were doing our best to live in a low-impact way and in tune with nature, or to be "harmonious" with the world around, to use a family term.

In the pages that follow, you'll learn about all that, but you'll also discover that as I grew older I fell off the eco trail for a short while. I didn't intend to, but it didn't take long before I could *feel* the difference, and it was the process of getting back on track that proved ultimately to be my most valuable lesson. I learned a lot about myself, and about how to get back to a more natural state of living, about what works and what in particular is easy for people who are just starting out and moving toward greener, more natural living.

I also learned that there is no such thing as perfect. My parents weren't perfect, I'm certainly not, and I won't ever expect you to be. Choosing to live more sustainably isn't one-size-fits-all and it's not all-or-nothing. It's about a series of small steps and changes toward greater health and harmony. I was lucky; my parents started taking those steps before I even came into this world.

My Upbringing

I was born at home, in my parents' bed. There weren't many naturopathic Ob/Gyn's at the time, and home births were not very common, but my parents found someone they trusted—someone who would make house calls and home deliveries—so that our first breaths wouldn't be in the sterile environment of a hospital. My older brother took a *long* time to come into this world. Dr. Vander Yacht napped on the couch off and on for the final six of the twenty-six hours that my mom labored. About two years later I was a little quicker, but without any meds at all my mom felt every moment of my birth. At the time, we were living in a small house in downtown Ann Arbor, Michigan. Ann Arbor, home to the University of Michigan, is a town made up of educated, liberal nature lovers. Not everyone there fits this snapshot, of course, but with over one-quarter of city residents employed by the university, definitely more so than average. The city is known for, among other things, an internationally recognized art fair and the "Hash Bash," during which possession of marijuana used to be punished only by a five-dollar fine. (The fine has since increased considerably.)

And it was into this offbeat Ann Arbor community that I was born. At the time, in July of 1976, my parents were already deeply involved in the booming natural products and natural foods movement, a movement that would later help birth the "green movement" of today. My dad, Tim Redmond, was raised in Birmingham, Michigan, an affluent suburb of Detroit, as the younger of two sons of a successful businessman. His dad, my grandfather, had founded a company dealing in industrial rubber in the auto capital of the world, Detroit, prior to the Second World War. He and my grandmother and the two boys lived quite a comfortable life in the postwar years. My dad went to college to study business but came out with a degree in English literature and education. So after college, rather than taking over his father's business, which would have immediately provided a certain level of prominence and comfort, Tim announced to his much-chagrined father that he wanted to "do his own thing" and that his intentions were to save the world . . . through food.

My mom, Pattie, was the daughter of an accountant/economist and a nursery school music teacher. For most of his career, my maternal grandfather worked for U.S. Steel in New York City. My mother grew up with two sisters in a home in Princeton, New Jersey, where dinner table conversations centered on serious matters like religion and politics, punctuated by a lot of girlish giggling. Pattie followed her older sister Judy to Ann Arbor in 1970 when Judy needed a nanny and my mom needed a break from college.

It didn't take long for Pattie's and Tim's worlds to intersect on the city sidewalks of Ann Arbor.

Around this same time, a Japanese man named Michio Kushi was beginning to teach about a lifestyle and food practice called macrobiotics. *Macrobiotics* is a Greek word meaning "great life" or "whole life" and was first used by the father of medicine himself, Hippocrates. Kushi's mentor George Ohsawa, the founder of macrobiotics, had in the early 1900s used a regimen of holistic living and pure, natural foods to cure himself of lung tuberculosis. He became resolute in his belief in the power of whole and living foods, and went on to teach others about this practice that he called macrobiotics. Ohsawa believed there was a second layer to "food is health," and that is that "health is the key to peace." He thought that if we could all return to a traditional diet of whole and natural foods, humanity would become more peaceful by reclaiming our physical and mental balance. Michio Kushi and a few of George Ohsawa's other early followers took his teachings to Germany, France, Brazil, and the United States.

And this is where I (or my parents) come back into the picture. Around the time my dad was making the announcement about his intentions to save the world through food, he was spending time in Boston training under Michio Kushi, learning the principles of macrobiotics and natural foods. Tim came back to Ann Arbor in 1970 and, in the entrepreneurial fashion of his father, cofounded a macrobiotic natural food business called Eden Foods. (One of his buddies and Eden cofounder at the time, coincidentally, was Mark Retzloff, who later went on to cofound Horizon Organic Dairy, the company that first brought organic milk to America's food stores.) Eden, now an internationally respected name in the organic food business, started off as a simple natural-foods buying club, then grew into a retail store, and grew again into a distributor and processor. In step with increasing demand from the burgeoning number of young back-to-the-landers and readers of Stewart Brand's *Whole Earth Catalog* and Robert Rodale's *Organic Gardening* magazine, my dad forged relationships with farmers and food producers who were growing and processing whole and natural foods that were synonymous with the macrobiotic diet. In the early 1970s, well before organic farming on a commercial scale really existed, my dad and his group had a vision for a company based on sustainable agriculture and the distribution of natural foods: whole grains, stone-ground flours, unfiltered oils, beans, seeds, nuts, sea vegetables, and other unprocessed, unrefined foods. "Real" foods, they called them. Their vision was to change the way America eats—to get Americans off Twinkies and Coca-Cola, and to create a better world through healthier living. At first there was just a co-op of people who wanted these foods, but that quickly changed and Eden Foods grew in 1976 to include a distribution warehouse and small fleet of trucks, located outside of town, and a restaurant and storefront in downtown Ann Arbor. My mom, by now married with a toddler and another (me) on the way, worked alongside my dad and honed her green thumb growing organic sprouts in the basement at home for our store and a few others around town.

And then I came into the world, making our little green family a four-some, and growing the Eden family business by another. My dad's original partner was his brother-in-law, and as the little company grew, the people working there generally related to each other as brothers and sisters and peers. We lived near one another, shared meals together, and played together as kids. Nate, my brother, smart for his years already at age six, was manning the register at the store, making change for customers. I had it much easier. I rooted raisins out of barrels, ordered up the "daddy's special" sandwich (a hand-fired whole wheat chapatti filled with hummus, Muenster cheese, cucumbers, and sprouts and sprinkled with Herbamare—a sea vegetable, herb, and salt mixture) in the deli, and wagged my chubby little fingers at the customers who came in to stock their healthy kitchens.

Our family was a good illustration for healthy living, yet every now and then meals of brown rice and vegetables were punctuated with a pint of Häagen-Dazs ice cream, a heavily sugared dairy food considered unbalanced and extreme in the macrobiotic diet. I imagine my mom and dad, still very young, in their kitchen with the curtains drawn, enjoying this infrequent guilty pleasure. While the ice cream itself was unbalanced and too "yin," having an occasional bite or two of forbidden fruit allowed them to *live* with balance, something very important in any naturalist's lifestyle.

Our Home

A few more years into this life, my parents wanted to have more children, and were starting to form a vision that involved raising their family in the country, with fewer modern conveniences but a greater connection to nature and the simplicity and freedom that it could bring. My mom's two sisters and their husbands, both involved in some capacity with natural foods and getting back to the land, were living in or near Ann Arbor at the time. One of her sisters decided to go in on a plot of land with my parents and my mom's parents, just recently moved to Ann Arbor from Princeton. My uncle David was a builder, so he and his team built the three passive solar, energy efficient, native white cedar–sided homes, on a cleared section of about twenty acres, with a lake and twenty-five more acres of woods and meadows surrounding. We were less than thirty minutes outside of Ann Arbor, but it seemed we had found a little piece of wilderness, just a marathon's distance from city life. My aunt and uncle and their kids moved into one house on the lake, and my grandparents moved into the other. We—my dad, mom, brother, and I—lived in the third house, on top of a small hill, just a short walk's distance from the other two homes. Eventually, two kids became four in our family, when my brother Joe was born a year or so after we moved in and sister Elizabeth followed four years after that.

If my upbringing wasn't already much different from your own, here are where the standout differences begin. We spent weekends in a small pop-up camper while we were building our home so we could all pitch in during the building process, and finally moved into the house when it had four walls and a roof. A ramp stood in for a lower set of stairs, a front door wasn't added until months later, the indoor plumbing wasn't fully operational the first month or so, and yet it was home. The house was a tri-level with a woodstove inside and solar hot water panels on a south-facing hill outside. The first floor consisted of my parents' bedroom, a bathroom, the kitchen, and, off the sitting area, a connected greenhouse on the south side of the house. The floors were solid hardwood, as was the beamed ceiling, and there were rough twelve-inch-square oak posts that went from the floor to the ceiling. The kitchen and sitting area were the heart of our home—with the woodstove serving as the main source of heat through years of harsh Michigan winters. The second level had a living room and wood-paneled den, and upstairs there was a bath, a big bedroom, an open reading area, and an office. The single bedroom became two bedrooms once Joe was born, and the office eventually became a third after Elizabeth joined us. It felt huge, spacious, and airy to me, but it wasn't so big at all compared to today's overblown standards or even a typical suburban home of the time.

The greenhouse was constructed of a glass roof and sloped glass walls. It served two important functions: a place to sprout plants from seeds so they could grow before being transplanted into the vegetable garden, and the second source of heat. Without a furnace, we relied on the woodstove and the collected solar heat from the greenhouse to keep us warm when the temperature outside dropped. In the colder months we would keep the door between the house and the greenhouse closed until midmorning, when the sun had been up for several hours and heat had started to gather in the greenhouse. I remember as a child watching the thermometer on the other side of the sliding glass door until it rose to a temperature higher than that of the house, indicating that it was time to throw open the door and let the heat flood in. Of course, as the sun began to dip down and the greenhouse was no longer warm, the door would be closed until the same time the next day. The most phenomenal part is that my parents designed the house so that even if it was only 2 degrees Fahrenheit outside, the sun's rays shining into the greenhouse would generate enough heat to flow into our home and keep us warm. In the summer months, because collecting the sun's warmth was not what we wanted, we draped a white canvas over the greenhouse roof to keep the heat from accumulating.

Our kitchen was stocked with healthy, unprocessed foods, mostly items my dad brought home; some of the rest we grew ourselves in one of our many gardens. My mom's primary focus, now with four kids and a home away from city conveniences, was raising a family on the most nutritious and simple foods possible in a nurturing, healthy environment. Dinners in the summer came mostly from the organic gardens. Everything from potatoes, greens, and corn to currants, melons, and herbs came from these gardens. We ate like kings and queens from late spring through mid-fall, and froze and jarred extras through the plentiful months so we could enjoy the just-picked freshness (and nutritious qualities "fresh" frozen can have) even after a chill set in.

With my cousins living just down the hill and my grandparents only a few steps farther away, it was a family affair of the best kind. We lived in a secluded family community where we could run barefoot from house to house, swap cucumbers for beets when one harvest was especially good, take picnics in the woods together, and ski through endless wooded trails in the winter. It was "simple" living at its finest.

Dirty Chores

But it had its share of hardships too. Maybe not hardships so much, but chores—dirty chores. I remember distinctly the job of taking out the compost. We had a stainless steel bowl that we kept on the countertop. It took us a while to decide to fit a lid to the bowl to keep the fruit flies from gathering and the slightly decaying food from smelling up the kitchen. It was my job to take the compost bowl from its home next to the kitchen sink and dump it in one of two locations outside: the bin by the back door or the heap at the far end of the vegetable garden. The bin was the convenient spot used most often for quick dumps from the kitchen. The heap was actually a pair of heaps where the aforementioned bin was dumped, as well as all of our yard waste.

I didn't mind trips to the heap because it meant that I got to linger in the mint patch on my way back, a soothing area that cleansed your nostrils and freshened your breath if you decided to nibble on a few of the gritty leaves. But it was a long way to walk carrying a stinky bowl full of gooey, ripe, decomposing kitchen scraps with arms too short to hold it a safe distance from my nose. Well before my age reached double digits, I had it all figured out. I could curl my upper lip up enough that it actually plugged my nose and, once at the pile, I'd quickly overturn the bowl, flinging the waste away from me a bit and, at the same time, jumping back to avoid the inevitable splatter on my bare feet. Then there was the *thump thump thump* that was required to get the stuck-on banana peels, apple cores, and lettuce leaves to unglue and drop into the pile.

Finally, with the dirty but empty bowl in hand, came the reward—that lovely, drawn-out moment of picking peppermint and spearmint leaves and placing them on my tongue, then sucking out the minty flavors. It seems like a small reward for such a big job, but I didn't mind one bit.

Low-Impact Living

My parents had this much figured out: take away the common comforts and conveniences of modern living and you quickly learn to fend for yourself. But, more than that, you learn to value and appreciate the smallest conveniences, rather than coming to rely so heavily on them. Your hands get dirty, your back gets sore, but you reap the reward daily. As kids, though we were small, there was a lot expected of us. Taking out the compost was just one of the many small jobs. We did dishes, pulled weeds, cleaned floors, raked leaves, picked vegetables, and performed a host of other tasks required to run a low-impact home. We also were only vaguely aware of a lot of the comforts that others had, so we didn't miss them.

My parents saw themselves as stewards of the land. We consumed less, which meant less waste; we ate few store-bought foods, which meant less processed products and chemical ingredients; we used limited amounts of electricity, water, and other precious resources, which meant we were helping to protect the land on which and *from* which we lived. While it sounds like a life of scarcity and deprivation, what we weren't short on was inspiration, enthusiasm, ideas, health, and happiness.

And what I didn't realize at the time was the impact that all of this was having on us kids. What seemed like an insignificant and dirty little job, carting the compost bowl to the compost pile, was actually my parents' way of assuring that their growing family was not only producing the least amount of waste possible (by turning kitchen scraps into free fertilizer instead of littering a landfill with them enclosed in plastic garbage bags) but that we were learning life skills and valuable lessons about protecting the earth in as many ways as possible.

Food

There are three things that I remember most strikingly about my childhood: faith, food, and family community. As Christians we had a strong faith, and we were taught to be honest, respectful, kind to others, and kind to the earth. Aside from that, though, food was the central focus of our life. We grew it, cooked it, shared it, ate it, talked about it, used it for healing, and, as it was also the source of my dad's income, counted on it for our health and livelihood.

That may sound grandiose, but it was true. Food is life sustaining, if you'll allow it to be. It has character, balance, sensitivity, and the ability to heal or harm, but it takes being in tune enough with your body to know which foods to eat in order to heal and *not* cause harm.

As you can well imagine, the foods we ate were quite different from what most people were eating at the time. While other kids my age were downing their Sugar Smacks and brownies, we adhered most closely to a macrobiotic diet, eventually adding in a little meat but sticking to meals involving cooked vegetables, whole grains like bulgur and brown rice, sea vegetables like nori and kombu, and magnificent stir fries and salads from our gardens. While my dad was out distributing natural foods for people across this country, my mom was in charge of our home kitchen. She made our baby food by hand, baked breads from scratch (even grinding her own flour), sweetened her homemade desserts with fruit juice or honey instead of harder-to-digest re-fined sugar, and canned and froze harvests from the garden and neighboring farms so we could enjoy fresh foods year round. She even became the inventor of our beverage of choice—"tea 'n' juice mix." As kids we naturally liked juice, or we thought we did, though I don't know that we ever had much of it straight out of a bottle. What she bought was always 100 percent real juice, but even that was too sweet for us, so my mom began the ritual of brewing an herbal (caffeine-free) tea in the morning—Celestial Seasoning's Red Zinger was a favorite—and then mixing it into the apple juice to create tea 'n' juice mix. The fruit sugars were cut in half and we loved it.

We learned lessons from food too. I remember going to friends' houses for overnights and play dates. And my mom would say to us, "Laura's mom is probably going to make those peanut-buttery caramel brownie bars" . . . foods we obviously didn't get to eat at home. And then she would assure us that it was okay to have one if we felt like it, but to pay close attention to how it made us feel: Did we feel hyped up at first and then low on energy an hour later? Did it give one of us a headache and make the other feel like tak-ing a nap? Did it make us bounce off the walls or hurt our stomachs? It was an experiential situation, like everything else in our lives. And later, when we returned from Laura's house, we would talk about why we don't eat foods like that in our family—because they *don't* make you feel great, they do your body no good, and so, aside from the occasional indulgence, they may as well be ignored. Because of this, I never felt deprived growing up. I experienced junk foods that other kids were eating and decided on my own that I didn't like them. Now, this doesn't mean that none of us ever got cravings, and we had plenty of opportunities to sneak chocolate milk in the school cafeteria or, better yet, a brownie or doughnut, but for the most part we chose not to eat it because we truly didn't want it. For the *most* part. I do remember a time a few years later, though, when Nate developed a dietary science experiment on a rat and decided to feed him nothing but powdered doughnuts to see what would happen to him. One evening a package of the powdered doughnuts, purchased specifically for the rat, was sitting on the table inside the front door so Nate would remember to take them to school in the morning. But come morning the doughnuts were nowhere to be found. It didn't take long to figure out that my younger brother, Joe, had let a sweet tooth and craving for junk get the best of him. He confessed to eating the doughnuts—the *whole* package—and we all had a good laugh over it.

By the time my life reached into the double digits, my dad's focus was beginning to spread beyond Eden Foods. He spent some time in Japan studying the local foods, in particular *tonyu*, milk made out of a soybean. By the late 1980s he was introducing America's first mass-produced soymilk to supermarkets across the United States. And a few years after that, he was developing a natural fruit and vegetable juice combination called Vruit (Veggies + Fruit = Vruit). My brothers and sister and I were the test kids for all kinds of new soymilk and juice combinations. We slurped down unmarked formulations of carob and vanilla soymilks and apple-carrot juice. I remember these "test days" distinctly. My dad would pull out his video camera, the size of a suitcase, and introduce each scene with his favorite saying, "The typical American family, around the table enjoying some soymilk." We were anything *but*! Even so, we sipped and shared our opinions, and believed wholeheartedly that the formulations for EdenSoy and Vruit were based on our opinions and favorites. The videos still come out at the occasional family gathering.

Family and Community

The other thing that I remember distinctly about my upbringing was the community sense we had on this little family commune. My mom and her sister helped each other so naturally with every element of daily life. One would do the run to the bus stop (it was almost a mile away) one day, and the other would do it the next. They would dress up as cleaning fairies and tromp through the woods to each other's houses to check on how the kids had performed their cleaning duties. (That never really inspired us to clean better; it just threw us into fits of laughter.) They shared food and trips into the city. As kids, being a good distance from town and our classmates, we spent most of our time playing with each other over the long lazy days of summer. And in the winter we got up many weekend mornings, put on our cross-country skis and warm gear, and gathered for long treks out in the pine forest.

Through all of this my grandma and grandpa (my mom's parents, who had retired early and moved from their Princeton neighborhood to join their kids and grandkids in the rural Michigan lifestyle) were there. I was a talkative child, especially as a toddler, so when my mom tired of hearing my endless chatter, she'd send me down the hill to Grandma's house. There I would sweep floors with her or help them both out in the garden, chattering away to their never-tired ears. My grandparents were both happiest in their garden. They had an enormous organic fruit and vegetable patch that measured about a third of an acre. And they spent their days tending to it. The two of them, my grandfather in particular, were environmentalists through and through. "Environmentalist" might not even be the right word, because it was simpler than that. They were stewards to God's creation, and the way they lived was guided by a sense of responsibility, an understanding that they didn't need to overconsume, and from a desire to live simply, off the land. They collected rainwater to use on their gardens, chopped up fallen trees for firewood, mowed with a turn-blade manual mower, and avoided chemical fertilizers and pesticides, which would poison their bodies and the earth, at all costs.

Lessons Learned from Grandma and Grandpa

My grandma patiently helped us learn how to sew, bake, can, play the piano, and distinguish a weed from a flower or a vegetable seedling, and through it all, she had a talent for listening to us talk for hours on end. She still does all of those things. My grandpa was quieter. He could tirelessly work for hours upon hours in his vegetable patches and beamed happiness when anyone would join him there or in his daily chores of running an efficient home. He told clever, witty jokes and loved nature in a way I didn't appreciate enough as a youngster. But today, seeing the throngs of people trying so hard to proclaim their love for "hugging trees," I know that he was a man ahead of his time. He was, as a T-shirt one of our neighbors gave him said, "outstanding in his field," quite literally and figuratively.

My grandparents understood the necessity of treading lightly on this fragile planet, and that you could achieve a respectable output even with very little input. My grandfather was an economist, so he would do the math and forecast the lack of resources imminent in our future with current consumption trends. He calculated exactly how long the water in his well could last, how many tomatoes he could grow if he continued or changed his methods, and how long our nation, in this bigger picture of a global economy, could sustain itself with and without significant change. And on his small patch in Michigan, he was making a difference.

They knew that they were inspiring a younger generation to continue down the path we were living at that moment, which was the second reason why they lived the way they did. They understood that by engaging us in their lives—helping in the garden; catching tadpoles in the rain barrel; storing rainwater in the crawl space; using urine and plants, instead of chemicals, to deter deer and pests; cooking and canning with foods grown there or in nearby farms; and, maybe most important, taking the time to explain each of these activities over a meal or a snack—we would become instilled with the same sense of responsibility and desire for nurturing the earth.

Propelled into Adulthood

Through all of this, my family didn't teach me only *how* to live green according to today's standards, they taught me *why* to live green. I grew up empowered by my parents and my grandparents with an understanding of the profound impact our daily actions have on the earth—the soil, water, and air—and ultimately on future generations. Today some people call it *green living*, but I have the perspective of a youth spent on a naturalist family co-operative, a *fresh living* perspective. In order to be healthy, raise a healthy family, and leave behind a healthy planet, you must think enough of others to make changes in your world today. Living selfishly for today, consuming and polluting, isn't going to get us there. I call it respectful living *and* healthy living; healthy both for us as individuals and for our future generations who will inherit our planet.

Though we thought we had discovered the fountain of youth in all those organic, living foods, life evolved, time moved on, and we each grew older. We eventually moved to a new house to be a little closer to town, got new neighbors and friends, discovered new pursuits, yet through it my dad continued to heed the call for responsible and healthy food production. His newest company, Blue Horizon Organic, was created with the belief that farmed sea animals are the next frontier for organic methods certification. My mom, who made sure four kids' bruises were treated with arnica, sniffles with goldenseal, and outlooks with a sunny disposition, always willing to embrace anything natural, healthy, or eco, found her own professional calling. Today she is a designer, helping clients create kitchens with as much warmth as the one she created for our family. My oldest brother, Nate, went off to the University of Michigan and then to Harvard. He works in investments, with a keen eye toward environmental businesses. Joe got a degree in horticulture and works for Whole Foods, helping to connect local growers and producers with consumers by way of the grocery store aisle. Elizabeth went to college to study art and design, with a focus on sustainable materials, and has since created a floor tile that generates energy using one's footsteps. And I . . . I went off to college to pursue theater and television and, being the daughter of free-minded parents, was allowed to do just that. I'll never forget the day I went for my college entrance interview. My goal was to get degrees in telecommunications and theater, and I wanted to do both in four years or less. I was sitting before the department heads of the theater program and was asked what my future goals were. I thought for a moment and then, out of nowhere, told them that one day I wanted to run my own theater. To this day I'm not sure where that answer came from, but its spirit rings true to my family background and my individual longings. One of the professors turned to another and said, "Sounds like we have an entrepreneur on our hands." They were right.

In my family, we learned that if the way that is right, true, clean, safe, and healthy isn't already paved—pave it. This has been my goal. It's why I created the first natural-living prime-time TV series in the United States just a handful of years ago, and a second one a year later, and it's why I am writing this book today.

I went to college and graduated with both degrees, in four years as I had hoped. And I did my best to live according to my upbringing. I remember heading into the student union club one of the first days of my freshman year. I was less than pleased to see that the offerings amounted to a few fast-food chains and a little store. So I started through the line with my friends and finally landed at a burger joint. I asked them if they could make me their signature burger; hold the sauce . . . and the burger. This was before the days of veggie burgers and gourmet salads at fast-food places, so after receiving some blank and confused stares, I explained that I wanted the bun and as many of the veggie toppings as they could load on there, but nothing else. What came back were some lettuce and tomato slices and pickles slapped between the two halves of a bun. The bun was white bread, of course, and the vegetables lacked the pigment they should have had, but it was probably safe and the best I would get until the kitchen opened in our dorm. I took it through the checkout line, where, after I explained what was in my paper wrapper, they told me they had no idea what to charge. I suggested ninety-five cents. And so, when our dorm kitchen was closed because it was a holiday or past hours, I knew I could get my signature burger, hold the sauce hold the burger, for a small price. It might not have been my mom's home cooking, but I was staying true to my parents' teachings—if the way isn't already paved, pave it.

After college I began to develop a professional career in television and had some success, earning two Emmy Awards as a producer on national sports documentaries. But sports weren't my calling; morning news was where my heart belonged. The truth is, as a kid in my house in the woods, I used to record "shows" into our little tape recorder, pretending I was the radio or TV host, doing everything from weather reports to commercials. When I went to college to get degrees in theater and telecommunications, it was with the goal of one day taking Katie Couric's spot on the *Today* show. I thought morning news was just the place for my happy disposition and my desire to change the world—one early morning viewer at a time. With this in mind I was thrilled when I got a call from the FOX affiliate in Indianapolis to join their morning news team. By this time I had met the man who would become my husband—a man who would adapt and change his lifestyle to fall in line with what was second-nature to me, and who would teach me so much about people and life. Ryan and I had just gotten married and it felt like the pieces of my life were falling into place. I had some of the most fun of my life working for that morning news show, and earned another Emmy for a teen special I created, but after three years of three a.m. wake-up calls, I began to see my health take a swift nosedive. With the stress of being in front of the camera for a three-hour *live* show every day and lack of sleep from those early morning wake-ups taking such a toll on my body, natural foods and a healthy home simply didn't offer enough protection against the vicissitudes of the television journalist's life. I could hardly walk into a grocery store or yoga class without first reclining my seat in the parking lot and taking a twenty-minute nap. I was, I came to realize, a half-version of my former self. I lacked energy, passion, strength, and, without all of that, some of my character. Looking forward to and desperately needing a slower, healthier life, I walked away from my "dream job" on that morning news program. I spent time with Ryan and our dog Makana and found myself going back to my roots in a deeper way than I had since I left home. I began to live more slowly, with time built in for daily meditation; I continued to eat whole and natural foods and began to once again sleep with the sun's natural cycle. And as I was getting myself back to that centered, healthy place, I couldn't help but hear the questions being whispered or shouted from *countless* people's lips: "I'm confused about organic milk!" "What should I be feeding my children?" "What should I use to paint my walls?" And on and on. So I began working on the concept for a TV series with practical advice on living green.

Since then I have been creator and host of two prime-time series on green living for the Discovery Networks, *Living Fresh* and *Get Fresh with Sara Snow*. I have been interviewed as a natural living expert for radio, television, and print publications. I have been the featured speaker at conferences, expos, and other events, declaring my message focused on simple steps toward living a greener, more natural life.

So why am I writing a book about healthy homes today? I was fortunate enough, as you can now see, to grow up in a healthy, low-impact "green" home. There is no doubt in my mind that I am a healthy person and a motivated activist because of it. Only a few years ago my husband and I were in the market for a new home. We were so tempted with the idea of building a brand new "eco home," complete with bamboo and cork floors, recycled-paper countertops, a roof covered with greenery and solar panels, and a great number of other cool green home features.

We envisioned the house out in the sticks with nothing around (quite like the way I grew up), a natural setting for our eco home. It was tempting but in the end my convictions won out. There is so much waste created every time a new home is built, and, though we live in a disposable society where people tend to have an "off with the old, on with the new" mentality, there are plenty of perfectly good homes that have already been built and are just waiting for someone to help them continue their life. My husband and I are avid recyclers, so we decided to recycle the ultimate—we recycled a home. We took a tired old home built in 1920 with solid bones but a weary interior, and we went to town on it. As subway tiles fell off bathroom walls and broke, we scoured reuse centers for matching ones to replace the broken few, rather than ripping the walls of tile down and replacing them with new. When we pulled the kitchen cabinets out to replace them, we recycled the old ones down to the basement, where they were reconfigured into a laundry room. In their place we outfitted the kitchen with healthy, solid-wood cabinets so as not to risk formaldehyde leakage. We replaced drafty windows with energy-efficient ones but left intact any that didn't need to be ripped out.

We made sure that every window, despite the layers and layers of paint that had accumulated over the years, could open to allow fresh air to infuse our inner sanctum. We installed compost bins out back and a recycling station in the basement; we filled a cupboard with non-toxic cleaning products and the pantry with organic and natural foods.

Afterwards, we stood back and realized that although it didn't have bamboo floors or solar panels on the ninety-year-old roof, we had recycled a beat-up house into an eco-friendly home. And that is something I'm so proud of. Though we don't have little ones running around in it yet, I know that come that day our home will serve as an inspiration to them in many of the same ways my childhood home did for me.

Trends Today

The lifestyle I was raised in is one a great number of people are striving for today. Green living is chic, desirable, and, as it becomes big business, it's also profitable. Everywhere you look, there are hybrid cars, organic foods, green street festivals where vendors sell T-shirts blazing slogans like "Green is the new black" or "Kiss me, I'm organic." It is amazing to see the transformation that has happened in homes and grocery stores across this country. In 2006 alone, organic foods saw the most impressive growth as a single broad category, generating a 20 percent increase in consumer sales, while organic coffee and tea sales jumped 23 percent and organic produce reached total sales of over $3 billion. Today more than half of all U.S. consumers say they buy organic products at least occasionally. The demand for organic food, beverages, and non-food products is expected to continue to grow at double-digit rates.

The trend goes well beyond food. Sales of energy-efficient compact fluorescent lightbulbs have experienced double-digit growth over recent years. Hybrid vehicles are still experiencing a tremendous increase in popularity, particularly in the Midwest, where sales went up 57 percent in 2007 as compared to one year prior.

All of these changes—new foods, new products, and newly motivated consumers—are fueling a growing industry that is generating headlines, revenues, and lifestyle changes. In just four years, from 2002 to 2006, sales of natural and organic products increased 56 percent, becoming a $56 billion industry. But we're still in the early part of the movement. Projections point toward organic food sales accounting for 5 percent of all U.S. food sales by 2010 (up from only 2 percent in 2003). Starbucks has long been a supporter of Fair Trade coffee, and recently stores like Sam's Club have begun converting their private labels of ground coffee to Fair Trade. Green fashion shows are popping up all over the country, including during Fashion Week in New York City, but at the end of the day, they're still heavily outweighed by conventional fashions strutting runways. Changes are happening and the movement toward greener living as a collective nation is taking shape. But individuals, as well as corporate CEOs and government officials, still have a lot of learning and changing to do. Thankfully, making those changes is getting easier every day with greater access to affordable green and natural products and programs.

Because I grew up in a naturalist home where environmentalism and healthy foods were such an enormous focus, I am fortunate to have the gift of perspective—perspective to see that living this way *is* entirely possible. Perspective *because* I've struggled to live between the worlds of conventional life and natural living. And perspective because I've watched as people have stalled out at the starting blocks, as they've wondered where to begin and how much of their life is going to be disrupted by doing so. Here's the truth: it's not always easy, it takes some work, and you're probably not going to be able to change everything overnight. But rest assured that I would never ask you to.

I have found that the greatest opportunity for change happens when someone discovers they are responsible for more than just themselves. This may happen when an adult takes in his or her parents, or a bachelor brings home a dog, or, more often than not, when a soon-to-be new mom first learns that she is expecting. Suddenly life—from the foods in the kitchen to the products in the laundry room—is about more than just you. It's about how all of those little things will affect another life, and you as the caregiver want to do it right. And quite suddenly you're willing to make changes, to spend the extra few bucks for organic milk and non-toxic cleaners and do the legwork to find the cleanest and healthiest everything. Whether you fit into one of these categories or not, you will learn from these pages.

How This Book Works

Throughout this book, I will walk you through steps you can take in every area of your home and life. I'll suggest incremental changes in the kitchen to get you eating the healthiest foods possible and to help you conserve resources like water and electricity. And I'll talk you through how and where to shop for the freshest, most nutrient-dense foods. We'll cover conservation and healthy body care products in the bathroom, natural cleaning in the laundry room, and creating a soothing, protective space in the bedroom. I'm even going to go so far as to touch on greener sex (yes, I just said "greener sex") in the bedroom. I've done my best to cover all areas of your home, from the home office, to the kitchen, to the garage, and have included checklists and other action-oriented charts to help you get moving in the right direction. What you won't find in the pages of this book, though, are specific product recommendations; instead I focus on the qualities you should look for in brands, with shopping guidelines and recommendations. You can consult my website, *www.sarasnow.com*, for more specific recommendations. I understand, though, that even the simplest and most enjoyable steps require some motivation, and because I've spent a lifetime around the pioneers and engineers behind so many natural foods and eco-lifestyle products, I want to share the inspirations I've gathered from them with you. So throughout the book you'll find *green-bar profiles* where I highlight inspiring people from inside the natural products industry and green movement, and some of what I have learned from them that I think might be inspiring to you.

This book is meant to be read either cover-to-cover in the room order I've designated, or chapter by chapter, in an order of your choosing. I've arranged the chapters in the sequence that I think makes the most sense, in terms of things people should and can most easily tackle first. But if you want to take on your garage first, by all means, skip to the back and read that chapter first.

My hope is that you'll take this book—underlining sections, scribbling in the margins, carrying it with you when you go to the store—as your starting point. The most rewarding feedback I can get is to hear from you that you read the book, maybe carried it around for a while, learned from it and then shared those thoughts back—with me, with your family, with the community. This is my wish for this book and you: that it will inspire changes in your life, just a few at a time, so that you are not overwhelmed by a need to change everything at once but you are encouraged to start somewhere. And to be honest, it doesn't make a whole lot of difference where you start. Just start—with a few simple changes this week and a few more next, until you wake up one morning and look around and realize that *you* are the picture of green, conscious living and that your home has become quite truly harmonious and healthy.

In the Kitchen

Reenie's Transformation

A few years ago, into the conference room at the production company responsible for my first Discovery series walked a successful, motivated woman, suitcase in tow and large coffee in hand. I immediately liked this driven, focused woman, but I saw in her the worn-out, "just trying to get a grasp on anything that's solid" look that I've seen in other new moms.

Just recently I sat across from this same woman. The change in her is palpable. Today she sits relaxed, centered, and grounded. She may sip herbal tea and munch on a granola bar, and she'll run the meeting or contribute, depending on what she's called to do. But if the conversation changes to kids, watch out. This woman has a story to tell, one that is about a life transformation, a shifted focus, an all-American girl turned greenie. Why the change? She had a baby, and that alone led her on a path of discovery toward a slower, more earth-focused way of living.

When I first met Reenie in that conference room, it was right after the birth of her daughter, Logan. Before this time she and her husband had enjoyed a life not unlike many other young married couples their age. They lived in a bustling suburb outside of Washington, DC, enjoyed great jobs, dinners with friends, and fun, active weekends. They weren't unhealthy by any stretch of the imagination, and they were only vaguely aware of the health issues that ran in the family. In truth, they both enjoyed the energy and sense of well-being that most people associate with good health. When Reenie found out she was expecting her first child, she and her husband, aside from the promise of sleepless nights, load upon load of laundry, and worries about childcare needs, didn't think much about the lifestyle changes that would come with becoming new parents. As time grew closer to delivering, though, Reenie began to think a little more specifically about her health and the health of her unborn child. She wanted, more than anything, to have a happy, bright-faced little boy or girl, and she decided that if it meant making some changes to her diet, she was okay with that. What she didn't realize was just how much and how quickly she would be willing to change once she saw the bright face of her brand new baby girl. "When Logan was born," Reenie tells me, "I vowed to learn as much as possible about the foods she eats, from how they would affect her growth to which foods would be the most beneficial to her well-being." If it had to do with the health of her baby, Reenie devoured the information.

Reenie is the perfect example of something I see every day. When it comes to making changes toward leading a greener and healthier life, the greatest opportunity is when an individual learns that she is responsible for more than herself. Most often that happens when a person or couple has their first baby. Suddenly they'll spend the extra for healthy products and go out of the way to visit health food stores or the organic aisles of their super-market.

Food Choices

When I was growing up, finding healthy and organic foods wasn't as easy as it is today. Today you can find organic milk and minimally processed meats at nearly any grocery store. You can find locally grown or prepared foods at a number of venues in your area. The shopping and basic sourcing for such foods has gotten much easier. So instead of "Where do I find it?" the biggest stumbling block for most people today has become "Where do I start?"

Let's dig in.

Organic Foods

Not that long ago the Environmental Working Group (EWG), a nonprofit and nonpartisan health and environmental research organization, put out a list it called the "Shopper's Guide to Pesticides in Produce." To create the guide, the EWG compiled and analyzed the results from over forty-three thousand tests that the USDA and FDA conducted between 2000 and 2004 to detect pesticide levels on and in common fruits and vegetables. From this data the EWG listed forty-four different fruits and vegetables (grapes were listed twice because they studied both domestic and imported) and ranked them according to which had the highest or lowest "pesticide load" when tested in the edible form. In other words, an apple was washed before being tested, a banana was peeled, etc.

The EWG's reason for their analysis of the government-collected data, and their ensuing "shopper's guide," was twofold. First, they believed that pesticides and other chemicals could have a harmful effect on people. Second, they wanted to give shoppers an easy reference guide for avoiding pesticides in everyday fruits and vegetables. According to an EWG simulation, people can lower their pesticide exposure by nearly 90 percent (fourteen pesticide exposures per day) by avoiding the produce items from their "dirty dozen" list.

USDA = United States Department of Agriculture

FDA = United States Food and Drug Administration

The result has become an often-referenced list of the twelve cleanest and twelve dirtiest (the "dirty dozen") fruits and vegetables.

The list is an excellent starting point for people wondering which produce to begin with when integrating in organic. This is not to say that you should never eat the items on the dirty list, only that they tend to be higher in pesticide residues, so if you're looking to lessen your exposure, these

EWG's Shopper's Guide to Pesticides in Produce

Dirty Dozen—*Buy These Organic*	Cleanest Twelve—*Lowest in Pesticides*
Peaches	Onions
Apples	Avocado
Sweet Bell Peppers	Sweet Corn (frozen)
Celery	Pineapples
Nectarines	Mango
Strawberries	Asparagus
Cherries	Sweet Peas (frozen)
Pears	Kiwi Fruit
Grapes (imported)	Bananas
Spinach	Cabbage
Lettuce	Broccoli
Potatoes	Papaya

From Environmental Working Group, *www.foodnews.org*

should be the fruits and vegetables where you try to buy organic first. And that perhaps the items on the "clean" list are ones where conventional is a little safer, providing you with an opportunity to save money by forgoing the organically farmed varieties for these few items.

That's *if* you're looking to avoid pesticide exposure. And I certainly think you should—so let's look at *why* it's so important to avoid the pesticides in the first place.

I d e a s   t o   G r o w   O n

Save some money by sticking with conventional when it comes to foods on the EWG's "Cleanest Twelve" list. Bananas, avocados, and aspara-gus are just a few.

The Health Side

The USDA's Pesticide Data Program (PDP) routinely checks samples of produce for pesticide residues. Samples often contain multiple residues, and soft-skinned fruits like peaches and leafy vegetables like lettuce or spinach tend to have more residues than foods with thicker skins or a hard outer shell or peel. According to PDP tests, 90 percent or more of conventionally grown apples, peaches, pears, and strawberries have pesticide residues. In fact, Americans under the age of twenty consume pesticides in about 200 million servings of food a day across the country. On average, children are exposed to around five *different* pesticides through their food and drinking water every day.

While it is difficult to point to pesticides as the sole cause of any disease, the consensus among many public health scientists is that pesticide exposure, especially in combination with other variables, could trigger developmental problems and other illness in otherwise healthy people.

I don't know about you, but if something in and on certain foods could lead to developmental problems and illness, then I'm going to find a way to eat around it.

Factor in the Kids—All of this becomes particularly important when you recognize that kids eat, per pound of body weight, more food than adults every day. Plus their variety is limited. So when a child eats a food that contains residues, the dose they receive is much higher than the dose you or I might get from that same food. Couple that with the fact that children's bodies don't have the ability to metabolize chemicals as quickly or as completely as adults' do, so the chemicals remain *in* kids longer, posing greater risks.

The good news is that making even a small change in the foods you feed your family can have a big impact. Here's a great example of that. In 2006 a scientist from the Harvard School of Public Health tested twenty-three school-aged children for levels of organophosphate (OP) insecticides. OP is a class of insecticides used across the globe and is considered to be *the riskiest* one out there. For the test the kids were put on an organic diet. Their urine was tested *before* going on the organic diet, *while* on a diet of only organic foods, and *after* returning to their conventional diet. Every single one of the kids tested positive for OP toxins in their urine while eating a diet of conventional foods. But after only five days on a diet of all-organic foods, the OP insecticide marks very nearly disappeared completely. The test proved what researchers suspected: that a diet of organic foods can provide a dramatic and immediate protector against organophosphate pesticide exposures.

Ideas to Grow On

Wondering how to start integrating organics into your child's diet? Change out those foods that your kids eat the most of first for maximum impact, ditching the conventional in favor of its organic counterpart.

The Good Stuff

Further research has shown that organic foods not only have *less* of the bad stuff (harmful chemical residues), they also have *more* of the good stuff: more taste and more healthy nutrients. Certain fruits grown under identical environmental conditions, with their only difference being the presence of chemical fertilizers and other conventional growing methods, actually tested *tastier* in their organic form. Organic strawberries, for instance, showed more intense color and higher sugar content—adding up to tastier—than their conventional counterparts. And because fruits and vegetables tend to grow and ripen more slowly on organic farms, where yield levels aren't as high (thus resulting in more nitrogen in the soil), the plants can have higher levels of certain key vitamins and minerals.

Fruits and vegetables, both conventionally and organically grown varieties, are exceptional sources of disease-preventing antioxidants (such as vitamins C and E, lycopene, and carotene), which promote good health and help us feel fuller. But the organic variety may be as much as 30 percent higher in antioxidants.

Antioxidant-Rich Foods

• Fruits—apples (with the peels), avocados, blueberries, blackberries, cherries, cranberries, pears, pineapples, plums, prunes, strawberries, oranges, kiwis

• Vegetables—artichokes, broccoli, red cabbage, spinach, potatoes (with the peels), yams (sweet potatoes)

• Beans—black beans, kidney beans, red beans, pinto beans

• Grains—oat-based foods

• Nuts—almonds, hazelnuts, pecans, pistachios, walnuts

• Herbs—cinnamon, cloves, ginger, oregano, turmeric

• Beverages—coffee, green tea, red wine, some fruit juices

• Desserts—fruits, dark chocolate

Three great reasons to buy organic foods whenever possible: higher levels of vitamins, minerals, and antioxidants; more flavor; *and* lower levels of pesticides. Sounds like a good argument for organic production methods, don't you think?

The Environmental Side

The other side to the organic food coin is environmental preservation. Organic farming protects and conserves water resources by eliminating polluting chemicals and nitrogen leaching. It supports biodiversity by growing a variety of crop species, rotating season to season, and including heirloom varieties. Cover crops, manures, composts, and rotating crops are all used to build healthy soil and naturally control weeds, insects, and disease. A primary focus of organic farming is building healthy soil as the foundation of the food chain. So each time you choose organic foods, you're not only choosing food that tastes great and keeps you healthy, you're supporting people who are protecting our present and future environment.

So where do you find organic fruits and vegetables? There are two primary channels—your grocer and your local farmers—and both should be embraced.

Finding Organic Foods

If you've shopped in any mainstream grocery store in the last few years, you've probably come across the little green and white USDA ORGANIC label. It's on individual apples, peaches, and zucchini; packages of meat, cereal, and grains; jars of spaghetti sauce and jams; cartons of eggs and milk; and countless other items.

The presence of that little label means the item or individual ingredients in a product have been closely monitored during their growth and processing according to strict regulations set in place by the USDA's National Organic Program (NOP), which was created and empowered to oversee these regulations by the Organic Foods Production Act (OFPA), established by Congress back in 1990. The NOP is the governing body responsible for the national production, handling, and labeling of organic agricultural products and for overseeing the certifying agents who deem a product acceptable according to the USDA organic standards.

A government-approved certifier must inspect any farm where organic food is grown or any company where organic food is processed or handled to ensure that the farmer and food processors are meeting all necessary rules according to the USDA organic standards.

What are those standards? That the food was grown or produced without irradiation, sewage sludge, or genetically modified organisms; that it contains no prohibited substances (this includes toxic and persistent chemical inputs like pesticides, herbicides, fungicides, and synthetic fertilizers); that meat, poultry, eggs, and dairy products came from animals that were given no antibiotics or growth hormones; and that an organic feed was used for all livestock.

The primary goal of organic agriculture is to optimize the health and productivity of people, plants, animals, and soil life. Healthy soil is the foundation of organic farming.

But the term "organic" can be admittedly a little tricky, because there are a number of different products that can carry the USDA organic label for a number of different reasons.

As of October 2002 there are four USDA-approved designations or "callouts" for labeling certified organic foods, based on the percentage of organic content. Let's take cereal for example. One brand of cereal might contain 100 percent organic ingredients, a second might consist of at least 95 percent organic ingredients, a third might be made with 70 percent or more organic ingredients, and a fourth have less than 70 percent organic ingredients. Each of these will carry a different label. If a product contains less than 70 percent organic ingredients, it may list which ingredients are organically produced on the back or side panel of the package but there can be no organic claims on the front of the package. As a consumer, you can look for the name and address of the government-approved organic certifier on the package of all products that bear the USDA ORGANIC seal.

Aside from grocery stores, the other fantastic place for finding organic foods is a farmers' market. In recent years the number of farmers' markets has grown from around 1,500 to somewhere around 5,000. There is likely a farmers' market not far from your home. In talking to people, though, I've learned that there is confusion over what is and what isn't organic at the market. People often assume that the foods they find at their farmers' markets are always organic. In truth they often are, but not always. And the reason for that is because many small farmers who would love to have the USDA ORGANIC certification simply can't afford the time and cost-intensive requirements. Many of the vendors at your local market may farm according to organic standards and practices, but they're prohibited from using the recognizable label on their sign or products because they haven't been properly certified. But between you and me, while that label is very important, especially for a global or national food program, it doesn't mean the whole world when it comes to your local food. If the farmer is growing without chemicals and according to other "organic" practices, then he's a friend of mine and should be a friend of yours too.

USDA Organic Categories

• "100 Percent Organic"—may proudly display the USDA ORGANIC seal. The product must be 100 percent organic by weight, not including water and salt. No synthetic ingredients are allowed by law. A cereal could be called "100 Percent Organic Granola," for instance.

• "Organic"—95 percent of the content by weight (excluding water and salt) is organic. These products may carry the USDA ORGANIC seal. The cereal could be called "Organic Granola."

• "Made with Organic Ingredients"—at least 70 percent of the content is organic. The remaining 30 percent must come from the USDA's approved list. May not display the USDA ORGANIC seal. The front of the product may display "Made with Organic" with the specific organic ingredients listed. For example, the cereal could be called "Granola—made with organic oats, organic oil, organic flaxseed, and organic almonds."

• Less Than 70 Percent Organic—may list specific ingredients that have been organically produced on the ingredient panel. May not display the USDA ORGANIC seal. May make no mention of the word "organic" on the package front.

Of course, there will be farmers (or vendors offering artisanal products like bread and jam) at the market who do use chemical fertilizers, pesticides, and synthetic ingredients. That's why the absolute best part about a farmers' market is that it puts you in touch with the growers of your food. Unlike at a grocery store, where Mr. Heinz and Ms. Tyson are nowhere to be found, you can actually speak with the men and women who grew, harvested, and transported the food. You can ask questions to find out exactly what sorts of practices they use in the cultivation of their crops. This is what I recommend—that you spend some time getting to know your local farmers. Walk up to them at the market and ask, "Do you spray your crops with chemicals?" "Do you grow a variety of fruits and vegetables?" "Is your beef grass fed or do you feed it a grain mix?" "What type of grain mix?" "Are the berries in your blueberry jam organic, and what else do you put in there?" And so on. As long as the seller doesn't appear too harried, and the line of heirloom-tomato-crazed shoppers isn't too long, take advantage of your chance to talk to a man or woman of the earth—the real deal. As you get to know your farmers, you'll find that there are most certainly one or two with whom you identify and will happily support. Once you've found these farmers, buy all that you can from them.

Ideas to Grow On

Get to know your local farmers and food producers to feel safer about the foods you're eating. And get the whole family involved in the process. Farmers' markets are a great learning and inspirational space for kids.

Many farmers today are growing a wide variety of outdoor crops, but also are expanding acreage in greenhouses to extend the growing season. This means you can get baby lettuces before the last frost, and crops that would typically fruit and then "bolt," like lettuce, can be planted over and over to assure a long season full of freshly grown fruits and vegetables.

Beyond farmers' markets, CSAs are a fantastic way to get local and seasonal, organic produce.

> CSA = community-supported agriculture

This is a system by which you become an actual member of a farm. You pay an upfront cost at the beginning of the year or the growing season, and in exchange, you get a weekly share of the farm's crops.

In the CSA that I belong to, our weekly shares of just-picked produce are available on Thursdays. I can pick up my produce box at a number of locations around town, or for a little more, I can have mine delivered when the farmer's wife and daughter do their afternoon run of deliveries. Because I travel and am busy, I choose this option. Every Thursday afternoon, from mid-spring until early fall, I get a box brimming with organics picked that morning: greens like romaine, red leaf, green leaf, and Bibb lettuces, Swiss chard, kale, and spinach. A great variety of herbs, heirloom tomatoes, summer squash, cucumbers, carrots, beets, peppers, and other vegetables that you might not typically buy at the store, like turnips and rutabaga, also find their way inside.

The beautiful thing about a CSA share is that you never really know what you're going to get, so you're forced to get creative with recipes and try foods you might not otherwise try. Many CSA organizers send out a weekly newsletter with recipes and crop information; some even include stories from the farm or interviews with field workers. As a member, you get to feel like you're a part of a larger community, focused around food and the earth. And the best part about the whole thing is that, in a very direct way, you are supporting a local farmer and, at the same time, serving your family the freshest foods possible.

Eating Locally

When it comes to the food choices you will make in the kitchen, beginning to implement organics regularly into your diet is an extremely important one. But equally as important is enjoying local foods.

The average American meal travels around fifteen hundred miles to get to the table. This means that when you sit down to your dinner of chicken, broccoli, and potatoes, each of those foods has traveled on average nearly fifteen hundred miles, by boat, train, plane, or truck, to get from the farm where it was grown to your dinner plate. Those are some well-traveled foods that have resulted in a considerable amount of wasted fuel as well as valuable nutrients and freshness.

Picture this. A tomato grows on a vine until it is plump and red, at which time the farmer picks the tomato and packs it in a crate for sale. That tomato,

DRAKE SADLER

Shortly after the 1967 "Summer of Love," Drake Sadler, a young hippie by many standards, left behind Haight-Ashbury and moved with friends into a cabin in the woods of northern California. It was during his first winter that he found himself on a walk, detouring to follow the sound of a baby's cry. He came upon a woman in her home making a stinging nettle "tea" for herself and her colicky baby. She offered him a cup. Thinking she was crazy to drink a tea made from a stinging plant, he headed for the hills. But later on, while browsing through Jethro Kloss's classic book *Back to Eden,* about natural living and herbal health, he regretted turning down this woman and her odd culinary use of the plant.

Hungry to learn more, Drake went back to the woman's cabin in the woods and asked her to teach him. Rosemary was a third-generation Armenian herbalist who had learned the craft of herbal medicine from her grandmother; that day she and Drake began a life and a business together. They started mixing and brewing herbal teas that offered alternative health solutions for dozens of common ailments—constipation, the common cold, restlessness, and so on. Evenings around the campfire were spent coming up with fun names for their teas—names like Throat Coat, Mother's Milk, and Smooth Move. With a first run of just ten thousand bags of medicinal herb teas, Traditional Medicinals was formed. Before long, demand for their teas began to increase and Drake, realizing that his little project just might turn a profit, decided it was time for him to leave behind his nine-to-five job and focus solely on TM and the medicinal herb teas he and Rosemary were creating together. But to do so, he had to leave behind a job he was equally passionate about—working for a community action group, waging war against poverty.

And here's where Drake's story gets really interesting. Despite the success of his company over the next thirty years, despite the focus

continued

and energy he put into creating a sustainable business that would care for the earth as much as its customers, despite efforts to use wind power, recycled materials, composters, and solar panels, Drake never lost his passion for finding ways to alleviate poverty. Instead of working on the front lines of poverty in California, he began to look at the communities and families in the villages across the globe where his herbs came from—communities in Guatemala where he would source his lemongrass, in Rajasthan for senna, and so on. Ninety percent of medicinal plants, he found, were not cultivated. Instead they were indigenous to a region and collected by workers who were more often than not living in extreme poverty. By dealing with them directly as the source, Drake found himself once again working against poverty, proving that a social and economic business structure could exist. But more than exist, it could thrive. And when a business like that does thrive, it isn't just good for the company, it's infinitely good for the people, families, and communities that that business supports.

It's not enough, Drake says, for a consumer to see that a product is healthy, natural, or even organic; they must get to know the company, practices, and ideals behind the product. What I have learned from Drake is to find those companies that have a triple bottom line—a goal of social and environmental performance as well as financial. If a company can focus on the "people, planet, and profit," then we as consumers can do the same. ∎

and crates full of other ruby reds just like it, are loaded onto the back of a truck, then possibly a plane, and a truck again as it makes its way to your grocery store. Once in the store, it heads for the cooler, then is gradually arranged for you to come by sometime within the next few days and buy it. You buy the tomato for a fresh caprese salad you're planning. But by the time you get the fruit home, it has spent days in transport and in the produce department of your grocery store, and it's mushy, the skin is broken, and it has oozed all over the gallon of milk it sat beside in the grocery sack. There is no hope of this tomato seeing its way onto a plate.

To keep that from happening, farmers often pick their produce well before it has ripened, when a tomato is still a little green and firm. It is then packed away for shipping and is flash-ripened through a synthetic process before hitting the store shelves. Doesn't sound very natural, does it?

Ideas to Grow On

The average food item travels fifteen hundred miles to get from farm to table. Buy local foods at your farmers' market, supermarket, or CSA to cut down on your food miles.

Farmers' Markets and CSAs

Now envision the same picturesque setting with the farmer heading out into the field one morning and picking the plumpest, brightest tomatoes. These tomatoes are at their peak ripeness, with all of their valuable nutrients immediately available in the fruit. Instead of spending days in transportation, the tomato goes directly with the farmer to the market where you buy it the very same day. To complete the story, you also find some fresh basil with leaves the size of a child's hand and mozzarella cheese from a local dairy, and you're able to plate a caprese salad more beautiful and tasty than you imagine any in Italy would be.

Farmers' markets are fairly easy to find today, in high school parking lots, city parks, or downtown main streets. To find a farmers' market or a CSA in your area, search the site *www.localharvest.org*. There you can find them according to your zip code.

Aside from these two primary sources of local foods, it's worth mentioning that supermarkets today are finding that they suddenly are competing with farmers' markets and farm stands and, as a result, are making tremendous strides toward offering more local foods, from blueberries to potatoes, to their consumers. In fact, Wal-Mart announced plans to spend

$400 million on locally grown produce in 2008. This is good news not only for you, the consumer, but also for the local farmers as well. Encourage this to continue by buying up local foods whenever you see them in the store.

Ideas to Grow On

When fruits and vegetables are plentiful, buy extras to can or freeze so you can enjoy the local freshness even in the dead of winter.

Locavores

There are all sorts of clubs and clever names for people who enjoy and adhere to a diet of mostly locally grown foods: *locavores* and *100-mile dieters* are two of the most common. Have some fun with it. Once you discover a few great sources for local foods, start to integrate as many of them into your everyday diet as possible. Maybe have a "Loving Local Foods Day" once a month and eat *only* foods that were grown and produced within fifty or a hundred miles of your home. Throw a dinner party and encourage guests to bring an appetizer or dessert made from in-season, locally grown foods. You'll be surprised at what you can come up with.

Of course, certain foods are nearly impossible for most people to get locally. Foods like salt and other spices, baking soda, wheat and other grains, and the baked goods and ingredients derived from them may not be grown in your region. But you should be able to find eggs, meat, fruits, vegetables, and many dairy products like milk, cheese, and yogurt from close-by sources.

Grow Your Own

Of course, the absolute best way to get fresh and local foods is to grow them yourself. When I was young, our two huge gardens brimmed with a great variety of fruits and vegetables. When it was in season, we ate most meals from our gardens, and in the winter we continued to enjoy our harvests through foods we had canned and frozen.

Today I don't have the space or the luxury of being home enough to grow many foods for my husband and myself. This is why I rely so heavily on our CSA. But I do always grow a select few vegetables and a variety of herbs: basil, oregano, thyme, sage, chives, parsley, rosemary, and tea herbs like comfrey, chamomile, mint, and echinacea. I do this not because I can get whole meals from my modest garden patch and containers, but because I believe that foods taste better when you've labored over them. And dishes always have more flavor when they've been seasoned with just-picked herbs.

It doesn't matter how much space you have. I took advantage of a small patch of earth along the kitchen wall of our house. And I put other things in pots and containers on an outdoor potting table and the patio. If you have a patch of land, plant some vegetables and a small herb garden. If you have only a few pots, do one full of lettuces and another full of herbs. If you only have a windowsill, plant a few herbs in small pots. The amount of space you have really doesn't matter, what matters most is what you plant (plant what you like to eat!) and how you grow it (without chemical fertilizers). Get the kids involved. One of the best lessons you can teach your children is where food comes from, so that they grow up understanding that a tomato doesn't come from a can on a grocery store shelf, but from a vine that grew and ripened its fruit in the sun.

I d e a s   t o   G r o w   O n

Grow only those foods that your family enjoys eating. If you grow what you like to eat, you're more likely to tend it and to cook with it.

When you have fresh ingredients, whose flavors are so abundant, meals don't need to be complex. One night I tossed together a few diced tomatoes and chopped basil—both locally grown—two cloves of garlic, and a pinch of salt. I simmered the mixture for about ten minutes in a skillet before pouring the sauce over a whole grain pasta. It was a tremendously good dinner, full of flavor, with so few ingredients, and prepared in well under twenty minutes.

Surround yourself with good foods and the inspiration will come.

Shopping

Shopping the grocery store these days can be tricky. Whether you shop at a supermarket or one of the big-box stores, it's easy to be tempted by the dedicated aisles of cereals, chips, sodas, snack foods, cookies, and other nutrition-challenged foods. When you shop instead at a combination of farmers' markets and smaller independent natural foods stores, there may be less choice but there's also less temptation.

There are two things that I recommend to people when it comes to grocery shopping: shop the perimeter and shop often.

Shopping the Perimeter

Think about the layout of your grocery store. The produce is probably at one end on an outer wall, and the frozen and refrigerated foods are at another end, also on outside walls. The middle section of the store is reserved partly for cleaning products and paper goods, while the majority of it is filled with packaged and processed foods (I use the term "food" lightly here). These range from cereals, crackers, and canned foods to boxed cake mixes, diet cookies, and soft drinks. Where once there was a small section of an aisle dedicated to breakfast cereal, there are now stores where entire aisles are full of sugary o's and enriched flakes. Where once it was easy to walk in and come out with the fifteen items on your grocery list, now you're tempted by the onslaught of new products claiming they can make your brain smarter, your skin brighter, your body leaner, your cholesterol lower, and, though they won't tell you this one, your pocketbook thinner. People who shop these massive grocery stores come home with foods they never intended to buy, because they lingered too long in the wrong aisles or were tempted by the promises screaming to them from packages on every shelf.

Ideas to Grow On

Try leaving your cart at the end of the aisle to avoid filling up with unneeded foods.

If you must shop this sort of store, stick to the perimeter as much as possible. Forget the habit of going up and down each aisle. Instead head immediately for the produce section, where you'll fill your cart with nature's bounty. Next head to the refrigerated case for your milk, eggs, cheeses, and other chilled necessities. Roll through the frozen section for things you might need here. And finally, quickly grab only what you *need* from the other aisles. If you're able to (if you don't have a toddler riding along with you), leave your cart at the end of the aisle and just walk yourself up to grab the items that you need. Without your cart there as a catchall, you'll be less likely to grab food items that you don't actually want or need.

Shopping Often

The second rule of thumb in grocery store shopping is to shop often. I know too many people who do a once-weekly Sunday afternoon trip to the grocery. Or worse still, a biweekly trip. They get all of their produce and packaged and frozen foods in one trip. But within days the produce is gone or going bad, leaving them with only packaged or frozen foods to last them until the next designated shopping day rolls around.

Instead, the way I shop is to hit my markets on a daily or every-other-day basis. I buy the foods I immediately need and nothing else. This way we always have fresh produce in the house and I can shop for foods that will inspire the meals I make that night or the next. When you get into the habit of shopping often, you'll find that trips into the grocery store no longer take hours upon hours. They become efficient in the time spent and the foods that you buy. Produce doesn't go bad and you don't stock up on unnecessary foods for fear you'll run out. You buy what you need when you need it.

> **The Four Rules of Healthy Shopping**
>
> 1. Shop the perimeter.
>
> 2. Shop frequently.
>
> 3. Know how to decipher labels.
>
> 4. Read the packages.

Label Hunting—Reading Between the Lines

Shopping the grocery store today can be a little like reading the menu at a fine French restaurant, full of superlatives painting pictures of happy cows and meandering chickens. But do package claims always tell the truth about what is under the cellophane wrapper or inside the cardboard carton? They *often* do, but, unfortunately, not always. Here is a look at some of the more common labels and how to decipher the truthfulness of them.

> *Greenwashing* is a phrase applied when a company or group unjustly claims an environmental virtue. As more and more consumers look for environmental and sustainable products, it's a marketing technique more frequently employed, and one the consumer needs to be increasingly on the lookout for.

Organic Animal Products—When it comes to animal products (beef, chicken, eggs, dairy), you have two primary choices: organic and natural. We've already talked about organic for most food items, but it's a little more involved when an animal comes into the picture. The term "organic," if used with a regulated USDA ORGANIC label, means that the animal was fed a 100 percent organic diet and was raised without the use of any antibiotics or synthetic hormones. Antibiotics are given to animals on conventional farms to prevent and treat disease (often a result of being raised in close confinement), and synthetic hormones are administered to encourage quick maturation, and, in the case of cows, quick and maximum production of milk.

The hormone used for cows is called Recombinant Bovine Growth Hormone, also known as rBGH or rBST. Many countries, the United States aside, have banned the sale of rBGH milk because it's suspected to pose serious dangers to human health and may jeopardize the general welfare of dairy cows.

Eating organic beef or drinking organic milk ensures that you are not ingesting these avoidable hormones and antibiotics. And it also means that you're not taking in any unnecessary chemicals by drinking milk from a cow who was fed a meal that was sprayed with chemical fertilizers and pesticides. From an environmental perspective, that's great news as well. It means that countless acres of grain and corn were spared chemical sprays in order to raise organic feed for these organic cows.

Eating organic meat can also reduce your risk of coming into contact with mad cow disease, because one regulation of organic meat is that the cow was not given a feed made from animal by-products. This is another example of buying organic for what *isn't* in a product, rather than what is.

In a simple sense, organic is your safest choice, especially if you don't know the origin of the product. If you're buying your milk or chicken or eggs from a grocery store rather than from Farmer John down the street, by choosing a product with that green and white USDA ORGANIC label you know what you're getting.

Natural Animal Products—Your second choice, when it comes to animal products, is to buy natural meat and dairy items. "Natural" typically means that it was raised without the use of hormones or antibiotics, but probably not fed an all-organic diet. Unfortunately, you can't fully assume any of this to be true when you see the word "natural" on a label, because it's a largely unregulated term. But seeing the word on a food package is reason to pick up the item and read a little further. If the grower raised their animals without antibiotics or growth hormones, they'll certainly say so on the label. Some producers like to be clever with their labels, like "We raise happy cows that are spared from antibiotics or rBGH," so read closely.

Reenie, whom you met earlier in this chapter, could see early on that her family of three was going to be consuming a lot of dairy (they're big fans of yogurt, milk, and cheese), so she committed to buying only organic or natural dairy and meat products. This was the first change she made on her grocery list, before forgoing conventional fruits and vegetables in favor of organic alternatives.

Antibiotic Free—About 25 million pounds of antibiotics are given to cattle, pigs, and chickens every year to encourage growth and prevent disease. The diseases the farmer works to prevent are often stress-induced because of the animal's poor living conditions. All told, animals on farms are given seven pounds of antibiotics for every one pound used to treat human infections. There is widespread concern with the part that farm antibiotics play in promoting antibiotic-resistant bacteria in humans.

The term "Antibiotic Free" is allowed by the USDA on labels of meat or poultry products if and when sufficient documentation exists that the animals were raised without antibiotics.

Hormone Free—The label "Hormone Free" should only ever be seen on packages of beef, since, according to the USDA, hormones are not allowed in the raising of hogs or poultry. Therefore if you see the claim "No hormones added" or "Hormone Free" on the label of pork or poultry, it should be followed by the phrase "Federal regulations prohibit the use of hormones."

On beef packages, the label "No hormones added" is allowed if and when sufficient documentation exists proving the claim. This claim, like "Antibiotic Free," is regulated by the USDA.

The hormone most often used, as mentioned in the section on organic animal products, is called Recombinant Bovine Growth Hormone, also known as rBGH or rBST, the name-brand version made by the agricultural corporation Monsanto. The hormone was approved for use in milk production in 1993 and is used as a way to increase a cow's production of milk by as much as a gallon per day. But taking the hormone often means that the cow needs to be given extra antibiotics, and milk from such cows has been linked to cancer and other issues.

Avoiding milk from cows treated with hormones is as simple as reading the label. And it's a step I recommend every person take, especially if they are new to the world of natural and organic foods.

Worth noting is the fact that many dairies are now giving up rBGH following pushback from consumers. As groceries (mainstream as well as niche) begin demanding more and more hormone-free milk for their knowledgeable consumers, dairies are altering their practices to meet this order. This is a vivid example of how your buying decisions *can* influence production on a much larger scale than you may realize.

Seafood Options—Sustainable and Organic—Because there are currently no USDA-approved standards for organic as it relates to aquatic animals, including fish and shellfish, it is important to read labels and to ask questions at the fish counter to be sure you are choosing a seafood option that was either farm-raised in a clean manner (this might be called "organically farmed") or wild-caught sustainably. Because of dwindling supplies of many of our favorite edible aquatic creatures, a good deal of the seafood we eat today is farm-raised. This is acceptable as long as it is done in a clean (hormone-, antibiotic-, and preservative-free) and environmentally friendly (with water purity standards, wildlife and habitat conservation, etc.) manner.

Some seafood companies are sourcing their fish and shrimp from organic farms in countries where the production *is* certified according to one of the European organic aquaculture standards, and until the USDA forms their organic standards for seafood, this is an important thing to embrace. Packaging in the United States will read "Made with organic shrimp" or "organic salmon" or something along those lines. When seafood is farmed organically, it generally means the fish or shrimp is hormone and antibiotic free, and that it was raised on organic feed in clean water ponds that weren't overstocked. All of this indicates that these fish ponds do not pollute the oceans or surrounding areas with waste and other by-products.

Fifteen years ago most people had never heard of *aquaculture*, but today, with a steady demand for healthy seafood, the domestication of seafood for human consumption is in place to keep grocery stores and restaurants supplied with fresh fish and shellfish. In fact, seafood farming is a growing reality that will take a tremendous amount of pressure off the oceans' dwindling stocks of wild fish and will relieve some of the environmental damage done by trawling and other seafood-harvesting methods.

The National Organic Standards Board (NOSB) has recommended to the USDA a set of regulations governing organic aquaculture and is in the process of collecting public and industry input before moving into the final process of making it law. Regulations are expected to go into effect in 2009, at which time you will be able to find seafood bearing the USDA ORGANIC seal.

I d e a s   t o   G r o w   O n

On fish, you'll find labels for fresh or frozen. "Fresh" means the fish never went below 26 degrees Fahrenheit. But because fish is often flash-frozen right on the boat, you should feel free to embrace frozen fish.

The other option, aside from organic seafood, is to buy "Sustainable Seafood," which can apply to either farmed or wild-caught fish. The Marine Stewardship Council has a seal, licensed by seafood producers, that encourages environmentally responsible management of wild fisheries throughout the world, helping to guarantee the longevity of our fish supply. Often the gathering methods of wild-caught fish are destructive to our environment, like trawling or dredging, which can dig up the ocean floor and destroy natural habitats. Other fishing methods result in too much wasted by-catch. By asking the appropriate questions at the fish counter, you can be sure the fish was caught in a sustainable manner or farm-raised in a sustainable, clean, and possibly organic farm.

An organization called FishWise has created a system of green (best choice), yellow (okay), and red (avoid) tagging for retailers at their seafood counter, according to the Monterey Bay Aquarium's Seafood Watch ratings of seafoods below. This list can also be downloaded as a wallet-sized tip sheet that you can carry with you when you go to the grocery store or a restaurant. Find the guide at *www.seafoodwatch.org.*

Monterey Bay Aquarium's Seafood Watch
Sustainable Seafood National Guide

GREEN/Best Choices	RED/Avoid
Arctic Char (farmed)	Chilean Seabass/Toothfish
Barramundi (U.S. farmed)	Cod: Atlantic
Catfish (U.S. farmed)	Crab: King (imported)
Clams (farmed)	Flounders, Soles (Atlantic)
Cod: Pacific (Alaska longline)	Groupers
Crab: Dungeness, Stone	Halibut: Atlantic
Halibut: Pacific	Lobster: Spiny (Caribbean imported)
Lobster: Spiny (U.S.)	Mahi Mahi/Dolphinfish (imported)
Mussels (farmed)	Marlin: Blue, Striped
Oysters (farmed)	Monkfish
Pollock (Alaska wild)	Orange Roughy
Salmon (Alaska wild)	Rockfish (Pacific)
Scallops: Bay (farmed)	Salmon (farmed, including Atlantic)
Striped Bass (farmed or wild)	Sharks
Sturgeon, Caviar (farmed)	Shrimp (imported farmed or wild)
Tilapia (U.S. farmed)	Snapper: Red
Trout: Rainbow (farmed)	Sturgeon, Caviar (imported wild)
Tuna: Albacore (U.S., British Columbia troll/pole)	Swordfish (imported)
	Tuna: Albacore, Bigeye, Yellowfin (longline)
Tuna: Skipjack (troll/pole)	Tuna: Bluefin

Used with permission of the Monterey Bay Aquarium Seafood Watch Program.

Free Range—"Free Range" is a label or slogan often seen on eggs, chicken, and other meat. It causes confusion for a lot of people who assume that it means the animals have spent a good part of their lives roaming outside, free to run and ramble as they please. This isn't necessarily the case, though. The

USDA *does* regulate use of the term "free range" on poultry products, directing that the chicken be given access to the outdoors for an "undetermined period each day." It *does not* mean that the chicken is necessarily well traveled or even that she has spent any of her day outside of the coop. The door to the coop may have been open for some time every day, but it's up to the chicken whether she leaves her cozy roost and ventures out. If she was given access to the outdoors, she can be called a free-range chicken. "Free roaming," incidentally, often means the same thing.

Doesn't sound like a label that carries a lot of weight, does it? Don't be too quick to judge. It is, again, a label that implies the best of intentions, and those intentions might be true if you know the producer. If you're buying chicken from a local farmer who claims his birds are free range, ask him how much time they spend outside and then you be the judge.

Cage Free—"Cage Free" is another label you may see on eggs, and it means that the hens were permitted to roam, typically in barns but not necessarily outside. It is not a term regulated by the USDA.

Local—We already touched on the "local" label and the importance of buying it when possible. Buying local cuts down on the harmful emissions caused by transporting foods, often as much as two thousand miles, to your plate and ensures a greater degree of freshness and nutritional value.

You'll find local foods most often in the produce section of your grocery store, and the foods should be clearly marked, often with a large sign that might read "Local squash from Hobby Farm; Prairie City, Oregon" close to it. Many grocery stores also carry shelf-stable foods such as spaghetti sauce, pasta, honey, and soap that are made locally. These foods should also be clearly marked, often with a hangtag on the shelf.

Frozen—"Frozen" is not a hard term to figure out when it's on a package of peas or blueberries. But is it okay to buy? Absolutely! And here's why. Most produce that is picked fresh and delivered fresh to you was picked well before it ripened. The producers, thinking ahead, knew it would take anywhere from two to seven days to reach your plate. If this strawberry, let's say, was picked at its peak ripeness, it would be rotten well before it reached your morning cereal bowl. Instead, it is picked before it has a chance to ripen, then it is either chemically ripened sometime before you buy it or it ripens somewhat on its way to you. When a strawberry is picked for freezing, it is picked at its peak ripeness, right when the color is vibrant and the juices sweet. It is immediately flash-frozen and set aside for the moment you decide to take it home from the freezer shelf and defrost it for a smoothie or a strawberry cobbler. When you do, you are getting a strawberry that is full of the nutrients it developed right at its ripest. Choose frozen organic produce and you're in the money.

Ideas to Grow On

Better even than buying frozen is freezing your own. When your farmers' market is overflowing with strawberries, blueberries, or even tomatoes, buy extra and freeze them. You'll be able to enjoy locally grown produce in the dead of winter.

Biodynamic—Biodynamic agriculture is a method of farming that goes beyond organic regulations, adding another level to nongovernmental certification. You'll find "Biodynamic" on the labels of wine, fruits, vegetables, and some animal products. The Demeter "Biodynamic" label has been monitored by the Demeter organization, the only certifier for biodynamic farms, processors, and products in the United States, since 1928. Biodynamic farming incorporates principles similar to organic farming—goods are produced without synthetic pesticides and fertilizers, without animal by-products, and without genetic engineering—but then goes well beyond. Biodynamic agriculture is considered a "spiritual science," incorporating principles of cosmic rhythm that involve the timing of planting and harvesting according to the sun and moon phases, as well as an added emphasis placed on building the strength of the soil, the relationship of humans to farm animals, and the community of farmers and farm workers.

Fair Trade—"Fair Trade" is a term you'll see on food labels, most frequently in the cases of coffee, tea, and chocolate. It is one of my favorite labels and one that I use as a purchasing decision-maker nearly every time I'm faced with it as an option. Here's how Fair Trade Certified works. Long-term relationships are formed with the farmers and producers of food (or other items like flowers and wine) in developing countries. By doing business directly with the producers and artisans, and thereby bypassing any middle-men, the Fair Trade business can guarantee workers fair wages and safe working conditions. With newfound wages in their pockets and a reason to continue to grow and produce more of their crop or other good, the farmers and producers are empowered and motivated to invest in their businesses, their communities, and the health, educational, and nutritional needs of their families. The "Fair Trade Certified" standards, as regulated by the non-governmental organization TransFair USA, prohibit genetically modified organisms, synthetic chemicals, the deforestation of virgin forests, and soil erosion, and it promotes soil fertility and the conservation of water and other natural resources. In following these practices, Fair Trade businesses protect the environment as well as the people who live in and around it. Aside from food products, you can find non-certified fair trade goods like jewelry, clothing, and other decorative items.

Natural—"Natural" is a term that understandably confuses many people. "Natural" seems to imply very good things but, unlike the word "organic," it is not a regulated term—meaning there is no code of federal regulation governing the use of the word "natural" in food labeling, so it can't always be trusted. Back in the mid-1970s a small group of the larger natural food distributors in the country gathered several times, as my dad tells me (he was there), to try to define what "natural" was. Because of all the gray areas, the task proved too daunting; the issue was eventually abandoned. Unfortunately for consumers, the USDA hasn't had any better luck than the industry, as it's extremely tough to write strict regulating code for that descriptor.

The USDA's Food Safety and Inspection Service does have *some* regulating definition, however general, over use of the word "natural" on meat and poultry packages. With these products you're guaranteed that the meat or poultry in question contains "no artificial ingredients or added color and is

Fair Trade Certified

Fair prices: Democratically organized farmer groups receive a guaranteed minimum floor price and an additional premium for certified organic products. Farmer organizations are also eligible for pre-harvest credit.

Fair labor conditions: Workers on Fair Trade farms enjoy freedom of association, safe working conditions, and living wages. Forced child labor is strictly prohibited.

Direct trade: Importers purchase from Fair Trade producer groups as directly as possible, eliminating unnecessary middlemen and empowering farmers to strengthen their organizations and become competitive players in the global economy.

Democratic and transparent organizations: Fair Trade Certified farmers and farm workers decide democratically how to use their Fair Trade Certified premiums.

Community development: Fair Trade Certified farmers and farm workers invest their premiums in social and business development projects like health care, new schools, quality improvement trainings, and organic certification.

Environmental sustainability: Fair Trade Certified strictly prohibits the use of genetically modified organisms (GMOs), promotes integrated farm management systems that improve soil fertility, and limits the use of harmful agrochemicals in favor of environmentally sustainable farming methods that protect farmers' health and preserve valuable ecosystems for future generations.

only minimally processed," which means it can only be produced in a manner that does not fundamentally alter the raw product. The label may also explain the use of the term "natural" with descriptions such as "no added colorings" or "no artificial ingredients."

Here's what I recommend. When you see the word "natural" on a label, whether it's a package of beef or a box of cookies, take a moment to pick up the package and read further. Find out why the producers felt it was an appropriate description for their food. Is it because they don't use chemicals on their crops or treat their animals with antibiotics? Is it because they use only whole grain wheat in their crackers or unrefined sugar in their cookies or don't use artificial preservatives or flavorings or colorings? If so, these are probably safe products to buy. Seeing the word "natural" on a package, as with many other food labels, is simply a reason to pause and read on, allowing yourself to make an educated decision about the food before you buy it.

What to Avoid

As if all of that isn't complicated enough, I'm going to throw just a few more things into the pot. There are a few key ingredients that you should be able to pick out on a product's label and avoid whenever possible.

Reading Labels—What to Avoid

- High-fructose corn syrup (HFCS)

- Monosodium glutamate (MSG)

- Trans fats

- Genetically modified (GM) foods

High-Fructose Corn Syrup—High-fructose corn syrup is lurking in the strangest and trickiest places these days. It's in sodas, fruit juice beverages, and other sweetened foods like yogurt, but it's also in unlikely foods like ketchup, barbeque sauce, and even bread. As is the case with most foods, there are two reasons to buy or not to buy: health and environmental. The environmental factor of high-fructose corn syrup is interesting. Corn, when grown conventionally as it is for HFCS, requires more fertilizers and insecticides than other crops. So as more and more corn is grown to produce the syrup that Americans have become accustomed to consuming on a daily basis, more agricultural chemicals are being used, polluting our water and soil.

The health effects of consuming HFCS are clearly negative: it leads to an increase in triglyceride (a type of fat) and LDL (bad cholesterol) levels, and has been linked to diabetes, obesity, and metabolic syndrome. The reality is that high-fructose corn syrup is cheap to produce, which is why, as the number one soft drink sweetener, it's so prevalent. Most Americans consume over 130 calories a day, and some as much as 700 calories a day, from HFCS alone. To avoid it or at least cut back on your consumption, start reading labels of packaged and processed foods, and cut back on soft drinks in favor of 100 percent fruit juices instead.

Monosodium Glutamate—Also on the list to avoid is monosodium glutamate, more commonly known as MSG. MSG is a flavor enhancer used in processed meats, canned vegetables, and soup, and probably most commonly, Chinese food. MSG can trigger headaches, heart palpitations, chest pains, and shortness of breath. Decades ago the FDA ruled it as an ingredient "generally recognized as safe," but many disagree and controversy certainly still surrounds it. To avoid the issue, many Chinese restaurants now advertise their MSG-free menu. According to FDA regulations, when monosodium glutamate is added to foods, it must be listed as a separate ingredient on labels. (Many people only know MSG from its abbreviation; it is important that you know the full name and read ingredients lists before making purchases.)

Saturated or Trans Fats—With coronary heart disease one of the leading causes of death in this country, it's not difficult to get on board with avoiding trans fats in your daily diet. Trans fats are found as an ingredient in foods made with or fried in partially hydrogenated oils, such as crackers, cookies, pie crusts, and other snack foods, as well as margarines and shortenings. Trans fats have been shown to raise levels of the bad (LDL) cholesterol and lower levels of good (HDL) cholesterols. Eating foods prepared with trans fats has been shown to contribute to heart disease and stroke and has been associated with a higher risk of developing type 2 diabetes.

Also called "partially hydrogenated oils," trans fats are created when hydrogen is added to liquid vegetable oils to make them more solid. Trans fats have been favored by food companies because they are inexpensive to produce, have a long shelf life, and give foods a desired texture and taste. Fast-food restaurants have used trans fats for years because oils *with* trans fats can be used over and over in a deep fryer.

Since 2006, food manufacturers have been required to list trans fats on the nutrition panel of packaged foods, making them easy to avoid. Pay special attention when shopping for chips, crackers, cookies, and other snack items. California has banned trans fats, as have the cities of New York and Philadelphia, with others sure to follow suit. The anti–trans fats consumer movement has paid off nationally as well, as many fast-food chains and food producers like McDonald's and Kraft, to name just a few, have moved toward eliminating trans fats altogether.

Genetically Modified Foods—The four primary genetically modified (GM) plants are soy, corn, canola, and cotton. GM foods are sometimes also called GE (genetically engineered) or "nanofoods." They are modified to be able to stand up to strong weed killers and to make them resistant to insects. And though a good deal of controversy still surrounds GM foods, a growing list of accounts of allergies and reactions to them is enough to make one wary. In the United Kingdom, allergies relating to soy (the ingredient most associated with GM foods) increased dramatically soon after GM foods first came to market. Because genetically modified soy contains a certain protein not found in natural soy, it's not all that surprising that a skin-prick test performed on men and women produced allergic-type reactions to GM soy but not to natural soy. While many benefits are attributed to the genetic modification of foods, the simple fact is that, in spite of assertions to the contrary from chemical and seed suppliers, it's just too early in the study of GM foods to know what the long-term effects will be. Even so, according to most estimates around 70 percent of the processed foods (cookies, crackers, soup, soda) in supermarkets today contain genetically modified ingredients. While there are ongoing conversations about whether GM foods should be called out as such on food labels, the USDA prohibits the use of genetically modified food ingredients in organic foods. So one sure way to avoid GM foods is to buy organic, especially in foods containing corn, soy, and canola or cottonseed oils.

Conservation

The best diet in the kitchen certainly *starts* with the foods you eat—moving toward greater amounts of organic and local foods that are grown sustainably and are free of undesirable ingredients like high-fructose corn syrup, MSG, trans fats, genetically modified foods, and pesticides. But another extremely important diet involves your activities in the kitchen and weaning yourself of excessive water and energy use. Below are a few ways to cut back on both so you and your home can grow healthier together.

1. Skip the pre-rinse. *Consumer Reports* advises that pre-rinsing your dishes before placing them in the dishwasher is no longer necessary, especially if you have a newer dishwasher model. You can save time and up to twenty gallons of water for each load of dishes. By making sure your dishwasher is completely full before you run it, and opening the door to let your dishes dry on their own, you'll be maximizing your water and energy usage every time you run your "kitchen's best friend."

2. Your refrigerator can be the biggest energy sucker in the home, but it doesn't have to be. To optimize its energy use, make sure your refrigerator is reasonably but not too full. Too much stuff can prevent it from functioning properly, but leave it too empty and the fridge has to work extra hard to do its job. If your refrigerator tends toward bachelor-style empty shelves, fill empty containers and pitchers with water to help use up some space. Use that water for drinking and cooking later on. Make sure hot foods have cooled before you stow them in the fridge, and be sure both the refrigerator and freezer are at their proper temperature settings—the fridge should be set at 37 degrees and the freezer at 3—for an optimally efficient machine.

3. When it comes to packing up your leftovers, there are a couple of options that are better than the plastic standbys, for your health and the planet's. Plastics can leach harsh chemicals into your food, especially when food is reheated in the plastic. Most plastic containers have a number inside a triangle on the bottom, and in general, numbers 1, 2, 4, and 5 are safer than numbers 3, 6, and 7. A better option is to store your leftovers in glass, ceramic, or stoneware containers with lids. While you're at it, avoid the temptation to use a plastic bag or paper towel for every little kitchen job. Opt for wax paper bags and reusable cloth towels instead.

4. Go vegetarian, for at least one day out of the week or one week per month. Farmers require forty times as much water to produce a pound of beef as they do to grow a pound of potatoes. Cows are responsible for the consumption of a lot of antibiotics, and they produce a *lot* of methane, which is the second worst greenhouse gas. Eating only vegetables for at least a portion of your diet means you are asking less of the environment and its most valuable resources.

5. And my favorite tip—start a reusable bag collection and carry them every time you go to the grocery store, farmers' market, or (for the super committed) department store. Americans use close to 100 billion plastic bags every year and less than one percent of these are recycled! Plastic bags are made from polyethylene, a petroleum by-product and nonrenewable resource. You could drive a car for a mile and use the same amount of oil it takes to make less than fifteen plastic bags. Plastic bags sit forever in the landfill, and as they begin to break down they release tiny fragments that work their way into our waterways and slowly begin destroying our aquatic life. Larger pieces of plastic trash make their way on their own into our oceans and rivers. There is currently a trash island, mainly plastics, in the middle of the Pacific Ocean that is the size of Texas. All of this trash floated there, swirled together, and has remained there because it has no other place to go. And the worst part is, this trash island is a killer being. Every year about a million seabirds and a hundred thousand marine

mammals and sea turtles are killed by ingestion of or entanglement in plastics.

What about paper bags? They're often made from virgin-growth trees (ancient trees that are cut down just to be turned into paper towels, bags, and other disposable paper products), and even when they are manufactured from recycled paper, their manufacture requires four times the amount of energy used to produce a plastic bag. Plus only 20 percent of paper bags are recycled.

The answer to the paper-versus-plastic riddle is neither. A reusable bag of any kind uses little resources, especially when spread out over all of its many uses, and wins the battle hands down.

If you must use a disposable bag, choose one that you can reuse a time or two. Many people use plastic bags as garbage can liners, and so on.

Top Five Tips for an Efficient Kitchen

1. Skip the pre-rinse.

2. Stock an efficient refrigerator.

3. Pack leftovers safely.

4. Choose vegetables over meat.

5. Use reusable bags, again and again.

Taking Action in the Kitchen

When you start shopping for healthier, safer food products, you'll need to build extra time into your trips to the grocery store for label reading. Picking out turkey for sandwiches may not be as simple as selecting the honey-roasted turkey breast on special. You'll want to read the package labels to see if there are additives and how the animal was raised. You'll want to pause over the apple display to decide whether the organic apples or the locally grown ones are the right choice. You'll want to pick up the cartons of eggs and decipher the verbiage to determine which were raised most humanely with the greatest amount of nutrients intact. All of this takes time at first, but is well worth it.

While Reenie's transformation eventually went well beyond the kitchen, the hardest part for her was the constant overhaul of the foods they eat. "Sometimes life is so busy," she says, "between working and raising a family. But it does pay off to stop and think about the consequences of what you're putting into your body." What Reenie has experienced is an extremely important lesson in the transformation toward living a healthier life: understanding that what you eat has an amazing ability to feed and nourish your body or to profoundly harm it.

Reenie now knows what to look for when she shops for food—what's good for her family and what isn't. She and her husband are healthy, and given that they're constantly chasing a happy, rambunctious toddler around the house, it's safe to assume that her daughter Logan is feeling good too. For Reenie, the greatest surprise in changing her food habits came in the opportunity to share her reasons for certain food choices with her family. When she was growing up, her family thought junk food was part of the food pyramid. Now that her mom is helping in the daily care of Logan, Reenie is constantly explaining to her mom why she switched certain foods in Logan's diet, like conventional milk to organic milk, and chose the organic macaroni and cheese over the old standby. In order to explain these things, Reenie must first understand the reasons herself.

But beyond these extremely important food lessons, Reenie has also learned another important lesson. It's the "go with the flow" mantra, and in my opinion it is one of the most important lessons anyone can learn when making changes in their life to live more naturally. Here's how it goes: *Do what you can, when you can.* Make one change this week and another next week or next month. Do not open your cupboards, berate yourself for all of the wrong choices you've been making, and then vow to pull each item out, read the label, and if it doesn't meet your new set of standards throw it in the trash. This will be overwhelming (and wasteful) and is probably not a task you'll stick with. Instead, when something runs out, consider more thoughtfully what you will replace it with. The next time you go to the store, think about which items you could get from the farmers' market instead and read closely the labels of the items you do put in your cart. And when you find yourself at a friend's house for dinner or a kid's birthday party, don't worry too much over the foods they are serving. Pick your way around things you don't want to put into your body, but be a little flexible. No one likes an ungracious guest. Use this opportunity to tell others about the changes you've been making and inspire them to do the same. But be careful not to soapbox or alienate yourself. While we are what we eat, we don't want them to think we're eating sour grapes.

In the Bathroom

The Bathrooms of My Childhood

Today people do a lot of things besides just the expected in the bathroom. Thirty-some percent of us read our mail in there (paper or email), almost 20 percent listen to music, 15 percent talk on the phone, and 3 percent of us watch TV. In fact, according to some estimates, 88 percent of people use at least one electronic device in the bathroom. Can you imagine electronics in the bathroom of your childhood? I can't. My childhood bathroom was simple—simple but controlled. We had a family potty mantra: *If it's yellow, let it mellow; if it's brown, flush it down.* (I'm sure this isn't the first time you've heard that phrase, and please don't think less of me for it, because it does still make me giggle every time I say it out loud.) We did a lot of things to conserve water in our house: we turned it off when we brushed, we shared bathwater—just adding more hot water before the next person got in—and we avoided flushing when not completely necessary. From an early age, we learned that a little tinkle was no reason to flush and that doing so would mean wasting precious gallons of water. If, for example, I went number one at 10 a.m. and the bowl had been empty when my little five-year-old self skipped up to it, I'd "let it mellow." Someone else might come along a half hour or hour later and do the same. The water in the bowl is still pretty yellow. By person three, however, the water starts to turn a distinctively darker color, now beginning to resemble "brown," and this was the signal that it was now the appropriate time to flush.

Of course, a number two instantly turned the water brown and required

an immediate flush. Failure to do so generally resulted in bickering and fin-
ger wagging from siblings.

I remember when we first built our simple "kids'" bathroom. We only had
two bathrooms—the main and "master" bath downstairs and the second,
shared among four kids, bath upstairs. When we built the house, we did most
of the tile work ourselves. Or, I should say, my parents did. I remember
vividly when the upstairs bath was being tiled. And while I was too young to
actually lay the tiles myself, I could help peel the paper backing off the mesh
of smaller tiles that made up the twelve-inch-by-twelve-inch squares. I
hoarded these paper backings because I had a plan for them. While most of
my friends had special diapers for their Cabbage Patch dolls, I had a doll but
no diapers. These flimsy and, in my memory, somewhat waxy paper squares
were perfect. I had watched my mom diaper my younger brother enough
times to know that by folding the sides in toward the middle I could get it to
look like a diaper. I'd lay my doll on top so it covered her bottom and front,
then safety pin the sides together. I was a recycler even then.

As my stack of paper diapers grew, the tiles covering the floor also grew
until the bathroom was soon wall to wall in an intricate blue and white pat-
tern. The walls were painted pale blue, and a toilet, tub, and sink cabinet
were installed. A small wall cabinet was hung and beside it, eventually, a tiny
mirror. The most interesting thing about all of this, as I look back, was the
placement of the mirror. Walk into any bathroom and the mirror is almost always over the sink, so that as you wash and dry your hands you can scruti-
nize your face, your hair, the arch of your eyebrows, or, I don't know, maybe
the curve of your lip. Our mirror, however, was on the side wall. As we stood
at the sink to wash our hands or brush our teeth, instead of looking at ourselves, we looked out a window at the front drive and the woods beyond. We
were surrounded by nature in that home, even as we spent time in one of the
most intimate rooms in the house.

In designing the bathroom this way, the focus was placed not on ourselves
but on the world beyond our own. In my bathroom today I have two side-
by-side sinks connected by a countertop. There *are* cabinets with mirrors
above each, but between the two cabinets is a window. As I get ready in the

morning, I can look out that window for the birds that I hear chirping and watch as winter makes way for spring.

Bathroom Conservation

Which is why, as I stand in the bathroom, I think of the countless reasons why we must conserve water, and the many, many ways that we can. Although water covers about 70 percent of our planet's surface, less than one percent of that is safe and available for human use. That one percent must be shared among countries and continents and between the many residential, agricultural, commercial, industrial, and environmental needs we all have. In the United States alone we demand 26 billion gallons of water every single day. Thirteen percent of that is for residential use, with each person in the country averaging as much as a hundred gallons of water per day.

I d e a s   t o   G r o w   O n

Think before you flush. In many parts of this world, families must survive on a daily ration of water equal to one flush of a standard American toilet.

Because water consumption has increased threefold across the planet in the last fifty years, people everywhere are suddenly feeling the pinch. In the United States over the last five years, nearly every region of the country has experienced water shortages. According to the Environmental Protection Agency, at least thirty-six states are expected to experience local, regional, or statewide water shortages by the year 2013.

Saving water, whether in the bathroom, the kitchen, or anywhere else in the house, is necessary for two reasons: to preserve our collective health and to safeguard your personal finances. By cutting back, you'll end up saving money on your water and gas or electric bills. How? Just connect the dots between energy use and water use—hot or cold. According to the U.S. EPA, running your faucet for five minutes uses nearly the same amount of energy as letting a sixty-watt bulb run for fourteen *hours*. Just as you see the savings add up when you raise (in the summer) or lower (in the winter) your thermostat a few degrees, you should save a few bucks on your utility bills when you use less water.

As for health-saving benefits, when water levels in reservoirs and aquifers (underground layers of gravel, sand, or other permeable materials from which groundwater can be extracted) become too low, concentrations of pollutants and other natural contaminants increase, which can pose a threat to human health.

Conserving Water in the Shower

Here's a question for you: How long are you in the shower each day? Three minutes? Five? Ten? If you're like many people, you have no idea. But there are three primary areas in the bathroom where you can cut down your water usage, and the most obvious is the shower.

A standard showerhead uses anywhere from four to seven gallons of water per minute. Assuming you take a ten-minute shower, and you have a very average five-gallon/minute showerhead, you're using fifty gallons of water per shower. That's a lot, by the way. Now, let's say you can cut your shower time in half. You'll be saving twenty-five gallons every shower. Twenty-five gallons of water every single shower! If we figure that you're showering once a day, that's over nine thousand gallons of water saved every year.

Set a Timer

So how do you start cutting back? Sometime before your next shower find a stopwatch or timer. An old egg or kitchen timer will work beautifully. Before you step into the shower, hit start. Go about your normal routine, being careful not to speed your way through. When you finish, hit stop. This is your base time. Now the next time you shower, you'll set the timer to go off (*bzzzzzzz*) just one minute shy of your base time. Keep an eye on the clock so you don't get caught with shampoo in your hair when the alarm bell sounds.

Over the course of the next week, work your time down so that you're comfortably showering in five minutes or less.

The easiest way to keep your eye on the minute hand while you lather and rinse is to pick up one of the new nifty shower timers that suction-sticks to your shower wall.

Average Water Use

50–75 gallons—water used per day per person

400 gallons—indoor water use per day for an average family of four

50–75 percent—percentage of indoor water use that occurs in the bathroom

4–7 gallons/minute—amount a standard showerhead uses

2.5 gallons/minute—amount a low-flow showerhead uses

0.5–5 gallons/minute—amount an average faucet uses

1 gallon/minute—amount a faucet aerator reduces

4.5–7 gallons/flush—amount a pre-1980 toilet uses

3.5 gallons/flush—amount a 1980s (1980–1992) toilet uses

1.6 gallons/flush (or less)—amount a low-consumption toilet uses

---

Install a Low-Flow Head

Swapping out your old conventional showerhead for a low-flow model is another fantastic way to cut water consumption while you shower. A typical low-flow showerhead uses two and a half gallons of water or less per minute. So if your showerhead is using three or more gallons per minute, it's a prime candidate for a proxy. You can find easily installed low-flow showerheads at your area hardware store.

To find out how much water your shower flows, place a bucket under the showerhead and let it run for one minute. Then measure how many gallons have been dispensed. Try placing a standard five-gallon bucket under the showerhead. You might be surprised to see it overflowing after a minute of the shower running.

Ideas to Grow On

Skip the bath and opt for a five-minute shower. A full bathtub can use as much as fifty to seventy gallons of water. If you still prefer to take baths, be sure to plug the drain immediately, adjust the water temperature as the tub fills, and turn off the water when the tub is only half full.

Conserving Water in the Toilet

Believe it or not, toilets use more water than any other appliance in the home. They account for over 25 percent of in-home water consumption. If your toilet was purchased before 1992, you could save thousands of gallons every year by replacing the toilet with a newer model.

In fact, a family of four using an older, less efficient toilet will use an extra 14,000 to 25,000 gallons of water each year.

Toilets are rated based on their "gallons per flush" (gpf). Most toilets today are fairly water efficient, but models manufactured before 1980 used (and if they're in your house they still do use) as much as 5 to 7 gallons of water per flush. In 1992 "low-flow toilets" became the standard, with the federal government requiring that toilets use 1.6 gallons per flush of water or less. If you're unsure how much water your toilet uses, check under the tank's lid.

There are even more efficient models available today. High-efficiency toilets use between 1.2 and 1.3 gpf, while dual-flush toilets do one better. If you've never seen a dual-flush, they're clever. Many industrial buildings have the type where the lever on the side of the toilet goes *up* for liquid waste and *down* for solid waste. It's a little awkward because you have to think before you use your foot to press *down* on the lever, but it works. Other dual-flush models have two buttons on the lid. You press one for "number one" and both buttons if you've gone "number two." Clever—one for one, two for two. It's easy enough for a toddler to remember.

The beauty of these dual-flush toilets is that they have two different gallons-per-flush rates, 1.6 gpf for solids and between .8 and 1.1 gpf for liquids.

Make Your Toilet Flush Less

If, after a check under the lid, you find that you have an older, less efficient toilet model but are unable to replace it immediately, there is a simple way to make your toilet more efficient.

Take a water bottle, a small milk jug, or any other plastic container, fill it halfway with pebbles and the rest of the way with water, then put the cap back on. (The pebbles serve only to make the container heavy enough so that it won't float to the top of your toilet's water tank.) Then submerge the container into the tank of your toilet. This helps to actually displace the water so it takes less to fill up the tank, thereby using less water per flush.

Stop the Leak

A simple toilet leak can waste as much as two hundred gallons of water per day. That's the same amount of water used to wash ten loads of laundry in an Energy Star efficient washing machine.

But leaking toilets are hard to detect, because an easy-to-spot puddle on the floor isn't usually the indicator. Instead, the leak typically happens between the toilet tank and the toilet bowl, releasing a steady drip of water into the bowl and thus down the toilet's drain. To check for a drip of this kind, drop about ten drops of food coloring into the toilet tank. After ten minutes take a look in the toilet bowl. If the coloring has crept from the tank to the bowl, your toilet has a leak.

To fix it, you'll probably need to replace the flapper valve or flush valve. This is a doable project for an adept DYIer, or one for the plumber.

Conserving Water in the Sink

A typical bathroom sink faucet uses anywhere from two to six gallons of water per minute. Leave it running while you brush and you could be wasting hundreds of gallons a month. Turning off the water while brushing your teeth is not a new concept. We've been told to do that for years and years, but sometimes bad habits form and bad habits are hard to break. The same goes for shaving or washing your hands or face. Best to shut it off while you lather, brush, or shave.

Ideas to Grow On

Look for "WaterSense" appliances for the bathroom. A label regulated by the Environmental Protection Agency, it indicates products that are 20 percent more water efficient than counterparts.

Stop the Drip, Slow the Flow

The slow, steady drip of a leaky faucet can wreak havoc on your sleep at night, but also on your water bill. A leaky faucet can waste gallons over the course of an hour or a day, depending on the frequency of the drip. No matter how steady the drip, it's water wasted. It's best to call a plumber and put a stop to it. If you suspect that your faucet is a guzzler, look for an easy-to-install faucet aerator that will cut down on the amount of water flowing from the faucet. Or replace it with a new "WaterSense"-labeled faucet. If every home in America installed a WaterSense faucet or aerator, we would save over 60 billion gallons of water each year.

Personal Products Overhaul

Truth or dare? Truth? Do you peek in the vanity or medicine cabinet when you use someone else's bathroom? Be honest, because most do. I have to admit, I sometimes do. It's not because I'm curious what pharmaceuticals someone is taking; that wouldn't even interest me. It's because I wonder what types of products they're using. Are they safe and clean products, free of chemical ingredients, or are they conventional cosmetics loaded with perfumes, parabens, and petroleums?

Long ago I quit buying the majority of my hair and beauty products at the drugstore, salon, or mall. Gone are the days of grazing the cosmetic counters at department stores. I'll be honest and say that I flirted with this type of shopping right out of college, but it didn't last. As more and more research surfaced about the harmful nature of some of the newer ingredients, I went back to the shampoos of my childhood. Today the products I buy to care for my physical person are as carefully thought out as the foods I buy to care for my internal health. And more often than not, they're all found in the same place—my local natural foods store.

It is certainly worth noting, though, that as more and more mainstream companies begin cleaning up their products, the offerings at conventional beauty stores and cosmetic departments are improving dramatically.

Whether you're shopping at a health food store or with an eagle eye in a mainstream beauty department, picking out natural cosmetics, body lotions, and hair care products can be confusing and daunting. This is because the key benefit to natural products often is what the manufacturers *don't* put in them. But how do you know what to avoid? And how are you supposed to remember it all when you're standing in the aisle surrounded by people who look like they live their lives in these stores?

Maybe what makes it all so confusing is that you're not sure when to trust a label. Especially when nearly every product out there is trying to stake some sort of "natural" claim. Who is regulating all of this?

Ideas to Grow On

Look to your health food store for a great selection of personal care products.

Smart Shopping

One of the most confusing things in natural cosmetics today is the use of the term "organic." The USDA (but not the FDA) regulates the term "organic" as it applies to *agricultural products* in cosmetics and body care and personal care products. If a personal product (cosmetic, body care, or personal care product) contains agricultural ingredients (farmed ingredients) that meet the USDA's National Organic Program's organic production, handling, processing, and labeling standards, it may be certified organic. Once certified, a product can be labeled according to the same four organic categories as food and other agricultural products.

Organic Labeling on Cosmetics and Personal Care and Body Care Products

Only "100 Percent Organic" or "Organic" products can display the USDA logo.

• "100 Percent Organic"—contains only organic ingredients (excluding water and salt).

• "Organic"—contains at least 95 percent organic ingredients (excluding water and salt). The remaining 5 percent must be nonagricultural substances on the approved National List, or agricultural products, also on the approved National List, that are not commercially available in organic form.

• "Made with Organic Ingredients"—contains at least 70 percent organic ingredients. The product label may list up to three of the organic ingredients or "food groups" on the display panel (for example, "made with organic chamomile, lavender, and cardamom").

• Products containing less than 70 percent organic ingredients may not use the term "organic" anywhere on their main display panel. But they may identify the specific ingredients that meet USDA organic certification on their ingredients panel.

But natural isn't so easy. While many products use the word "natural" on their labels, use of that term hasn't historically been regulated. So even products labeled "natural" or "herbal" may contain harsh preservatives or other ingredients that can be harmful to your body and to the environment.

Suddenly shopping for shaving cream just got a lot more difficult. Let's simplify it again.

Responsible Purchasing

There are a number of considerations to take into account when contemplating a certain body care product.

First—question not only whether the product will work, but will it work without side effects?

Second—where did all of those ingredients come from? Were they mined responsibly or grown sustainably, organically, or biodynamically? At the very least, they should be as close to nature as possible and harvested in a way that protects the earth's natural resources.

Third—what is the product's afterlife; what will be the environmental reaction when this product rinses down the drain?

Finally—am I being a responsible consumer by buying this product? That might seem a little heavy but it's important to think about, especially in our personal items like cosmetics and fashion. Does the company I'm supporting by buying this product use workers in unfair labor conditions? Do they test

---

Responsible Cosmetic Buying

- Find a product that works, without harsh side effects.
- Check to be sure the ingredients are truly natural in origin.
- Consider the product's "afterlife" and environmental impact.
- Find one that is fairly crafted and fairly traded.

on animals? Or, instead, were villages and communities supported in the making of this product?

Olowo-n'djo—I recently met a gentleman, a beautiful, warm man who grew up in Togo, West Africa. Olowo-n'djo Tchala told me the story of growing up in poverty in a village in Togo. The girls there often don't attend school and the boys do only if they're fortunate enough. Though life there may lack many of the comforts you and I are able to enjoy each day, it was a home to him for a very long time. In fact I bet if you asked him today, though he now lives on the West Coast of the United States, he would still call Togo home.

A few years ago, while he was still living in his hometown of Koboli, Togo, he met the woman who would become his wife. Rose was there as a Peace Corps volunteer from the United States. Soon love prevailed, and he found himself leaving this village to travel back to the States with her so she could finish her education. Shortly after their arrival in Washington State, Olowo-n'djo looked around for a way to support his community back home and fulfill the need for education that so many young girls there have. He and Rose turned to a special natural product they knew well from Togo, and that had become popular in many African-American communities here. They started a business making skin and hair care products using the shea butter from his native land. Rather than export the shea butter himself, he organized a Fair Trade shea butter cooperative, in which members craft shea butter using traditional techniques, then ship the product to Washington State, where Rose formulates it into their finished products.

By paying the cooperative members fair incomes, Olowo-n'djo Tchala has been able to help these women sustain their families, funneling income, and therefore health, back into the community. More girls now have the opportunity to go to school, and women perfect and teach the art of their craft to the next generation of women. Buying a product from a company like Alaffia is better consumerism at its finest. Your dollars are supporting a business that supports and grows individuals and communities.

Each time you, the consumer, walk into a store, you have the option to buy a product manufactured in a factory by workers who may or may not have been treated fairly, or you have the option to buy a product like the one made by Olowo-n'djo Tchala and his wife, Rose. By buying products like theirs you are directly supporting and empowering African women.

Know the Ugly Side
Every day, the average person uses ten cosmetic or personal care items on their body, and those ten items combined contain over 125 different ingredients. This is scary when you consider that over 10,000 of the chemical ingredients in personal care products are considered carcinogens, pesticides, reproductive toxins, endocrine disruptors, surfactants, degreasers, and plasticizers. That means that any one of the ingredients you are putting on your skin every day could cause anything from cancer to hormone disorders.

The ingredients in skin care products are specifically designed to penetrate the skin, so they can deliver the results they claim on their packaging. And penetrate they do. We inhale, absorb, and ingest a portion of *all* of these product ingredients. In fact, your skin, the largest organ in your body, absorbs 60 percent of what you put on it. In other words, 60 percent of each of those ingredients is absorbed directly into your bloodstream, affecting your organs, your hormones, and, most certainly, your health.

Today studies are linking off-kilter hormone levels and industrial chemicals in breast tumor tissue with the chemicals in personal care products. And that's only the beginning of it.

What many people are shocked to learn is that the FDA does not require that cosmetics be tested for safety before being sold. Aside from color additives, the FDA doesn't require health studies or any sort of testing on personal care product ingredients that show up in the marketplace. That means that anything can be put into a body lotion, shampoo, or mascara without first undergoing any sort of health study.

Instead, a panel funded by the U.S. cosmetic industry is the group responsible for reviewing the safety of cosmetic ingredients for products sold in the United States. Without another set of checks and balances, this sounds to me like a group that *could be* slightly biased and persuaded to label a product as safe, just for the sake of better sales.

What this means is that there are hundreds of products being sold with potentially unsafe ingredients, and many more with ingredients for which basic safety data does not even exist.

The Environmental Working Group conducted a study of over 23,000 cosmetic and personal care products sold in the United States and found that nearly one in thirty products failed to meet at least one industry or governmental cosmetic safety standard. Over 400 products contained ingredients that, according to safety panels run by the cosmetic industry, were unsafe when used as directed on the package, but because the FDA doesn't have authority to require further safety checks, they continue to be put on store shelves anyway. Beyond that, more than 750 products actually *violated* U.S. industry safety standards or the safety standards of other countries. And, maybe the most disturbing of all, 98 percent of all the 23,000 products tested contained one or more ingredient that had never been publicly assessed for safety.

For years the European nations exceeded the United States in their ingredients scrutiny. They banned thousands of ingredients that were still allowable here in the U.S.

Know the Friendly Side

Then, a few years ago, as awareness of harsh and often dangerous ingredients was beginning to build, a number of mainstream companies came forward and vowed to adhere to European guidelines and remove ingredients from their products that have been shown to cause cancer, gene mutation, and birth defects. In effect, they have made changes to rid their products of the most dangerous ingredients.

The best thing to do when shopping for cosmetics is to get to know the companies from which you're buying products. Find out what their standards of efficacy and safety are. Then support those that you feel the best about. It's exciting to hear about the large mainstream companies that are cleaning up their products, and at the same time, it's good to know about

MARK BLUMENTHAL

Mark Blumenthal is an herb enthusiast, to put it mildly. He has spent the better part of his life studying herbs and medicinal plants, and has become one of the world's most oft-quoted herbal authorities. He is the founder of the American Botanical Council, founding editor of *HerbalGram,* and author or editor of a number of books, articles, and other texts. He *is* the Herbal (or *Herban*) Cowboy.

Mark today is a cautionary advocate for self-medication. Cautionary only because when people make the decision to self-medicate, they must, says Mark, also self-educate. Once they do that, though, a whole world opens up in which certain strong herbs can be used in place of pharmaceuticals and other common products people have in their medicine cabinets or bathroom vanities.

I did a segment with Mark for my Discovery Health TV series. Mark showed a young couple (husband and wife lawyers) how ordinary items that he found in their bathroom cupboard could be swapped out for plant-based alternatives: ginger for nausea, parsley for mouthwash, peppermint for headaches, chamomile for cramp relief, and slippery elm for a sore throat. It was so easy that I think the onetime naysayers were actually willing to give it a try.

But that is because Mark was able to answer the question first to most people's lips, "Is it safe?" People are afraid to self-medicate, and rightly so! They don't know what herbs they can take and how much. They don't know what might interact with something else. And with a lack of good research to prove the safety and efficacy of herbs, people have a hard time overcoming those obstacles to favor the natural alternative.

But when Mark looks around at the growing state of today's green movement, he is encouraged, because he figures that the more aware people become of the environment, the more aware of and concerned they will become with the products they put on and in their bodies.

continued

Our bodies, Mark believes, should not be seen as disconnected from the environment and the water, soil, and air around us.

And it is in this vein that Mark spends his days researching and publishing, in hopes of reaching the fringe people with a message of self-medication and self-*education*. ■

the smaller companies (like Aubrey Organics, Burt's Bees, Ecco Bella, Kiss My Face, Dr. Hauschka, Weleda, and others) that have been doing the same for years. You can find the full list of cosmetic companies that have vowed not to use a number of suspected or known harmful chemicals according to the Environmental Working Group's research at *www.safecosmetics.org*.

Know the Red-Light Ingredients

Another way to go about it is to know the "red-light ingredients," those that you want to avoid, and then spend time reading the labels of products before you make a purchase. Reading labels is always a good idea, anyway. If you see one of your red-light ingredients, put it back on the shelf.

Here's a look at ten ingredients you should avoid whenever possible.

1. Fragrance—The cosmetic industry has had it easy when it comes to fragrance. They can put "fragrance" in everything from shampoos and soaps to serums and creams, and yet they don't really have to tell us what it is. They can list it as "fragrance"—a chemical concoction to make a product smell a certain way—while in truth that one word is a curtain behind which hundreds of potentially harmful ingredients blended together may be hiding.

According to the Environmental Working Group, synthetic fragrance contains neurotoxins and is among the top five allergens in the world. Over twenty years ago the National Academy of Sciences pointed to synthetic fra-

grances as a top chemical category worthy of "high-priority" status for neurotoxicity testing. Testing has found that musk xylene and musk ambrette,
two common ingredients used in product fragrance, can cause brain damage
and neuropathologic changes in lab animals. Synthetic fragrance has also
been linked to allergies, immunotoxicity, and neurotoxicity.

The really bad news is that fragrance is in all types of products. But the
good news is it's not a necessary ingredient, and a pleasant aroma can be
achieved in a product without its use. Think twice about any product with
the word "fragrance" or "perfume" in the ingredients. Look instead for products that are scented with plant extracts and essential oils.

2. Phthalates—Phthalates (*tha-lates*) are a chemical group used to add
flexibility and dissolvability to other ingredients. They're common in perfumes, where they help create a long release of the fragrance, and in hairspray, where they create flexibility so the product doesn't make your hair
too stiff. In nail polish, phthalates prevent chipping. Phthalates seem so helpful, right? Hardly! Research has uncovered their dark side. Phthalates may
cause organ damage and have been linked to liver toxicity. Women should
avoid exposure to phthalates during pregnancy. Studies have indicated that
boys exposed to phthalates in the womb may be at risk for certain developmental and reproductive issues.

There are a number of common beauty product ingredients that have
been researched for their estrogenic properties, meaning their ability to
mimic the female hormone estrogen when present in our bodies. Synthetic
chemicals that behave this way are called *xenoestrogens*. A great deal of research today has pointed toward the danger of exposure to synthetic estrogenic chemicals, including estrogen drugs for menopause, because they can
encourage certain types of cancer, including breast, ovarian, and uterine cancers. While many women have begun shying away from estrogen replace-
ment therapy (ERT), they're often not aware that estrogenic chemicals may
be lurking in body care products.

Phthalates are one such source. Phthalates can build up in a person's
body fat, accumulating over time, where they then begin to disrupt the

metabolism of estrogen in the body, which can, in turn, contribute to certain types of cancer.

In 2000, the United States Centers for Disease Control (CDC) studied the types and amounts of toxic chemicals in people. While they found seven different types of phthalates alone, every person tested had type DBP (dibutyl phthalate), the most toxic form of phthalates. Upon further investigation they found that the age group and gender heaviest with DBP in their body was women between the ages of twenty and forty. These are women in prime childbearing years, carrying around heavy loads of a chemical known to cause birth defects and reproductive disorders, especially in boys. And why? Because these women had worn nail polish and sprayed their hair with Aqua Net? The CDC couldn't say with 100 percent certainty, but they pointed to cosmetics and personal care products as the likely offender.

Phthalate Labeling

Dimethyl phthalate (DMP)

Diethyl phthalate (DEP)

Dibutyl phthalate (DBP)

Di-2-ethyl hexyl phthalate (DEHP)

Diisodecyl phthalate (DIDP)

Diisononyl phthalate (DINP)

All of this is not to say that you have to give up being pretty. But maybe you can give up some hair sprays and nail polishes that are great offenders. I'm okay with chipped nails if it means a healthier inside.

Because products are not always clearly labeled, look for products, like nail polishes, that present themselves as phthalate free.

Ideas to Grow On

Find nail polish free of the three most harmful ingredients: phthalates, toluene, and formaldehyde. Many today are labeled as such.

3. *Parabens*—Parabens are an extremely common type of preservative. They are used to extend the shelf life of shampoos, lotions, toothpastes, hand soaps, shaving gels, and a number of other products, and their use dates back to the 1920s.

There are multiple classes of parabens; the four most common are methylparaben, ethylparaben, butylparaben, and propylparaben. Individually or collectively, they inhibit the growth of mold, bacteria, and yeast in a product.

Parabens are a known hormone disruptor. I explained earlier the way that chemical ingredients can cause estrogenic activity in the body. Parabens fall into this category; they are xenoestrogens, with a potential to cause cancer because of the way they mimic estrogen in the human body.

Parabens are also scrutinized for their relationship to breast cancer because of a 2004 study published in the *Journal of Applied Toxicology*. The study found an alarming five types of parabens present and intact in eighteen of twenty tested breast cancer tumors. The lead researcher on the study publicly stated that the nature of the parabens indicated that they had been absorbed through the skin (as opposed to ingested, inhaled, or otherwise taken in), probably by way of lotions, deodorants, and the like. The FDA and European Union have further studied parabens and now regard them safe for human use. But many people, myself included, still reserve some caution against the chemical preservative.

The good news with parabens is that they're easily detected on a product's ingredients list (labeled as methylparaben, benzylparaben, etc.) and, therefore, easily avoided. And many companies are spending countless hours and research dollars developing natural, non-toxic, plant-derived preservatives to use in place of parabens. Look for products without parabens in the ingredients or, as many products now have, a proudly stated "paraben-free" declaration on the package front.

4. Petroleum—"Petroleum" is a word we're all too familiar with today. We hear almost daily about the price of oil. We know we need to conserve it and make efficient use of it, since petroleum provides fuel for our cars, controls the temperature in our homes, and is useful in the manufacturing of plastics and medicines. But we don't often think of petroleum as it relates to our beauty products. The truth is, though, petroleum, or petrolatum, is found in a number of products from lip balms and lipsticks to moisturizers, conceal-ers, hair relaxers, and sunscreen.

Petrolatum often contains a contaminate known as BAHS, which is shown as a possible carcinogen, contributing to many types of cancer, in-cluding breast, skin, and gastrointestinal.

Also under the petroleum category are petroleum distillates. They're used as an antifoaming agent or solvent. These have been listed as a possible hu-man carcinogen, and studies have proven their ability to cause damage to human lungs. The European Union has banned the use of petroleum distil-lates in cosmetics, but they still appear here in the United States in mascaras and other products.

5. SLS (Sodium Lauryl/Laureth Sulfates)—SLS stands for sodium lauryl or laureth sulfates, and in all truth it probably isn't as harmful as the previous listings. SLS is made by fusing sulfate and lauric acid together. It's a foaming agent, a surfactant, that is in an estimated 90 percent of foaming products, from soaps and shower gels to toothpastes. But sodium lauryl/laureth sul-fates are harsh chemicals that can cause skin irritation. The small molecular makeup of SLSs penetrates the skin easily and can lead to dryness, irritation, and other forms of dermatitis.

SLS makes my list because it is one that affects me very directly, so I'm sure it affects others as well. For a number of years when I was growing up, I suffered from canker sores in my mouth. Often I'd get two or three in the same area that would quickly grow together into one large open sore along my gum line. I tried eliminating so many types of foods from my diet—from citrus to nuts—to prevent the painful lesions from forming. But nothing seemed to help. My naturopathic doctor eventually suggested that I seek out a toothpaste that didn't contain sodium laurel/laureth sulfates. On a mission to try everything, I hit the store shelves and flipped through well over a dozen toothpaste tubes before I found one that didn't contain the harsh ingredient. I have been canker sore free ever since.

6. *Mercury*—Mercury is another ingredient that we're hearing a lot about these days. The mercury-based preservative thimerosal (now banned from children's vaccines) has become the target of many angry parents of children with autism. Mercury and thimerosal have been recognized for their damaging effects on the human nervous system and the brain, potentially contributing to the advance of Alzheimer's. It has also been shown to cause organic system toxicity and liver damage, with a possible link to Lyme disease.

Given all of this, it's hard to believe that mercury is still an allowable ingredient in U.S. cosmetics. It is, however, turning up in products such as lip and brow liners, lip glosses, some moisturizers, and mascaras.

7. *Formaldehyde*—The word brings to mind preserved frogs in fifth-grade science classes, not fancy cosmetics in slick packages. Formaldehyde is a colorless, flammable gas at room temperature, with a distinct and pungent smell. It is used in the production of fertilizer, paper, and some resins. But it's also a preservative that shows up in cosmetics, most often in eye shadows, mascaras, and nail hardeners. Formaldehyde is a known human carcinogen.

Formaldehyde is found in consumer products that range well beyond cosmetics, including the pressed woods that are used to make inexpensive cabinets and bookshelves. Japan, China, and Europe all restrict formaldehyde's use in consumer goods, but it remains an allowable ingredient in the United States.

8. *Skin Whiteners*—*Hydroquinone* is the ingredient name to be aware of here. Hydroquinone works to lighten the skin by inhibiting the production of melanin pigments. Hydroquinone is a known animal carcinogen and is toxic to the skin, brain, and reproductive and immune systems. Though it's

banned as an ingredient in the European Union, it is still allowable in U.S. cosmetics.

Hydroquinone is found in over a thousand face creams, particularly those with anti-aging claims, lipsticks, sunscreens and products containing SPF, and eye creams. And you'll almost certainly find it in any product claiming to lighten skin pigmentation (dark spots) or dark circles.

I d e a s   t o   G r o w   O n

Instead of skin whiteners and eye creams containing hydroquinone,
try cool tea bags or cucumbers to brighten your under-eye area.

9. Lead—Lead has gotten a bad rap, and rightly so. Studies linking lead to brain development disorders in children have resulted in restrictions in its use. Lead paint has been banned from the walls of homes since 1978. Unfortunately, it is still an allowable ingredient in cosmetics. Lead acetate is a possible human carcinogen and is known to disrupt reproduction and lead to neurotoxicity. And while it's not showing up with nearly the frequency of many of the other ingredients on this list, it is found in some black hair dyes and a select few other products.

10. Certain Sunscreens—The case of sunscreens is a confusing one because there are two issues at stake: harmful ingredients in sunscreens and ineffective sunscreens that don't provide adequate protection.

A lack of sufficient protection from products claiming to block UVA and UVB rays is a widespread concern. A study by the Environmental Working Group showed that only 14 percent of the products on the market are "safe and effective." Furthermore, products that claim to stay on and stay strong all day often don't, simply because the key sun-blocking ingredients lose their effectiveness over time. While "water resistant" may be a truthful claim, "waterproof" is false labeling. And though some products claim to be SPF 50 or SPF 45, they are only slightly more effective than SPF 30 sunscreens.

The difference in types of blockage is really quite simple. Blocking UVB radiation protects from sunburn, and blocking UVA radiation helps protect against skin damage, aging, and, potentially, skin cancer. But the FDA doesn't require UVA protection in a marketed sunscreen, and of the nearly one thousand that the Environmental Working Group tested, only one in five provided protection from UVA and UVB radiation, with safe ingredients.

Ideas to Grow On

Don't be fooled by false sunscreen claims. Choose an SPF 30 that blocks UVB and UVA rays, and apply the sunscreen often. A zinc- or titanium-based sunscreen is the healthiest choice.

The safety issues of sunscreens go beyond a lack of adequate and effective protection. Many sunscreens release free radicals in sunlight, and these can damage DNA and cells, encourage the aging of skin, and possibly elevate the risk of skin cancer. Others have estrogenic properties that can disrupt your body's hormonal system.

The best thing to do is shop for zinc or titanium sunscreens that have little chance of absorption through the skin. And try to stay away from sunscreens in a powder or spray form, as this makes it easy to inhale tiny particles.

What to Do

The bottom line is we are now finding out all sorts of things about the dreadful effects of many synthetic and chemical ingredients. Things once thought to be safe later turn up to be extremely dangerous, even deadly. So the way I look at it is this. You don't have to give up your lipstick and your shampoos or even your perfumes. You just need to *replace* them with products free of harsh chemical ingredients. Yes, they may be a *little* harder to find. And on occasion they may be a little more expensive (though I've known women to spend hundreds on a bottle of face lotion and I've never seen a natural product retail for that much). In the long run, isn't it worth it?

How do you find these products? You can pay a visit to my website, *www.sarasnow.com*, where I do offer some recommendations. Or spend a few minutes in the cosmetic and personal care aisles at Whole Foods or other natural foods stores. Not everything you'll find there is completely free of all of these ingredients, but I know you'll be encouraged when you find that a number of products, from blush and mascara to face scrub and eye cream, meet your new standards for healthy and safe. Other mainstream stores like Target and Sephora are beginning to offer "green" and "organic" products as well, making them even easier to start using as early as today.

Cut Back

Starting today, one of the best steps you can take is to simply cut back on the number of products you buy. It's very tempting to pick up a new lip gloss or nail polish color every time you run to the store, but is it necessary? By buying less, you'll care more about the products you actually choose to bring home.

Paper Products

And, because I think we should end on a lighter note than the declining state of our beauty products, let's talk TP. The bathroom is a great place to start thinking about cutting back. If your guest bath still stocks neat little disposable towels for your guests to use, use them up and hang a towel. Your guests won't mind and the forests will thank you.

Many of the big-brand bathroom paper products, like toilet paper, facial tissues, and hand towels, are still made from virgin trees. These are 100- to 150-year-old-trees that are cut down just so they can be turned into disposable paper products for you. In fact, if every home in the United States made the decision to replace one roll of virgin toilet paper with a recycled paper one, nearly 425,000 trees would be saved.

If you're a little worried about using recycled goods in the bathroom, you don't need to think twice about it. Recycled toilet paper has never spent time on another's bum before coming into your bathroom. In addition to the pioneering green companies like Seventh Generation, an ever increasing number of big-time consumer product companies have jumped on the bandwagon and offer recycled alternatives to their leading brands. Think of your favorite brand and more than likely you'll find a roll with some recycled content.

You, like I, only have one body. I pay so much attention to the foods that I put *in* my body that I would be remiss if I didn't pay just as much care to the products I put *on* my body. We spend a lot more time in the bathroom than one might think, so it's a great place to take some basic conservation measures.

In the Bedroom

When my husband and I remodeled our home, we did a fair amount of work in each room, but paid close attention to two rooms in particular: the kitchen and the bedroom. The kitchen is the soul of every home. I'm sure it's the case in your house as well—where you catch up after work, where the kids do their homework, where you succeed and sometimes fail in replicating a recipe you saw somewhere, where you snack and hydrate and fill your tummies. But where the kitchen may be the soul of a home, the bedroom is the heart.

We spend at least as much time in the bedroom as in any other room in our house. Though most of those hours aren't spent awake, it's bedroom air that we breathe while we slumber and the bedroom environment that we count on to ease us into those important regenerative hours. But for too many people the bedroom becomes a repository for books, computers, and exercise equipment, detracting from its ability to be a soothing, healthy, romantic, and even sexy environment. If you use the space beneath your bed for storage, you become subconsciously aware of that clutter when you don't need to be. Stacks of newspapers and unnecessary electronics are distracting in a room where focused serenity is most important.

In my bedroom our shared closet is orderly, the attached bathroom serene and free of unnecessary chemicals, and our bed and other furnishings are simple, healthy, and soothing. Here's how you can create the same.

Creating a Healthy Bed

You probably spend anywhere from six to ten hours a night sleeping. That's a third of each day spent in the bedroom. It's unlikely you can say that about any other single room in the house. And where do you spend those six to ten hours? You spend it with your face flat against a pillow and mattresses. Now that you're taking so much care with the foods you put *in* your body and the products you put *on* your body, it makes sense to take as much care with the environment you put your body in and the materials by which you are surrounded.

Mattress

Start with the mattress. Most mattresses are chemical wastebaskets, full of formaldehyde (a classified VOC—volatile organic compound—that has been shown to cause cancer in lab animals), pesticides, chemical solvents, and flame retardants. Chemical flame retardants contain polybrominated diphenyl ether (PBDE or pentaBDE), a toxic chemical linked to hyperactivity and neurobehavioral modifications. Though banned in Europe, this is still allowed in most parts of the United States.

Better alternatives are mattresses made with organic cotton, organic wool, or latex. Organic mattresses generally involve an organic cotton outer layer with organic wool on the inside, sometimes with a latex or metal coil spring center. Latex mattresses, on the other hand, are solid latex with a cloth outer layer. Latex, though it makes some people think of plastic and unhealthy matter, is actually a very healthy and natural material; it comes from the milky sap that is naturally excreted from certain plants and trees like milkweed, rubber trees, and poppy plants. And latex or rubber is naturally antimicrobial and dust mite–resistant, making it a perfect sleeping surface for people with asthma, allergies, or other sensitivities.

The fact that the wool and cotton in these mattresses is organic means that it was grown without the use of any chemical fertilizers or pesticides, making it a healthier material for your bed, and for the environment in which it was grown. But organic wool goes one step farther. On its own, wool is naturally fire retardant, and many wool mattresses and bed pads are infused with essential oils like eucalyptus and lavender to help them naturally repel dust mites as well.

A mattress is a big investment under any circumstance. If you've recently plopped down a big chunk for a new mattress, you may not be able to spring for a new set anytime soon. So if you're not in a position to be able to replace your current, conventional mattress right away, you can start by covering your existing mattress with an affordable organic cotton or organic wool barrier cloth. This will form a protective layer between you and the chemicals your mattress may be emitting.

If you are in the market for a new mattress, in general latex mattresses cost about the same amount as or a little more than standard mattresses and can be found, quite surprisingly, at many conventional furniture stores today. Organic cotton and/or wool mattresses take a little more searching (there are great online natural bedding stores from which you can order) and can run close to double the cost.

Pillow

Your pillow, if filled with synthetic materials, could be just as harmful as your mattress. Even if you're not able to switch out your mattress, a great place to start is to swap your pillow for one filled with organic wool or shredded rubber, both of which will help regulate your body temperature and repel dust mites.

Headboard and Footboard

The best option for a bed is one made from sustainably harvested wood or bamboo and sealed with a non-toxic sealant. If you're not in the market for a new bed, give your existing frame a good sniff test. If it smells like chemical finishes, try refinishing it with a non-toxic paint or finish. And if your bed and other bedroom furniture are made with pressed wood or particleboard, be aware that the glue used in them could be leaching formaldehyde into the air you're breathing. If that's the case, seal any exposed areas with a non-toxic sealant and get some fresh air into the room to allow those chemicals to outgas outside of your four walls.

Ideas to Grow On

To check to see if your furniture is made with pressed wood, look at the underside of your bed rails or the peg holes in closets and cupboards. Any exposed areas where you can see the thin layers of wood should be sealed over with a non-toxic sealant.

Bedclothes

Your bed coverings, from your sheets to your blankets, comforters, and pillowcases, should be as carefully thought out as the T-shirts and sweaters in your closet (I'll get to that later in this chapter). Look for silky sheets made from natural bamboo or organic cotton and blankets made out of organic wool. You'll find explanations on organic cotton and other natural fibers like bamboo below. Vintage quilts are an excellent option from a health perspective as well as an environmental responsibility standpoint.

Healthy Bed Checklist

Latex, organic cotton, or organic wool mattress

Organic cotton or organic wool barrier cloth

Shredded rubber and/or organic wool and cotton pillows

Natural bamboo or organic cotton sheets

Organic wool blankets

Vintage and secondhand blankets or quilts

Developing Healthy Sleep Patterns

How much sleep do you get each night? If you're like most Americans, 65 percent of us, then you're sleeping less than the recommended seven to eight hours a night. Sleep is often treated as a luxury rather than a necessity. Although we might think we are being productive by working late into the night and getting up early in the morning before the kids or the emails start their cries for attention, lack of sleep and chronic sleep loss can contribute to elevated stress hormone levels, a slowed metabolism, a compromised immune system, and an increased risk of heart disease, diabetes, and high blood pressure.

A few years ago I was working as a morning news anchor and reporter. This was my dream job and I felt like I had been training for it all of my life. (I know now that I had actually been training for *this*, what I'm doing today, rather than that, but hindsight is twenty-twenty.) For three years I set my alarm clock for three a.m. For three years I dragged my tired body up and into the shower while the skies were still pitch black and the only people on the streets were the previous night's revelers. I would pull into the dark parking lot of the TV station by four o'clock and spend the next two hours reading scripts and getting camera-ready. From six until nine o'clock my coanchors and I would do the three-hour live broadcast. At nine we were off the air and I would spend the next three or four hours in meetings, out shooting stories, or simply trying to keep my eyelids open at my desk. Around noon or one I would leave, with the whole afternoon and evening wide open ahead of me. The only problem was I could hardly go anywhere without laying my seat back and taking a twenty-minute nap in the parking lot first. I couldn't fix dinner without a nap, and dinner out with friends required a three-hour nap. Then, because I'd taken that afternoon siesta, I was able to enjoy the evening with my husband but unable to get back to sleep until close to ten or later. Five or less short hours later my alarm would go off and I'd start it all over again. I knew it wasn't good for me, but I would argue with myself that I loved my job and was doing my part to make people smile in the morning. Finally, after three years of this,

I couldn't do it any longer. My body that had always been well cared for was now being taxed beyond its abilities. I won't go into details, but suffice it to say that things that should have been working like clockwork quit. My overworked body and brain were screaming for a breather, and I had no choice but to listen.

The environment in which we sleep is important, but simply making the decision to go to sleep so our bodies get the full benefit of eight regenerative, recuperating hours is paramount. There are a few simple and decisive steps you can take to make your sleep environment more conducive to getting the rest you need.

Light

Light is one of the most important factors to influence the quality and duration of your sleep. It's important that you get enough exposure to natural or artifical bright light during daytime hours and, as daytime turns to twilight, begin to dim the lights throughout your home as bedtime approaches. If you or your children prefer to sleep with a nightlight for security or comfort, use one that emits a very low wattage. If you're in a neighborhood or city with a lot of artificial light outside your window, which has become harder to avoid even in semirural areas, invest in some heavy drapes or shutters to block out unnatural night light. A good rule of thumb is this: if you can see your hand at night, your bedroom is too bright. When you awaken during the night to use the bathroom, keep the lights off or dimmed; exposure to a bright light could prevent you from drifting quickly back into a deep slumber.

I d e a s   t o   G r o w   O n

For a good night's sleep, keep your bedroom dark enough that you can't see your hand in front of your face.

Noise

Unnatural noise can be as disturbing and sleep preventing as artificial light during the night. Remove any loudly ticking clocks or other noisemakers from your room, close the drapes to block out outside sounds, or invest in a soothing water fountain to create white noise and cover up unwanted sounds.

Of course, there are times when it won't be possible to create a perfectly quiet bedroom. Crying babies and sick kids will disrupt that, but rest assured that this is temporary and that serenity and quiet will one day be restored.

The Three Essentials to a Restful Sleep Environment

1. Light—dark enough so you can't see your hand

2. Sound—as quiet as possible, with any disturbing sounds covered with a soothing fountain of white noise

3. Temperature—try for a cool 65 degrees

Temperature

Temperature plays an incredibly important role as well; although it's hard for anyone to say what the perfect sleeping temperature is, most experts say to try for around 65 degrees for the best night's sleep.

Closet Talk—Clothes and Shoes

We've all seen pictures of ultimate closets: filled to the gills with rows upon rows of neatly folded cashmere sweaters, trendy T's, and the latest designer jeans; hangers draped with dresses, tops, slacks; and then the shoes! Shelves set at a slight angle to properly display rows of flats—simple to embellished— practical pumps (and pumps that say a *lot* more), gym shoes and fashion sneakers, sandals, wedges, boots, and more. Let's be honest, we drool when we see closets like this in movies and on TV, but if we take a step back we can quickly see that, aside from the fact that it's not realistic and that our closets will probably never look like that, it isn't earthly responsible either. I don't mean to crush dreams, rather to give you permission to stop pining away for this "picture-perfect" closet. Each pair of shoes and blue jeans, each sweater and T-shirt, required a significant amount of resources and other materials— leather, cotton, silk, or otherwise—that were most likely grown and finished with a vast amount of chemicals. And how long will each of those articles stay in the closet to be worn and enjoyed? A season or two? A few items may be- come "classics" and live for thirty years, but most will not. That means that all of those resources went into creating clothes that are good for only a few years at best. Then what happens to the clothes? Maybe, hopefully, you'll get them to a secondhand store, a church thrift shop, or to Goodwill, where their life can be continued. And if not today or this year, eventually they end up in a landfill somewhere, taking up space, leaching chemicals back into the earth.

So much for the pretty picture of the dream closet, huh? Sorry about that. But as I talk you through it, I think you'll begin formulating your own picture about a prettier and more responsible closet. One not quite as big, filled with secondhand "recycled" clothes, organic cotton blue jeans, vegan shoes, and other clothes made from conscientious and eco-friendly materials. And don't worry, there's still room in this greener closet for your favorite items. Because, since eco *is* classic, items made from quality materials that will last a lifetime are allowed shelf space even in this eco closet.

Recycled and Reused

When I was young, my brothers and sister and I wore a lot of secondhand clothes. For me it was either jeans handed down to me by my brother, or dresses, corduroys, and shirts from my only girl cousin, who, lucky for me, was just a couple of years older and lived only a stone's throw away. There were four kids in my family and four in my cousin's family, so sharing everything, clothes included, made good sense. My mom also shopped for us at a now classic but then little-used clothing boutique in Ann Arbor. (I looked and was excited to see that the Woman in the Shoe is still in business today.) At the time, I thought my parents were penny-pinchers of the worst kind, and it took me a number of years to realize that instead they were conscientious consumers, finding it unnecessary to buy an item brand new when a slightly used version would work just as well.

Ideas to Grow On

Buy "recycled" secondhand clothes for growing babies and kids. Because babies grow so quickly, the items are usually only lightly worn.

Today vintage and used clothing boutiques are everywhere. They range from the type that will charge you forty dollars for a vintage T to ones where you can root through a box and buy them five for a dollar. It doesn't matter which of these you choose. The important thing is to understand that in shopping this way you are demanding less of the world and its assets and, in so doing, are becoming a responsible shopper.

Compare a T-shirt to a roll of toilet paper for a moment. You can either buy a standard roll made from paper that came from virgin-growth trees (solid, old trees that were undisturbed in their habitats until they were cut down for the sole purpose of making paper towels, toilet paper, and other disposable paper products), or you can buy a roll made from recycled paper. By making that choice, you are saving trees. Now think about the T-shirt. You can buy a brand new T-shirt from a designer shop or a discount box store; either way your T-shirt required fresh cotton and all of the energy and inputs necessary to grow that cotton. In fact, it takes a half pound of cotton to make one T-shirt. And that half pound took a lot of water and chemicals to grow. But buying a recycled T-shirt doesn't require any new cotton.

Where a roll of recycled-materials toilet paper differs is that it was made from a smattering of recycled content. A recycled T-shirt simply spent a part of its life on someone else's back. When you buy it, you are demanding no new cotton, no chemicals or labor to grow, press, spin, dye, and knit that cotton. The responsibility for those materials and resources are spread out over everyone who has worn and will wear the T-shirt.

A friend of mine started a business a few years ago called the Clothing Warehouse. He and his partner buy huge amounts of discarded clothing in bulk. After sorting through it all, they pull out the very best and highly fashionable items—the kinds of vintage garb rock and movie stars wear, like vintage T's, dresses, western boots, jeans, and so on—and attractively display their vintage clothing for sale in their Clothing Warehouse stores, stores that are now popping up in quite a few regions across the country. One day I pointed out to him the eco side to what he was doing for his customers. Sure, I told him, it's cool to buy vintage and to hit the town in a dress or a groovy 1970s poly shirt that you're almost certain no one else will own. But it's also very environmentally responsible to buy a secondhand clothing item, where the *only* resources that went into getting it to you were some detergent and water to help it smell less like the last owner, and fuel to transport it from collection site to resale location. It's not very often you can combine high fashion, reasonable prices, *and* environmentally friendly products! Usually you only get one or two of the three. Whether he initially

Where to Buy Recycled Clothing

• Online—everything from vintage items to "brand new with tags" that someone is looking to clear out of his or her closet

• Thrift stores—unique T-shirts, jackets, and other items

• Vintage shops—fashionably vintage items like concert T's, hippie shirts, bohemian dresses, etc.

realized it or not—and Mo is no dummy, so I'm guessing he did—he's pav-
ing the way for more and more people to shop for recycled duds in a very
fun and unique way.

You can buy recycled clothing at vintage shops like Mo's, but also be sure
to check out thrift stores and online auctions. Craigslist and eBay are great
places to land yourself secondhand high fashion items. But you'll also find a
great amount of never-before-worn clothing that someone is looking to clear
out of his or her closet. It's better that it goes to you than to the dump!

When you shop online for recycled clothing, it's worth taking a little time
to find out about the item you're buying and its condition.

Condition Descriptions

• *Mint condition* implies that the garment is in perfect condition and shows
no wear at all.

• *Excellent condition* means just that: the item may show a slight bit of wear,
but once you have it on it will only look like you've worn it once or twice.

• *Very good* indicates great item with a few flaws: stains, small tears, missing buttons, odor. Be sure to find out the details and determine if you can
live with them.

• *Good* suggests that the garment is wearable but may have greater flaws
than those mentioned above. Again, find out the details, and if you're
handy put a needle and thread to it to make it as good as new again.

Organic Cotton

I mentioned the amount of cotton that goes into growing one T-shirt (a
half pound), but what I haven't told you yet is the amount of chemicals it
takes to grow that much cotton. Though only a little more than 2 percent of

the world's farmland is used to grow cotton, cotton crops account for nearly 25 percent of the world's insecticides and more than 10 percent of the pesticides. More than $2.5 billion worth of pesticides (over 84 million pounds) are used on cotton crops worldwide every year. These pesticides kill cotton pests but also beneficial insects, and their damage doesn't stop there. In 2000 the Environmental Protection Agency cited seven of the top fifteen pesticides regularly used on cotton crops in the United States as "possible," "likely," "probable," or "known" human carcinogens. More than 50 percent of cotton field workers in Egypt in the 1990s experienced neurological and vision disorders and other symptoms of chronic pesticide poisoning. Farmers here and all across the globe must be experiencing the same.

And yet the farmers continue to spray to keep up with our hungry fashion appetites. But sometimes seeing the raw truth is all it takes for someone to lose their appetite. Here's the truth: to grow the cotton for just one conventional T-shirt takes one-third of a pound of chemical pesticides. That's a full pound of chemicals to grow the cotton for the three-pack in your dresser drawer.

Now multiply that one-third pound of pesticides by the number of T-shirts you have in your dresser or closet. Imagine how much it takes to grow enough cotton for a pair of blue jeans or a set of sheets. How about a shelf full of blue jeans or a linen closet full of sheets? A lot. Thankfully, like food, cotton can be grown with or without these harmful chemicals, and, like food, it can be certified organic if the growing and manufacturing processes meet a set of standards.

According to the Organic Trade Association, organic cotton must be "grown using methods and materials that have a low impact on the environment. Organic production systems replenish and maintain soil fertility, reduce the use of toxic and persistent pesticides and fertilizers, and build biologically diverse agriculture." Verifying that producers of organic fibers are using methods and materials allowable in organic production are third-party certification organizations such as IMO and SKAL, both accredited by the International Federation of Organic Agriculture Movements.

I d e a s   t o   G r o w   O n

Look for clothing as well as sheets and towels made from organically grown cotton. It's surprisingly soft and can come in a great variety of colors.

In 2006 the Global Organic Textile Standards (GOTS) were set to unite the international organic fiber community under one set of regulations. This is the highest internationally approved certification for finished organic-fiber textile products. The standards oversee all parts of a finished product, from the farming of the fiber through the spinning, knitting, weaving, dyeing, transportation, and selling of it.

Other fibers that can be grown or raised organically (some certified, some not) are hemp, flax/linen, soy, bamboo, wool, cashmere, and silk.

Other Eco-Fibers

There are a number of eco-fibers that you can look for to dress your body and your bed. These range from natural or color-grown cotton to bamboo and soy fibers. Here are a look at some of my favorites and those that you'll most easily find.

Organic cotton, as we've discussed, is grown without the use of toxic chemical fertilizers, pesticides, fungicides, and herbicides. Organic cotton can be certified according to standards set forth by the GOTS.

Color-grown cotton is grown in natural colors of muted greens, browns, whites, and reds. As a result the finished materials are not dyed. Color-grown cotton came into popularity only in the past decade but has its roots in the ancient Americas. For thousands of years, weavers cultivated tan, green, yellow, red, brown, and white cottons, resulting in blankets and garments that had color without being dyed. The quality of the color-grown cotton fiber wasn't up to the standards of modern consumers or textile machines until the 1990s, when a woman cultivated a longer-fiber version of the color-grown cottons, suitable for modern processing.

Green cotton is cotton whose fibers are neither dyed nor treated with chemicals like formaldehyde or chlorine bleach in the finishing process. It does not mean the cotton was grown without chemicals.

Bamboo is considered highly sustainable because it grows quickly and easily without pesticides. Bamboo is extremely durable and, when woven into a fabric, has a soft feel and a silk-like drape. It's also naturally antimicrobial, antifungal, and antibacterial, making it perfect for sheets and undershirts. Because of the recent popularity of bamboo for everything from sheets to headboards, there are some growers who are raising it in a less sustainable fashion (clearing forests to grow it and using chemicals to increase yield). As with everything else, know from whom you are buying.

Organic wool is from animals that have been raised organically, much the way an animal would be raised for food production.

Organic cashmere is from goats that have been raised organically.

Soy and milk fibers are just the tip of the iceberg of other innovative fabrics that are being made from alternative materials. Look for clothes, from designer couture to mainstream duds, made from soy, milk, and even seaweed fibers.

Fair Trade Clothing

Fair trade is almost as common in the closet as it is in the kitchen pantry. When something is labeled Fair Trade, it means that the farmers and, in the case of clothing and accessories, artisans and producers were given fair wages and safe and healthy working conditions. Look for Fair Trade items like ethnic shirts, beautiful scarves, handbags, and other accessories.

I d e a s   t o   G r o w   O n

"Fair Trade" and "handmade" are a couple of my favorite clothing and accessories labels. I love to know that a sarong, a scarf, or a pair of shoes was made by hand by a group of real people somewhere across the globe.

MARCI ZAROFF

Though organic food production is something that has been an area of focus for quite a few years now, organic fashion is somewhat of a younger industry. It's no surprise that a girl who was voted best dressed in high school, and who became a macrobiotic and organic advocate later in life, would be the first to coin the phrase "eco-fashion."

By 1996, Marci Zaroff had spent a few years running an organic food and beauty education center and was fed up with the limited amount of organic fashion products available to her. To fill in the "missing link in the wellness equation," she started a clothing catalog called *Under the Canopy,* focusing on style, ecology, and world health. Working with a freelance fashion designer, Marci was able to sell blankets, dresses, leggings, long tops, and T-shirts made from organically grown cotton. She was taking simple but innovative products out to people who had never considered "why organic cotton" before.

Marci's real zeal was found in working with the farmers and factories who supplied her with fine-grade organic cotton and fabrics. But she was constantly up against one hurdle—the lack of organic cotton to supply her growing business. So Marci, like so many others, turned to the Rodale Institute for help. She partnered with Rodale to aid conventional farmers in their efforts to transition from growing cotton conventionally to growing it organically.

By 2000, just four years after conception, *Under the Canopy* had grown to a distribution of a million catalogs a year and had secured the slot as apparel partner for Whole Foods Markets nationwide. From there the brand became more and more mainstream each year.

While fashion has always been a goal of Marci's, her real mission has been to increase the production of organic cotton and to change people's mindset from a "why would I . . ." to a "why wouldn't I buy organic fiber?" Because, with cotton being one of the most heavily

continued

sprayed crops in the world, farming it has become a major cause of air and water pollution. And it doesn't just hurt the planet, it hurts the farmers; especially in areas of India where cotton is the leading crop, farmers are getting sick from the pesticides that they are convinced they must spray on their crops.

Marci, now spokesperson for her extensive brand of organic cotton and eco-fiber fashions, is also an outspoken spokesperson for the organic cotton industry. Through consumer, retail, and media outlets, education is her focus, and her goal is to convince people that farmers' lives and the planet are at risk, affected by the choices we make each and every day. People are starting to make the organic decision when it comes to food, so why not cotton? asks Marci. The way she puts it, food is feel-good but fashion is cutthroat. Today, thanks at least in part to Marci, the two worlds are colliding. ■

Vegan Clothing

Vegan is a term that you'll hear in the closet as well as in the kitchen. Many people who adhere to a vegan diet, staying away from all animal products, also adhere to a strict vegan lifestyle. Most choose not to wear leather and some stay away from wool, cashmere, angora, and silk as well. Whether or not you practice veganism in the kitchen, you can still enjoy purses and shoes that are made from faux leathers and help to cut down on the demand for factory-farmed cattle and the environmental damage associated with raising them. Look for shoes and purses labeled "man-made leather," "synthetic leather," or "man-made materials." The downside? Many of these faux leathers are petroleum by-products, so you make the call.

Making Natural Whoopie

Let's be honest here. Going green is about making changes, sometimes fun, sometimes not. But it can't be all work and no play, and surely all of your hard work deserves the reward of a little green roll in the hay. When you really get down to it, creating a healthy environment in the bedroom goes beyond what goes in the closet and on the bed, it also involves what goes on *in* the bed.

Green sex might not be the first thing you think of when contemplating ways to tread more lightly, but experimenting with the wrong toys and lubes can take you down a slippery slope—er—wrong path.

Toys

We've already explored the hazardous risks of plastics and phthalates, with their dangerous links to cancers and reproductive disorders. But toys made for the most intimate parts of our bodies, ranging in shapes from spheres to rabbit ears, are often made with dangerous PVC and phthalate-softened plastics. Studies have shown that harmful chemicals, including phthalates, leach out of sex toys into our bodies when exposed to heat or fats, like fatty flesh (no matter how svelte you are, it's only natural that you've got some fat on your bones). While some measures have been taken to keep phthalate chemicals out of children's toys, the same hasn't applied thus far to adult toys. In fact, because these toys are often labeled "for novelty purposes only," they don't have to adhere to regulations that you might think would apply to something being used on and in the body.

Thankfully, certain companies are starting to make adult toys that are phthalate and PVC free. When you shop—as many people apparently do, since the U.S. market for sex toys is estimated to be close to $500 million— look for toys that are labeled phthalate or PVC free or toys made from alternative, safe materials like silicon, glass, and metal.

Also, keep in mind your goal of conserving energy and resources in the nooky nook. Some toys actually now come with solar cells or their own rechargeable batteries.

Condoms

Natural rubber or latex is a material that comes from a tree, so latex condoms are generally considered to be safe. What can make them dangerous is the lubricant you use with them or the way you dispose of them. Condoms are often flushed, rather than tossed, and as a result end up clogging pipes and polluting our waterways and beaches. Picture a condom, or the larger version—a plastic bag—floating underwater in the ocean. Both slightly transparent jelly-like items begin to resemble jellyfish or other sources of food to hungry sea creatures. But for those who mistake them as a protein source, the result can be harmful to deadly. For their safety and the sake of our planet's health, you're better off disposing of these disposables in the garbage can, rather than the toilet.

Some condoms are made from polyurethane, so be sure you're buying natural latex rubbers. And because latex condoms often contain a milk protein, they are unsuitable for vegans to use. But not to worry, there are a great variety of vegan-friendly condoms on the market today as well.

Oils and Rubs

The lubricant you use, whether for massage or otherwise, should provide moisture, glide, and if you feel like it, flavor. Look for lotions and lubricants free of synthetic fragrance, synthetic colors, synthetic flavor, and chemical preservatives. You'll find wonderful varieties made with shea butter, coconut and olive oils, and aloe vera. Be sure the product you choose is paraben-free and clear of petroleum ingredients.

Natural Aphrodisiacs

Finally, if you're looking for a little extra oomph, there are some natural and very green ways to get the blood pumping. A brisk walk around the block, a bike ride, or a Pilates or yoga session can work the right muscles and get your juices flowing. Certain foods and herbs have been known to help: kava kava root, ginkgo biloba, ginseng, and horny goat weed (who would have guessed) are among those. Of course, some good organic wine, organic dark chocolate, and natural candles will probably do the trick.

Hey, the birds do it and the bees do it, why can't we? It's only natural, after all.

In the Nursery

The Soupy Nursery

Not long ago, my friend Anne announced that she and her husband Jake were expecting. They were in the third month of their pregnancy and of course hadn't yet started to prepare, aside from deciding which room would become the nursery and telling all their family and friends that in six months' time they would be having a baby. A few months later my friends and I held the first of the couple's many baby showers. By this time Anne and Jake had given quite a bit of thought to how the nursery should look: the wall color, the bedding, the onesies, the rocking chair, and all the toys. Anne opened gift after gift from her registry and you could just see the wheels turning in her head as a picture of her fully decorated nursery began to take shape. Between that shower and her due date, she and Jake put a fresh coat of paint on the nursery walls, brought in new carpet for the floor, and bought and installed all-new furniture (crib, changing table, dresser, bookshelf, and cushy chair), complete with the sheets, blankets, and the stuffed animals they had received as gifts. As Anne and Jake took one last satisfied look, they saw the closet was lined with all-new clothes, a basket filled with diapers, a bin brimming with toys. Anne and Jake stood back, Anne absentmindedly rubbing her swollen belly, and declared that they were ready.

But there was something going on in that room of which they were unaware. The air in the little baby's nursery was slowly turning into a chemical soup. The furniture was releasing formaldehyde, the furniture finish and wall paint were seeping VOCs, the fabric finishes, stain repellents, and flame retardants from the upholstered chair, the carpet, and the mattress were all sending dangerous chemicals up into the air. Add to that the fragranced laundry detergent they had just used to wash all the bedding and new clothes and the chemical cleaning products they had used to make sure the room was spic and span according to their strict standards. And the plan, of course, was to bring their brand new baby home and lay her or him down in the room to sleep.

Okay, truth? This isn't the story of just one friend in particular. This is the story of what is happening in soon-to-be nurseries of my friends and other awaiting moms and dads all across the country. And it has me and a lot of environmentalists concerned.

Timing

Babies sleep on average anywhere from fourteen to eighteen hours a day, much of that time spent breathing in the nursery's air. Many scientists are coming to believe that children are more vulnerable in the face of environmental toxins and other hazards than adults. This is because pound for pound, infants and young children consume more food and water and breathe more air than we do as adults. Their air intake, on a body-weight basis, is twice that of adults. And before they turn six months old, babies will drink, pound for pound, seven times as much water and, by the time they're five years old, eat four times as much food. Their skin is more permeable and their still-developing internal organs and systems are less adapted to and less able to eliminate certain chemicals.

What all this boils down to is that you need to pay particularly close attention to the food babies eat, the water they drink, and the air they breathe. I know, it sounds a little scary, and truthfully it is. But there is a lot that you can do to make it better. Certainly, picking the right materials and design elements is crucial, but so is the timing of it all. To allow proper off-gassing time, do all major remodeling months in advance. Pregnant women and small children shouldn't be near the work.

> ### What Is Off-Gassing?
>
> Off-gassing is what we call it when volatile chemicals and volatile organic compounds (VOCs) evaporate at normal atmospheric pressure.
>
> Materials like paints, stains, insulation, carpet, plywood, particleboard, and so on can off-gas, and the evaporation, or off-gassing, can carry on for years. Look for further explanation on VOCs in the next chapter.

If you do have to buy conventional furniture items, simply allow them ample time (a few months is best) to off-gas either off-site or in a well-ventilated room long before you bring your baby home. Even blankets, diapers, and baby clothes should be washed ahead of time to remove any chemical residues from the manufacturing process. Be sure to wash these in a non-toxic detergent that is, at the very least, free of synthetic fragrances.

Ideas to Grow On

For a healthy environment, do any redecorating, furnishing, and cleaning at least a month before you bring your baby home. If that's impossible, let your baby sleep in a bassinet in your room while the new furnishings for her room off-gas elsewhere.

Paint

Applying the right shade of paint to your nursery walls can dramatically impact the feel of a room, making it bright and cheery or calm and soothing. There is a reason that waiting rooms are often green; it's because the right shade of green is a very soothing color. Pick your nursery color for the mood you want to project and emotions you want most to feel when you're with your precious little one.

Colors—What They Mean and What They Do

- **Blue:** Generally cool and calming. Too much blue can dampen spirits.

- **Brown:** Natural and earthy. Brown can stimulate an appetite.

- **Green:** Soothing and relaxing. Green signifies renewal, health, and growth.

- **Orange:** Vibrant and natural. Orange conjures memories of fall leaves.

- **Pink:** Typically delicate and feminine. Pink can be soft or playful.

- **Purple:** Royal and exciting. A purple room is said to enhance creativity.

- **Red:** Strong and emotional. Red can signify deep love or deep anger. Red may conjure up emotions that are too strong for a baby's room.

- **White:** Purity, innocence, and cleanliness. White goes with anything.

- **Yellow:** Warm and happy. Yellow signifies hope.

It may be that the walls in the room you've chosen as the nursery are already a nice neutral shade. If so, the best thing you can do is let them be and avoid repainting altogether. Why add more stress and work to your already busy life? Neutral walls provide the perfect backdrop for colorful pillows and wall hangings to add color and personality to the room. If you're already partial to whites, taupes, and beiges throughout your house, don't feel like you have to paint the baby's walls something bright and nursery-like just because all of your friends do. The nursery isn't just about creating a supportive environment for your child; it is also a place where *you* will spend a lot of time, and you want it to give off a vibe that will support your best moods too.

Picking a Paint

If you are planning to repaint, be sure to select a low- or no-VOC latex paint. Latex paints are generally healthier than oil-based versions. Choose paint in a light color or in one of the lightest shades of your selected color to help keep the room bright and cheery and to reduce the VOC amount in the paint. Because lighter shades contain less pigment, they also are generally lower in VOCs. If you're the pregnant one, let your nonpregnant spouse, partner, or friend paint the walls for you. Even though you're choosing the healthiest paints possible, these are still fumes you don't need to be breathing.

Be sure the room is well ventilated, with open windows and fans on, while the painting is taking place. And allow at least a month between the paint application and your due date so you're sure not to bring the baby home into a "paint-ripe" room.

Dealing with Lead-Based Paint

Many houses that were built before 1978 have lead-based paint throughout. If you suspect that the old paint on your walls and trim is lead based, take proper precautions to have it removed and your home properly mitigated. It

What to Do If You Suspect Lead Paint

• Watch for peeling, chipping, or cracked paint. Lead-based paint in good condition doesn't pose as great a risk.

• Have the paint in your home and the soil surrounding your home tested.

• Have blood tests performed on your family for lead poisoning.

• Contact a certified lead abatement contractor to remove, seal, or enclose all areas of lead-based paint.

is best to hire a lead abatement contractor to do the work for you. Because pregnant women and children are especially vulnerable, you'll want to vacate the property while the abatement takes place. Be on the lookout for cracking, chipping, or peeling paint, as this is when the lead can become airborne. Because it can become airborne, you should never sand or chisel away at paint that may contain lead. Areas where lead is most likely to be a hazard include door and window frames and sills, railings and banisters, stairs, porch floors, and outdoor railings and fences.

Floors

If you already have carpet in your nursery, it might be best to leave it as is and just have it thoroughly cleaned. But if you have the option, bare floors are superior because they can be cleaned easily and don't harbor dust mites or dander like carpet, both of which can contribute to allergies and asthma. If you would like to refinish your wood floors, choose a non-toxic sealant.

To absorb sound and create a softer, more cozy space, lay down area rugs that can be washed and aired out when needed.

The best rugs are those made from organic cotton, wool, jute, or even goat hair. Look for those that are undyed or colored using vegetable-based dyes. If you choose to lay down wall-to-wall carpet, select one that hasn't been

Keeping Carpet Clean and Safe

• Vacuum carpet with a HEPA (high-efficiency particulate air) filter vacuum twice a week to cut down on allergens like dust mites.

• Avoid humidity in the space to prevent mildew growth.

• Get rid of carpet odor by sprinkling baking soda before vacuuming.

• Avoid chemical cleaners whenever possible.

treated with stain repellents or other finishes. Traditional carpet padding contains a great number of chemical ingredients, so look for wool, camel, or goat hair rug and carpet pads.

Electronics

There has been a good deal of research that suggests that the electromagnetic fields (EMFs) generated by electrical appliances, electrical wiring, and power lines can have a negative effect on one's health, in both full-grown and child-sized bodies. The research is controversial in scientific circles, and still today there remains quite a bit of divide, with some people suggesting that certain frequencies are better than others, and other people recommending a reduction of appliance use altogether.

Whether you choose to explore the subject yourself or take it all with a grain of salt, the safest and most "harmonious" thing to do is to limit the number of appliances you have in your nursery. If you choose to use a baby monitor, position the monitor as far from the crib as possible, or at least three feet away, and be sure it is not plugged into the wall directly behind the crib. Keep all other electrical devices at least three feet from the crib and avoid leaving computers or cordless phones in your baby's room for long periods of time.

If You Use a Baby Monitor

• Keep the monitor at least three feet from the crib.

• If it's an option, set the monitor to "voice activation" so it doesn't transmit continuously.

• Don't plug the unit into the wall directly behind or below the crib. Use an outlet at least three feet from the crib's edge.

Just as you don't want a lot of technology and work reminders in your bedroom, the nursery will be a more balanced environment, conducive to sleep and peaceful feedings, without a lot of technology and other things to distract.

Furniture

From a design standpoint, the furniture you choose is as important as the color of paint you put on the walls. From a room health standpoint, it is at least as important. But it's also important to remember that babies don't need much. They need a place to lay their head, a place to be fed and rocked to sleep, a place to be wiped and swaddled, and maybe a place that will contain the toys and books that friends and families will give.

Buying Secondhand

For each of these items, there are two choices, to buy new or used. Buying used is one of the more environmentally sound things you can do. Remember,

What to Buy Secondhand

Crib	Stroller
Rocking chair	Toys
Changing table	Electronics and other gadgets
Bassinet/Bouncy seat	Bedding and clothing
High chair	

What Not to Buy Secondhand

Car seat	Mattress

buying secondhand is just a modest way to let someone know you are a world-class, heavyweight recycler! Secondhand baby items like strollers, furniture, toys, and baby monitors can be found online, at secondhand stores, or through newspaper ads or garage sales. Because babies go through so many stages so quickly, secondhand baby items are often only gently used. They can save you money and create a healthier nursery environment because you're not bringing in freshly manufactured items that have a greater chance of off-gassing into the room.

The two times when it is important to buy brand new is for your crib mattress (there have been links between secondhand mattresses and SIDS) and car seats (which may have damage to them that you're unable to see). For everything else, go for it! Just make sure particulars, like the spacing between crib bars, are up to current standards.

Buying New

When you buy new, there are a few things to keep in mind. First, you want to be sure the furniture is on the low-toxicity level: that it was stained or finished with non-toxic finishes or painted with low- or no-VOC paints. If the item is made from pressed wood or plywood, as a lot of furniture today is, be certain that the glues used to adhere the layers together don't contain formaldehyde, as many pressed-wood products do.

Formaldehyde is a colorless, pungent-smelling gas that can cause burning eyes, trigger asthma attacks, and may cause cancer. Urea-formaldehyde resins are used in the glues that adhere layers of wood together for plywood or particleboard, and at room temperatures, the formaldehyde (a classified VOC) emits toxins into the air. The degree to which formaldehyde off-gasses decreases over time. When an item is new, be sure there are no exposed areas of pressed wood. Simply use a non-toxic sealant to seal peg holes or shelf undersides where the pressed wood may be exposed.

If the item you are purchasing is made of solid wood, check to see if the wood was from a sustainably harvested forest or tree farm. Items made from reclaimed wood are also a great choice.

Beyond wood, there are a number of materials that furniture can be made from, including recycled materials like plastics and metals, and the ever popular eco superstar, bamboo. Bamboo is extremely fast growing and grows on its own with little or no chemical inputs. It is extremely durable and versatile, so you'll find bamboo in a variety of products from flooring to furniture.

Some of the greatest things coming out of baby furniture today are modular pieces. Cribs become toddler beds, then full-size child cots. Storage units go from toy bins to bookshelves. Changing tables become desks for your little ones to work and play on. The items in the room can last for years, changing and growing with the growing needs of your little one.

When buying new furniture check to be sure each piece is a low-toxicity item, made from sustainable materials, that will grow with your baby and last for years to come.

Mattress

It goes without saying that the mattress you choose is at least as important as the ones you choose for you, your spouse, and older children, so you'll want to be aware of issues surrounding mattresses, like chemical flame retardants that contain PBDEs (polybrominated diphenyl ether), specifically pentaBDE. PentaBDE is a toxic chemical that has been associated with hyperactivity and neurobehavioral modifications. Though this and other chemicals have been banned in Europe, they are still allowed in most parts of the United States.

Wool serves as a natural flame retardant; it and mattresses produced with organic cotton or natural latex with an organic wool outer layer are your natural choices. In some mattresses, wool is worked in throughout the mattress. Wool is mildew resistant, doesn't harbor dust mites or bacteria, and can help naturally regulate the body's temperature by insulating as well as wicking away excess moisture.

Mattress No-nos

• Flame retardants—chemicals like PBDEs, arsenic, antimony, and phosphorous

• Polyurethane foam filling—contains chemicals like formaldehyde, benzene, and toluene

• PVC plastic covers—toxic to baby and the environment

• Phthalates in mattress surfaces—associated with asthma, reproductive issues, and cancer

---

Textiles

Though cotton may be the fabric of our lives, as discussed in the bedroom chapter, it is also one of the most heavily sprayed crops in the world. The fact that the cotton in your home was sprayed with so many chemical pesticides and fertilizers means two things—those chemicals are coming home with you, and the earth's soil, water, and air have been polluted as a result of them. So for everyone's sake, choose organic cotton or other eco-fibers for all of your baby's textile needs. Look specifically for color-grown cotton, or fabric that has been colored with low-impact dyes. You'll be amazed to find organic cotton blankets and clothes at many big-box stores and large department stores today. And eco-friendly baby boutiques are popping up all over the country and the Internet. If there isn't a shop in your town, let your fingers do the walking and start to explore the wide variety for sale in online stores. While some of it is still more expensive than conventional baby clothes, the price is certainly coming down as availability goes up.

Baby Bedding

Organic wool is a wonderful option for a warm baby blanket, but cotton is still the fabric of choice for bedding. There are a number of companies making organic cotton crib sets and bumpers, as well as blankets and snugglies.

Of course, vintage is another great option for baby bedding. Even an old sheet cut to size will work. And a family blanket or quilt folded over a time or two is perfect for tummy time on the floor.

Baby Clothes

Organic cotton is the surest choice for baby clothes. Organic wool is warm and wonderfully moisture wicking, but not always as soft and cuddling as cotton. Thankfully, today there are a number of companies making everything from onesies to little party dresses out of organic cotton.

Toys

I'm guessing that your child doesn't reach for much of anything without promptly popping it into his or her little mouth. But whether the found object ends up there or not, it will still be close enough to your baby for him or her to breathe in any toxic fumes it may be emitting.

Most toys today are plastic and brightly colored, and involve some sort of mechanism that makes them spin or sing. But sometimes simple is better. In all honesty, your baby would probably be just as happy playing with an empty toilet paper tube.

Lead in Toys

If your toy has a color that is anything other than what you suspect the natural color of that substance might be, it could possibly contain lead, depending on its age and its place of origin.

Lead has been shown to be toxic if inhaled or ingested and has been linked to a number of additional problems, including ADD, learning disabilities, and memory loss, in children under six.

But like houses, toys made before 1978 may contain lead paint, so it's best to avoid vintage toys for your tots. Secondhand toys are absolutely fine, as long as they are post-1978. And your best bet for any new toy is to check the source of the item. If it came from China or India, notorious today for lead recalls, find an alternative.

This is probably going to limit the number of toys you buy pretty considerably. But this is an important issue for a lot of parents, so look for success stories and buying resources from healthy child and healthy parenting sites online.

Plastic Precautions

So many toys today are made from polyvinyl chloride (PVC) plastics. PVC, as a gas, is a known carcinogen. But PVC toys often contain lead as an additive, and soft, pliable plastic PVC toys (think rubber ducks, inflatables, and waterproof books) often contain phthalates to make them flexible. Phthalates have been shown to be hormone disruptors and can be released from a toy as it is handled and sucked on.

Spotting PVC Toys

Look for a number 3 on the bottom of a plastic toy as an indicator of whether it is a PVC plastic.

Some big-name toy companies today are swearing off PVCs and phthalates. These good guys include Lego, Gerber, Little Tikes, Early Start, Tiny Love, Sassy, Brio, and Ikea.

Healthy Alternatives

I know it's a little frightening to think about a toy landscape that doesn't include any flexible plastics, older painted toys, or anything from certain foreign countries. What that immediately means is that you may end up with fewer toys in your nursery than your neighbors. But let's think about that for a minute; that would probably be just fine. Fewer toys means money saved and less to keep picked up.

Wood makes a wonderful alternative to plastic for toys. Look for unfinished wood or wood finished with non-toxic paints, sealants, and varnishes. As an alternative to stuffed toys that are made from and filled with synthetic materials, look for cloth toys made from organic cotton, hemp, bamboo, or wool.

If you don't have stores in your area offering these healthier toy alternatives, shop online. You'll find a vast array of companies and websites selling healthy baby toys.

Less Is More

While simple is certainly better when it comes to toys, less is almost always more. But it's one thing to set a standard for the toy buying at home and another to expect adoring family and friends to obey your "less is more" mantra. Before you have your baby, and at each consecutive birthday party, consider setting some limitations and encourage gifts that are actions instead of objects.

A friend of mine tells me about how, though she and her husband are adamant about not overbuying for their little girl, her parents can't help themselves. She's trying to help Grandma and Grandpa understand that a date for ice cream means as much to their little girl as a new doll or paint set.

Ideas to Grow On

Set limits before your child's next birthday party. Encourage gifts that are actions instead of objects.

Diapers

The diaper debate—cloth versus disposable—is ongoing, and in truth there are varying opinions on which is more environmentally responsible. The reality, though, is that your baby will go through up to eight thousand diapers in his or her lifetime. So make *this* decision with your eyes wide open.

Better Disposables

Gel free   Nonplastic outsides

Unbleached

Better Disposables

The first disposable diaper, Pampers, was introduced by Procter & Gamble in 1961, and by 1971, only ten years later, disposable diapers were registered by one cleanup crew as the largest portion of litter on the sides of highways. By 1989, 18 billion diapers were being soiled each year, costing American parents $300 million annually and accounting for nearly 3.5 million tons of garbage, or 2 percent of all solid waste in our landfills. And the same estimates hold true today.

Today an unbelievable 95 percent of the diapers used are disposable, and most of those, at least those of the conventional variety, will take two to five hundred years to decompose in a landfill. That's a lot of diapers lasting a long time littering our precious earth. But that's not the worst of it. Disposable diapers contain a filler called AGM, which stands for "absorbent gel material." AGM has been linked to an increase in childhood asthma and a decreased sperm count in boys.

Today there are diapers that are considered biodegradable, but truthfully, nothing biodegrades well in a landfill. Your best choices are diapers that are gel free and unbleached.

New Cloth Alternatives

But then there are cloth diapers. There is no arguing that cloth diapers do take a considerable amount of water, energy, detergent, and time to keep in working order. So how do you conserve when using cloth nappies? Use a diapering service; they use less water and detergents than you will if you launder them on your own. If you're washing on your own, use cold water to save a considerable amount of energy and a non-toxic, fragrance-free laundry detergent.

Diapers made from organic cotton can be found today at many mainstream supermarkets and box stores.

Quite possibly the best news to hit the cloth diaper circuit as of late is the new shapes and styles today's cloth diapers are coming in. Sure, you can still find cloth diapers that are the standard rectangle made of a few layers of absorbent cotton. But there are newer diapers that are shaped like a disposable, tapered in the middle, to better fit your baby's bum. These same diapers often have elastic around the waist to hold them snugly in place and Velcro on the sides, so you no longer have to use safety pins.

They are convenient to use, like a disposable, but better for the landfill and your wallet because they can be washed and reused time and again.

Hybrids

Worth a nod are the few newer varieties of hybrid diapers. Shaped like a disposable, these have a reusable cloth exterior and an absorbent insert that can be dropped into a toilet and flushed down any standard household latrine. But just because they're flushed doesn't mean they're gone, so consider equally the eventual disposal of these inserts as much as any other.

Shared Diaper Duties

But an important thing to remember is that it doesn't *have* to be all or nothing. Just because your child's daycare or your in-laws aren't willing to do the cloth diaper thing doesn't mean you can't do it during the hours when you're home with the baby. Choose cloth diapers to use at home, but have a diaper bag full of gel-free, chlorine bleach–free diapers for when you do the drop-off or someone else takes over diaper duty. Something is better than nothing, and when it comes to diapers, it doesn't have to be all or nothing. *Sometimes* is just fine.

Food

Babies are notorious for doing four things—they eat, they sleep, they cry, and they poop. And the four are all so closely related. A well-fed baby, particularly a breastfed baby, will have poopie diapers with *consistent* and *minimal* amounts of waste. I'm sure you've also eaten the wrong thing and "remembered" it the next day as you "passed it through." The same thing happens to a baby, and it's not hard to miss when you're the one changing the diaper. Baby food selection takes some time and care, but is well worth it for so many reasons.

Breastfeeding

Highly nutritious, breast milk is widely considered to be a baby's most perfect food. Numerous studies have shown that babies who are raised on breast milk have fewer and less severe illnesses than those fed formula as infants. Breast milk has been shown to reduce incidences of diarrhea and bacterial meningitis, and lead to lower rates of respiratory, urinary tract, and ear infections. And breast milk is good for the new mom too, helping her shed extra baby weight and feel calm and relaxed. It also helps contract her uterus after delivery and reduces her risk of urinary tract infections and certain types of cancer.

It's important when you're breastfeeding to drink plenty of water to stay properly hydrated and to eat a variety of strong, nutrient-rich foods. Remember that the flavors you enjoy while you're making breast milk, your baby will also be enjoying. You are playing a part in shaping your baby's young taste palate, so choose your foods carefully.

On top of all of the other pros, breastfeeding is free, saving you thousands of dollars a year.

Formula

Whether it's a first choice or not, formula is a necessity for many babies and mothers. And while there are certainly a lot of unhealthy ingredients and waste in common formulas, there are plenty of greener, healthier choices. When picking your baby's formula, choose an organic formula and be sure to use filtered water to avoid extra chemicals and contaminants entering through your water. The American Dental Association recommends that you filter fluoride out of your water before mixing it into formula. A home reverse-osmosis system will do the trick. If your water isn't treated with fluoride, as most city water is, a simple carbon filter on the sink faucet or in a pitcher will suffice.

Though they're convenient, try to avoid single-serving options, because they create a lot of waste. Choose instead large containers that you can mix on your own.

Often, liquid and powdered formula are sold in metal cans that have a plastic liner containing the toxic chemical bisphenol A (BPA). This chemical has been linked to reproductive disorders and neurobehavioral problems in lab animals, at levels lower than that at which humans are exposed. A group of scientists from the National Institutes of Health (an agency of the U.S. Department of Health and Human Services) has expressed concern about the impact of BPA on infants' brains and behavior. Even so, many of the popular name-brand formulas, including Nestle, Similac, and Enfamil, use BPA in the linings of their liquid formula. Your best option, to avoid BPA exposure, is to stick with a powdered formula where the surface area of BPA-lined metals is significantly less. Studies show that babies receive eight to twenty times less BPA when fed reconstituted powdered formula over liquid formula from a metal can. While not all organic formula packaging is BPA free, much of it is. Take time to read labels and stick with a powdered formula to reduce exposure.

Healthy Baby Formula

• Choose an organic formula.

• Choose a powdered formula over liquid.

• Use filtered water.

• Avoid single-serving options.

Bottles

Whether your baby's bottle holds breast milk or formula may not even matter as much as the material the bottle is made of. Bottles made from the wrong type of plastic can leach harmful toxins like bisphenol A (BPA), a known hormone disruptor, into your baby's milk. Even small amounts of BPA have been linked to early puberty, hyperactivity, impairment to the immune system, and decreased sperm count. To stay in the clear, avoid any bottle that has the number 7 on it, or is labeled PC or polycarbonate. The best bottles are made from glass or polyethylene or polypropylene plastics.

Ideas to Grow On

In general, any plastic labeled with a 1, 2, 4, or 5 is safer, whereas 3, 6, and 7 should be avoided.

When bottle shopping, choose bottles that don't require any sort of liner. The liners in bottles are typically made from a more harmful plastic that can leach toxins, especially when heated. Many bottles don't require any sort of flexible liner.

Nipples are another area to watch out for. Keep an eye out for cloudy or brown nipples, typically made from latex. These should be avoided because they can potentially lead to latex sensitivities down the road, and because

Healthy Bottle Feeding

• **Avoid** polycarbonate bottles—they can leach BPA, a hormone disruptor, into juice, water, formula, or milk. **Select** glass, polyethylene, or polypropylene bottles instead.

• **Avoid** rubber or latex nipples—they can harbor bacteria and lead to latex sensitivities. **Select** silicone nipples instead. They're easy to spot because they're clear, rather than brown or cloudy like latex nipples.

• **Avoid** bottle liners—soft plastic bags—that can leach chemicals into the liquid. **Select** linerless bottles instead and always heat in a pot of hot water rather than the microwave.

• **Avoid** liquid formulas in metal cans—the lining of the can will likely leach BPA into the liquid formula. **Select** powdered formula instead in a container with as little metal as possible.

• **Avoid** unfiltered water from the tap when reconstituting formula, as it may contain fluoride. **Select** a reverse-osmosis filtration system for your home to remove fluoride. If your water doesn't contain fluoride, a carbon filter (on your tap or in a pitcher) will do the trick.

• **Avoid** any plastic product (bottle, nipple, or otherwise) that is labeled with a 3, 6, or 7. Especially watch for bottles that are marked with a 7 or "PC" (polycarbonate). **Select** any plastic product (bottle, nipple, or otherwise) that is labeled with a 1, 2, 4, or 5 instead.

they're more porous, so they are more apt to harbor bacteria. Instead choose new clear silicon nipples. Silicon nipples also come in bright colors, but I recommend the clear variety to avoid synthetic coloring agents.

Solid Foods

Around six months in, babies start to get a taste for, and the ability to handle, solid foods. At first the foods are easy—mashed bananas, avocados, prunes, rice cereal, and other mushy items. Then it becomes more complex as their teeth and palates expand. Jarred baby foods can be a great option, particularly if you're on the go. And today there are a wide variety of organic foods in baby food jars.

There are other options as well: frozen foods in single serving sizes that you can pop out and defrost for a quick and fresh-tasting meal, and refrigerated bowls that are neither frozen nor jarred, as if you've pureed them yourself only hours before.

Ideas to Grow On

Consider how the foods you're already cooking for yourself can be turned into baby food. It's simple to steam some extra vegetables or mash up some rice you've already cooked.

But still the best option is to make your own foods. Rather than thinking exclusively about what your baby might want to eat, look first at what your family is eating and try to turn one or two of those items into a meal for the baby. Steam a little extra broccoli or other vegetables or pull aside some lentils or fruit. Just be sure to pull your baby's foods aside before you add seasonings or spices, and try to feed your baby a good variety of foods, including organic fruits and vegetables, healthy natural proteins, and, as they're ready, other foods.

Feed Your Baby a Rainbow of Colors

• **Reds:** raspberries, strawberries, watermelon, apples, grapes, rhubarb, tomatoes, beets, and peppers. Reds maintain memory, heart, and urinary tract health and help lower cancer risks.

• **Oranges/Yellows:** peaches, tangerines, lemons, carrots, sweet potatoes, butternut squash, yellow peppers, and tomatoes. Oranges/Yellows benefit healthy hearts, eyes, and immune systems.

• **Greens:** apples, grapes, pears, limes, avocado, broccoli, celery, cucumbers, peas, spinach, and leafy vegetables. Greens are good for strong bones, eyes, and teeth.

• **Blues/Purples:** blueberries, blackberries, purple grapes, raisins, purple figs, plums, eggplant, and purple cabbage. Blues/Purples provide lots of antioxidants, good for anti-aging and a healthy memory.

• **Whites/Tans/Browns:** bananas, white nectarines, dates, garlic, onions, ginger, cauliflower, potatoes, and mushrooms. Whites/Tans/Browns help maintain heart health and cholesterol levels.

Selecting a variety of colors, called "eating a rainbow," is an excellent way to be sure your baby is getting a variety of vitamins and minerals. But it will never be more important than at this young age to feed your baby organic foods, free of harmful pesticides and other chemicals.

Body Care

The sweet smell and feel of a baby's skin is one of life's simple pleasures. You certainly would not want to undo what is naturally lovely by overcleaning or cleaning with the wrong products.

An Environmental Working Group study found that children are exposed to an average of sixty chemicals every day through personal care products. These chemicals are breathed in or absorbed through their skin.

Ideas to Grow On

Think before you buff, lotion, or puff. Excessive use of products could be one of your most harmful practices.

The most concerning of these chemicals are phthalates, which are potent reproductive toxins. Phthalates were found in three-quarters of seventy-two different name-brand products the Environmental Working Group and partners tested. When these products are used, the reproductive toxins are absorbed into the baby's body, where they can cause damage, especially to the reproductive system of baby boys.

Unlike in food, ingredients in personal care products are not regulated by the FDA for safety, so it is perfectly legal for companies to use ingredients that are known to be dangerous or risky toxins, like phthalates, carcinogens, and other substances.

But the one thing you can do to protect yourself and your baby is to read the ingredients label of every product you get your hands on, before you put it on your baby's precious body. There are a small number of ingredients that should be avoided whenever possible. While the following list may look intimidating, try not to let it overwhelm you. This is simply a compilation of research into some of the more dangerous baby care ingredients. Do your best to read labels and avoid those that you can. Many products will say when they are free from a particularly toxic ingredient like phthalates or parabens, so look for products labeled "phthalate free" and so on or thoroughly read the ingredients list before buying. Aubrey Organics, Avalon Organics, Burt's Bees, California Baby, and Weleda Baby are just a few of the

ROBYN O'BRIEN

Robyn O'Brien has never been one to shy away from a challenge or edge gingerly into a passion. She and her husband had four kids in five years, so she well understood the challenges of a busy household. She was the typical mom slinging Happy Meals into the back seat of the car and handing her kids tubes of blue yogurt in the afternoons. It was hard enough to get everyone to eat *something,* let alone a *healthy* something. But one day her life abruptly and irrevocably changed, over a plate of eggs. And suddenly she was thrown into a childhood epidemic that she hadn't even known existed.

The day her youngest was diagnosed with food allergies, she planted herself in front of a computer and started digging up all of the food allergy research she could find. She was shocked to learn of the silent epidemic of food allergies that was affecting so many young children. Her first reaction, she says, was to ask, "What in the world has changed in our food supply that a PB&J and carton of milk are suddenly considered loaded weapons on a lunchroom table?"

She quickly became a full-time mama bear on the defense. Ingredient labels on food packages had never mattered before. After all, she grew up with the same foods and never thought to question them; the general consensus was "we turned out fine!" But suddenly *labels mattered.* She started reading long lists of ingredients on packages of macaroni and cheese and Spaghetti-Os and found she couldn't pronounce half of them. It suddenly started to sound more and more like a food science experiment and less like, well, food. As Robyn read and researched these hard-to-pronounce ingredients, she also learned that many of the same ingredients had been banned in other parts of the world and she started to wonder who was going to step up and protect her family. It was going to have to be her.

With a new "you are what you eat" mantra ringing through her head, she found that once you start making informed and educated choices about choosing "clean foods" for your family, you feel inspired and empowered to help others as well. Her family broke their "convenience" food addiction to blue yogurt tubes and mac & cheese and started eating real, whole, and living foods. Amazingly and almost immediately, her children's behavior began to improve; they began to sleep better and perform better in school. One day her child stopped, looked up at her, and said, "Mommy, we didn't always used to eat this way." Robyn responded, "No, we didn't, sweet pea. Mommy didn't know!" To which he said, "Did you know that my tummy and my head always used to hurt?" Robyn vowed then and there never to go back.

And so AllergyKids was born out of Robyn's living room, her fears, her resolutions, and her family's steadfastness. An agency with a goal of preventing accidental, life-threatening food allergy reactions by funding research and making it easier to identify kids with allergies, AllergyKids launched a universal symbol that can be applied as a sticker to children's backpacks, lunch boxes, or overcoats, alerting cafeteria monitors, teachers, and other parents that this is an AllergyKid.

Driving Robyn still today are the studies that show that one out of every three American children suffers from allergies, asthma, ADHD, or autism, all told affecting 20 million children. Since the introduction of many new foreign substances into our nation's foods within the last twenty years (new chemicals, genetically modified ingredients, and so on), the rate of allergies has increased by 400 percent, asthma by 300 percent, and ADHD by 400 percent, and there is an increase of between 1,500 and 6,000 percent in the number of children with autism-spectrum disorders. Robyn believes food is at least *one* thing that should be blamed.

Robyn is just one woman, just one mother. But she figures who better to fight the fight for safer food and better labeling than the mothers of the one in three American children with diabetes, asthma, allergies, autism, or ADHD? She likes to quote poet June Jordan, who wrote, "We are the ones we have been waiting for." ▪

The 1, 2, 3 of Baby Body Care

Less is more when it comes to particular products and frequency of use. A washcloth with warm water and a mild simple soap applied to the necessary parts is all that is needed on a daily basis.

Avoid antibacterial products, as they may prevent your baby from developing his or her own natural resistance and can play a part in developing strong bacterial strains.

Choose fragrance-free products across the board.

---

baby lines that are free of many of these avoidable ingredients. All of these can be found at natural products stores, while many are starting to pop up in big-box stores now as well.

Baby Buying—What to Avoid

In a Variety of Products

Fragrance—neurotoxic substance, allergen, linked to hormone disruption

Parabens—hormone disruptor possibly contributing to cancer

Phthalates—hormone disruptor, linked to cancer

In Shampoos and Conditioners

DMDM Hydantoin—allergen, irritant, can form cancer-causing agents

Ceteareth—petrochemical, may contain cancer-causing impurities

PEG Compounds—petrochemical, may contain cancer-causing impurities

In Liquid Soaps and Body Washes

Triclosan—causes thyroid disruption, leading to disrupted growth hormones

DMDM Hydantoin—allergen, irritant, can form cancer-causing agents

In Baby Wipes

Bronopol—allergen, irritant, can form cancer-causing compounds

DMDM Hydantoin—allergen, irritant, can form cancer-causing agents

In Lotions and Moisturizers

PEG Compounds—petrochemical, may contain cancer-causing impurities

DMDM Hydantoin—allergen, irritant, can form cancer-causing agents

Ceteareth—petrochemical, may contain cancer-causing impurities

In Diaper Creams

BHA—leads to skin depigmentation

Boric Acid—tagged by industry safety experts as unsafe for infants

Sodium Borate—tagged by industry safety experts as unsafe for infants

In Baby Powders

Particulates—lung-damaging airborne particles

DMDM Hydantoin—allergen, irritant, can form cancer-causing agents

Sodium Borate—tagged by industry safety experts as unsafe for infants

In Sunscreen

Oxybenzone—allergen, causes cell and DNA damage with free radicals

DMDM Hydantoin—allergen, irritant, can form cancer-causing agents

Triethalonamine—allergen, irritant, can form cancer-causing agents

In Toothpaste

Fluoride—neurotoxic matter when swallowed, causes teeth stains

PEG Compounds—may contain cancer-causing agents

Triclosan—causes thyroid disruption, leading to disrupted growth hormones

Remember, don't drive yourself crazy trying to avoid all of these ingredients—you already have a lot on your plate! Just do your best to find the most simple and natural products for your baby's health.

Conservation

Think back to when you were young. Did your parents have two or more car seats—one for each vehicle in the garage? Did they have twenty-plus blankets so they'd never have to walk to another room to get one? Did they have toys in every shape, color, and size for you? Did you play with things that blinked and beeped? Did you have monitor cameras staring you down while you slept? The amount of excess that many parents today find themselves buying into is frightening. But you can keep your purchasing in check by simply making a pact to avoid overbuying and by pausing to question the validity and necessity of an item before making a purchase. This isn't only about saving your money or saving the environment from an unnecessary amount of consumption, it's also about creating a serene and peaceful environment for your little one.

I'm sure that, given the chance, you would "give the world" to your little baby. So do all you can today to protect that world, and it will be there for him as he grows old and passes it on, with the same love and care as you did, to his little one.

In the Living Room

My Recycled Living Room

I had a reporter visit me in my home not long ago. I greeted her at the door and made her a cup of tea before we went to sit in the living room for the duration of the interview. We had a nice two-hour-long talk about my home, my upbringing, my hopes and fears for the environment, my experiences, and my plans for the future. When the article came out, I felt honored by what she wrote. But within the beginning section of the article, she made an observation that I thought was interesting and funny—she gave an exact count of the number of plants in our living room—a number that she apparently thought was high! What a funny thing for her to have taken note of—but maybe not, when you consider that a different reporter once gave a count on the number of tea packages in my tea drawer.

The reason for the high concentration of plants in my home is that simple houseplants can be such an effective way to clean the air in your home and to reconnect you to living elements, even if you are someone who prefers to spend your time indoors. But as I walk room by room through my home, I see so many elements, beyond the dozens of living plants, that make it a healthy home. If yours doesn't feel that way today, I hope that it will someday soon.

Natural Decor

From your home's hardware to its software, there are green alternatives to nearly every article. And I can't think of a better place to talk about the in-home elements that can make your house pretty, comfortable, *and* green than in the living room.

Plants

A little while back NASA conducted a study with the Associated Landscape Contractors of America on the abilities of plants to help clean indoor air and rid it of common pollutants. The study was conducted for purposes of purifying air in orbiting space stations, but the results of the study proved to be applicable to traditional homes as well. Many homes today are as airtight as possible, as a means of conserving energy. But the result is that common indoor air pollutants, from furniture upholstery to floor stains, remain trapped inside the home. Synthetic building materials, furniture, paints, finishes, and cleaning products can emit organic compounds that have been linked to negative health effects. Together these create a phenomenon that occurs often in office environments but also in homes as well, known as "sick building syndrome."

> The process of products and materials emitting organic compounds and organic chemicals is called "off-gassing."

Trees and plants, as you probably know, convert carbon dioxide into oxygen through the process of photosynthesis, which combat the CO_2 emissions we're constantly causing. Indoors, the same principles may be at work and are the reasons why plants prove to be very effective at removing certain interior air pollutants. The point—simple green plants can neutralize the big bad in-home contaminants.

NASA wanted to learn not only how to rid indoor spaces of chemical pollutants, but which pollutants are the most harmful and how they get in there in the first place. While numerous chemicals can be found in indoor atmospheres at any time, three common toxic gases became the focus of the NASA study (these were noted because of their links to cancer and birth defects, among other things): formaldehyde, trichloroethylene, and benzene gases. These three enter our homes through everything from common cleaning products and paints to wood products. Trichloroethylene is most often used in dry cleaning but is also present in paints, inks, varnishes, lacquers, and many adhesives. Trichloroethylene has been named a potent liver carcinogen by the National Cancer Institute. Benzene is a chemical solvent present in inks, oils, paints, gasoline, plastics, and rubber. Formaldehyde is a universal chemical present in so many indoor settings. Urea-formaldehyde (UF) is found in foam insulation as well as pressed-wood products such as particleboard and fiberboard, which are commonly used in furniture and cabinets. UF resins are also used to treat common paper products like grocery bags, tissues, paper towels, and waxed paper, and are an active ingredient in laundry products like starch wrinkle resisters, as well as water repellents and fire retardants used on furniture. Formaldehyde comes also from smoke and heating and cooking fuels like natural gas.

Ideas to Grow On

Turn indoor gardening into a family activity and let your kids take turns watering the plants. They'll enjoy watching them grow.

While all of NASA's selected plants proved to be effective at purifying the air, primarily through their leaves (roots and soil bacteria play an important role as well), certain plants seemed more effective at removing certain toxins than others. For example, the bamboo palm, the dracaena Janet Craig, and mother-in-law's tongue all did very well in filtering out formaldehyde. Peace lily, gerbera daisy, and Marginata were effective in filtering trichloroethylene. And flowering plants like gerbera daisy and pot mums did exceptionally well in removing benzene, as did the peace lily, bamboo palm, and Warneckei.

To cover all your bases, try placing around your home an assortment of plants from the group of fifteen that are most effective at cleaning indoor air. These fifteen plants all grow well indoors because they don't require much sunlight or attention. You'll notice that gerbera daisies and chrysanthemums are on the list but are typically used as seasonal decorations, so they may be hard to find year round. Of course, if you have pets at home, beware that some plants can be poisonous to cats and dogs if they chew the leaves. You

The Top Fifteen Plants to Clean Your Home's Air

If your home is between 2,000 and 3,000 square feet, use a total of fifteen to twenty plants throughout.

Common Name	Latin (Proper) Name
Bamboo palm (reed palm)	*Chamaedorea seifrizii*
Chinese evergreen	*Aglaonema modestum*
Elephant ear philodendron	*Philodendron domesticum*
English ivy	*Hedera helix*
Ficus (weeping fig)	*Ficus benjamina*
Gerbera daisy	*Gerbera jamesonii*
Golden pothos (Devil's ivy)	*Epipiremnum aureum*
Heartleaf philodendron	*Philodendron scandens*
Janet Craig	*Dracaena deremensis*
Marginata	*Dracaena marginata*
Mother-in-law's tongue (snake plant)	*Sansevieria laurentii*
Peace lily	*Spathiphyllum "Mauna Loa"*
Pot mum	*Chrysanthemum norifolium*
Spider plant	*Chlorophytum comosum*
Warneckei	*Dracaena deremensis*

can find lists of poisonous plants online or you can ask your vet or at your local pet store.

Paint

People always say that the biggest bang for your remodeling buck comes in a can of paint. Nothing makes a room feel fresh and new like a fresh coat of color. But that easily recognized paint smell comes from a class of chemicals in the paint, called volatile organic compounds (VOCs).

VOCs are carbon compounds that turn to gases at room temperature, especially when they come into contact with sunlight. Formaldehyde, named a probable carcinogen, is a VOC common in paints.

VOC Stands for Volatile Organic Compounds

VOCs can cause headaches, muscle weakness, nausea, skin and eye irritation, and respiratory problems. Some VOCs may lead to more serious ailments and diseases, including cancer.

According to the Environmental Protection Agency, 9 percent of consumer product VOC emissions come from paints, stains, and other architectural coatings. They are second to automobiles as the largest sources of VOC emissions. Concentrations of VOCs in indoor environments are up to ten times higher than outdoor levels. And when you're in the act of applying paint to a wall, the concentration level can rise to a thousand times that of outdoor concentration levels. Long after the paint on our walls is dry, VOCs are polluting the air we breathe in our living rooms, kitchens, bedrooms, and nurseries.

For a healthy dose of wall color, choose a low- or no-VOC paint. Such products should be clearly marked and are now available at most major home and hardware stores.

Latex Versus Oil-Based Paints

Although a product may be labeled zero- or no-VOC, it does not mean that it's completely chemical free. Even zero-VOC paints are allowed to contain up to five grams of VOCs per liter.

Your best and healthiest bet is to choose a latex paint instead of an oil-based paint. Oil-based paints, though often used because they make walls and high-traffic areas easy to clean, are petroleum based and contain formaldehyde, benzene, toluene, and xylene. And because they take longer to dry than latex paints, they emit higher levels of VOCs for longer periods of time.

Because latex paints use water in place of petroleum-based solvents, they have lower levels of VOCs than their oil-based counterparts. Cleanup is easier with latex also, requiring only water instead of chemical solvents.

Low- and no-VOC paints have increased immensely in popularity over the past few years and are now widely available at paint stores, home improvement stores, and nearly all of your big-box stores. While you might see a small price difference today, the gap is lessening as the market for these paints expands.

Ideas to Grow On

Choose lighter colors for a brighter and healthier room. Typically, the darker the hue, the greater the amount of VOCs in the paint.

Natural Paints

A paint labeled a "natural paint" is often made with materials like lime, clay, linseed oil, citrus oil, milk, and chalk. Natural paints can give a beautiful old-world, textured look, and they're free of petroleum products and therefore emit very low levels of VOCs.

Milk paints are probably the healthiest of any paints out there. They are made from powdered casein, a milk protein that is mixed with pigment. Many people choose to mix their milk paint colors themselves, but you can buy premixed milk paint in a can. Because milk paint has a dull finish, many people prefer to seal it using a healthy water-based sealer.

Furniture

Unfortunately, a lot of the furniture today is made with unsustainably harvested wood, which is bad for our disappearing forests, or particleboard and other pressed-wood products, which are bad for our homes because of the formaldehyde that can leach from the glues.

Sustainable Wood

By some estimates, over 7 billion acres of forest, almost half of the world's original forests, have been cut down to meet our demand for wood and paper. Nearly 40 million acres disappear every year, destroying natural habitats, plant diversity, and, because trees absorb and store carbon dioxide, an important tool in reducing global warming.

A better option for wood furniture items are products made with FSC (Forest Stewardship Council) certified wood. The Forest Stewardship Council has been certifying well-managed forests and logging since the mid-1990s, requiring the protection of forests, limiting the logging of old-growth trees, and setting standards for fair labor. You can find FSC-certified wood products at many major retailers today.

Healthy Wood

Try to avoid furniture items made with pressed woods such as plywood and particleboard. Most of these use formaldehyde-based glues as the bonding agent. Formaldehyde, a probable human carcinogen, becomes a gas at room temperature, releasing into the air you breathe and polluting your home for years to come.

While VOC emissions from the formaldehyde will lessen over time, it's best to avoid the toxin altogether when possible. Today there are companies making furniture from pressed wood using formaldehyde-free glues. Ask questions of the seller or do research on the manufacturer before you buy.

Many of these companies promote their furniture as eco or green, so they're usually easy to spot on a showroom floor.

Ideas to Grow On

Check the unfinished edges of furniture to see if it is made from chip-board, plywood, or particleboard. Look at the back side of shelves, the underside of desk drawers, and the inside of shelving peg holes. Seal all exposed areas with a non-toxic sealant.

Bamboo

Bamboo can be a very sustainable building material because it grows quickly with little help. Sustainably managed bamboo forests produce a durable and beautiful building material perfect for floors and furniture. Look for items held together with non-formaldehyde glues and finished with no-VOC stains.

Upholstery and Finishes

Two important elements to consider, for home health and environmental factors, are the upholstery and finishes used on your furniture. Many

---

Healthier Furniture Finishes

• Look for furniture items finished with healthy paints and stains.

• Buy items that were stained at the factory. These will have done most of their off-gassing before you bring them home.

• If you finish it yourself, choose a well-ventilated area, use low- or no-VOC finishes, and allow it to fully dry before you bring it into your home.

wood furniture items are finished with paints and stains that are high in VOCs. And nearly all new upholstered items have been treated with fire retardants as well as fabric finishes to prevent stains and to make them waterproof.

Many companies today are upholstering in wool or organic cotton, and using non-toxic finishes that are low- or no-VOC paints and stains.

Recycled and Reclaimed

If all of this seems a little daunting—finding couches with organic cotton upholstery and dressers with non-toxic finishes—remember that as with clothing, one of the best choices you can make is to buy something that has already been around for a while. Even if the item was made with conventional materials, most of the harmful off-gassing has already occurred and your impact on the environment is lessened by not demanding a brand new item.

Choosing reclaimed items, like tables and chairs from antique shops or flea markets, can save the environment but also save you money. So many of my furniture items are secondhand. I have tables from flea markets, items from antique shops, and things that I literally found on the side of the road. And because my mother-in-law loves to redecorate, I get to give new life to her old pieces.

Heirlooms and antiques are often higher quality than their contemporary counterparts, offering you a piece of furniture that will last through the wear and tear of your busy household. While acquiring antiques may not save you any money, buying secondhand is often much less expensive than buying brand new, making it a responsible choice for so many different reasons.

A childhood favorite in my house growing up was a rocking chair that my parents happened upon on a farm in Michigan. It was sitting outside of a chicken coop, covered in droppings and grime, but they could see past that. It was well designed, and made of solid, beautifully knotty wood, and with a little TLC it became a lovely piece of furniture. It has held a place of honor in my parents' kitchen for well over thirty years.

Ideas to Grow On

There is no shame in buying secondhand items—it's good for the environment and your pocketbook. Shop flea markets, garage sales, and online.

Furniture can also be brand new but made from recycled materials. Though many of us have gotten very good at recycling, we haven't gotten as good at buying products made from all of that recycled material. Recycled-content furniture is often made from recycled plastics, cardboard, wood, and other materials like seatbelts and metals. You'll find furniture like this mostly at specialty boutiques. But, as always, a lot of this can be shopped for online.

Candles

With the proper paint on the walls, plants on floors and tables, and furniture on which to relax, all that's left to create a beautiful and healthy living room is some natural decor. Decorating with candles is an inexpensive and eco-friendly way to brighten a room. You can use a single candle or an arrangement of short and tall tapers that may even eliminate the need for electrical lighting. Your best bets are soy or beeswax candles with lead-free wicks, which burn cleaner than conventional candles. If you're attracted to candles for their fragrance, choose ones that are scented with essential oils.

Ideas to Grow On

Making your own candles can be a fun family project. Melt soy wax into an old mason jar, insert a lead-free wick, and you're done. Or roll beeswax around a clean-burning wick to make natural tapers for your dining room table.

TIM REDMOND

Whether on a living room sofa or a city sidewalk, around a dinner table or a boardroom table, Tim Redmond has spent the better part of thirty years convincing others about the benefits of whole and natural foods. But the road hasn't always been easy. Early on, Tim Redmond walked away from the prospect of a lucrative career following in his father's footsteps for a loftier and more personal goal: he wanted to change America through food—simple, wholesome, natural food. After contributing to the natural and organic foods scene by co-founding Eden Foods, Tim moved on to beverages, delivering the first mass-market soymilk to the United States. He dabbled with tofu ice cream and vegetable and fruit juices, and most recently landed himself in the deep, deep sea of organic seafood. Murky waters indeed as he now finds himself once again working with the U.S. government to shape the organic food standards for a whole new category. As you now know by the pages of this book, Tim is my dad. His mission, thirty-some years later, remains the same—to change America through the foods we eat.

So what, aside from this, makes Tim someone you may find inspiring? Tim is a man who has never stopped developing, growing, and teaching. Fifty-plus years ago Tim was a kid, wet behind the ears, with balled-up white bread as a snack in his pocket. And as he grew he recognized that foods like the white bread in his pocket and on the plates of people around him—foods processed almost beyond recognition—could one day lead to a nutrient-deficient subset of society. So Tim rose to the occasion, and through his company he began distributing some of the first natural and organic foods. Thirty years later people now have plenty of options for whole grains, healthy oils, nuts, seeds, and other unrefined, natural, and organic foods at their disposal. They have options for nondairy milk alternatives. And soon they'll have easy options for organically farm-raised and sustainable seafood. But at

continued

least a portion of that may not have happened if he had taken the easy way out, or if he had stopped caring about people and the way they lived.

At one point in college Tim made the decision not to finish with a business degree but to study to become a teacher instead. In many ways Tim has spent his years teaching, but instead of lecturing students sitting behind desks, he's used the world and its sidewalks as his classroom. I've overheard him teaching people on street corners about better food options and arguing environmental policy over the dinner table. I've watched him dole out samples of "health foods" to junk food addicts, and haul cases of his newest products on family vacations so newfound friends could try something they might otherwise never experience. And I've spent a lifetime listening to countless little lessons about food, soil, health, and nature. And the big surprise—I've never tired of it. Instead I learned the greatest lesson of all—how to teach and inspire others without berating or intimidating them.

It's an important lesson to learn as an adult, I think, especially as you become excited about something new like the natural foods and environmental movement. It would be very easy to get on a soapbox at every opportunity and to make others feel small for the changes they're *not* making. But where would that get any of us? Instead quiet persistence and unfailing encouragement seem to be key. It's worked for Tim—one of the natural industry's pioneers, innovators, and teachers—so it can probably work for you too. ■

Conservation

Conserving energy and resources *and* money in the home can take place in one of two ways. By eliminating the need for "new" all of the time, you'll cut down on the materials and other precious resources used to meet your

consumer demands. And by practicing basic conservation methods, like turning off lights when you leave the room and turning down the thermostat
when you're away, you can turn your home into an energy-efficient eco
home.

Lightbulbs

I've never advised anyone to run out and replace all of the lightbulbs in
their house with compact fluorescent bulbs, but I do recommend that as
the bulbs in your house expire, you replace them with CFLs (compact
fluorescent lightbulbs) or other energy-efficient bulbs like LEDs (light-
emitting diodes), until *eventually* your whole house has been converted.
Either one will use considerably less energy to run than standard incandescent bulbs, making them more environmentally friendly and better for
your wallet. While CFLs are extremely easy to find today, LEDs are a little less common. Watch for that to change in the coming years, as many
people think these will end up being the more highly favored efficient
bulbs.

CFL Savings

Many people balk at the price of CFLs compared to standard lightbulbs.
Consider this, though. A CFL today will cost you around three dollars but it
will burn strong for about ten thousand hours. It takes only twenty-seven
watts to generate the same amount of light as in a one-hundred watt standard bulb. That amounts to seventy-three watts less. And because a standard
bulb only lasts about a thousand hours, you would need ten standard bulbs
to do the job of one CFL.

So let's say you buy your CFL for three dollars and it costs twenty-two
dollars in electricity to power that bulb over its life span of ten thousand
hours. Altogether it will cost you twenty-five dollars for ten thousand hours
of electrical light. Now, let's say instead you buy a standard bulb for fifty
cents. You'll need ten standards to last as long. So now you've spent five

dollars in bulbs (ten bulbs times fifty cents each) and it will cost you another eighty dollars to power the bulbs for the same ten-thousand-hour span. If you light with standard incandescent bulbs, you're spending eighty-five dollars for ten thousand hours of light, versus twenty-five dollars for a CFL. Plus, by using CFLs instead, you're requiring less energy and fewer materials, amounting to less waste.

> CFL stands for *compact fluorescent lightbulb*. A CFL is often shaped like a glass curlicue with a standard lightbulb base at the bottom. In general, CFLs last ten times longer and use 75 percent less energy than standard incandescent bulbs.

Where to Start

If you're looking for a place to start, start with the bulbs in hard-to-reach places like ceiling fans and front door fixtures. No one likes replacing those every few months, and with a CFL you won't have to. Next, switch out the bulbs that you burn the most, especially any that are sixty-watt bulbs and up.

CFL Disposal and Cleanup

Because CFLs contain a trace amount of mercury, they require special disposal methods. Many large home improvement chains now have recycling collection zones for CFLs. Visit *earth911.org* to find a CFL recycling center in your area.

If one of your compact fluorescent lightbulbs breaks, certain precautions should be taken when cleaning up the spill to avoid exposure to the mercury inside.

Cleaning Up a Broken CFL

1. Have people and pets leave the room, and don't let anyone walk through the breakage area on their way out.

2. Open windows and leave the room for fifteen minutes or more.

3. Turn off the central forced-air heating/air-conditioning system, if you have one.

4. Scoop up glass fragments using gloves or stiff cardboard.

5. Use sticky tape to pick up small fragments and powder.

6. Wipe down hard surface areas or vacuum carpeted areas.

7. Immediately dispose of the vacuum cleaner bag.

8. If the break occurs on a bedspread or clothing, discard those items.

Heating and Cooling

Temperature control, simply heating and cooling your home, likely accounts for more than 50 percent of your home's total energy use. In many houses it is as much as 70 percent. A well-insulated and properly managed house can amount to significant savings on your heating and cooling bills and prevent hundreds of pounds of CO_2 emissions.

Thermostat

Simply adjusting your thermostat is one of the most effective ways to conserve energy around the home. No matter what your typical degree setting is, by adjusting it just one degree (one degree down in the winter and one up in the summer), you'll save about 3 percent in your home energy costs. And that's just one degree. Two degrees saves about two thousand pounds of carbon dioxide emissions over the course of a year. Generally, I encourage people to work their way toward a two-to-five-degree adjustment throughout the year.

If you don't already have a programmable thermostat, installing one is simple and it will go a long way toward saving energy at night and when you're gone during the day. Keeping the heat turned down five degrees for just four hours a day (that's half a standard workday, so if you're typically gone from nine to five, this will be a piece of cake) can save you 6 percent in heating bills.

Windows

Windows, particularly ones of the old, leaky variety, can account for 15 percent of a home's energy loss. Depending on the condition of the windows, replacing them with more energy-efficient windows might be your best option. If cost is a factor, consider just applying basic weather stripping around the window frames or investing in storm windows to add a layer of insulation in the colder months.

In my husband's and my nearly-ninety-year-old home, we were selective with the windows we replaced. Many were still in great shape and I couldn't stand the thought of the waste that would ensue by replacing all of them. Instead we strategically replaced the windows in the kitchen, the sitting area off the kitchen, our bedroom, and the attached bathroom and closet. These are the rooms that we inhabit the most, where a drafty window would feel unpleasant and the ability to open the windows and have screens in place in the warmer months was necessary. The remaining windows got a good dose of TLC with new weather stripping and a lot of vinegar and water to clean them off.

Insulation

If you're planning to replace insulation or to add insulation to a finished attic space or uninsulated existing walls, one of the best options is made from healthy, recycled cotton. Unlike fiberglass insulation that requires a mask and fully covered arms and legs to install, the recycled cotton insulation is healthy enough to lie down on and take a nap. Take one good look at this insulation and you'll see by the leftover Levi tags that the primary material used is recycled denim.

Your living room is probably your family room. The room where you watch TV, play games, and enjoy time together. By choosing cleaner options for the furniture and decor, installing plants, and adjusting your thermostat, you can turn it into a healthy and energy-efficient space.

In the Laundry Room

Busy Families

He takes the longest showers!" came the shout from three of the four kids that make up the Baxter clan. Four kids regularly fighting over a bathroom and you better believe they'll be able to tell you who takes the longest showers. I just wouldn't have guessed it to be their preteen son. The only daughter and princess of the family, maybe, but the middle boy wouldn't have been my guess. Okay, so he likes a rub-a-dub-dub in the tub, who cares? Well, as the eco-expert charged with helping this family detox their energy consumption habits, I did. I visited the family to film an episode of my series *Get Fresh with Sara Snow* and discovered a lot of areas where I'd easily be able to help this family of six. They were running the dishwasher way more often than necessary, they drove a car much bigger than their needs required, they left lights and appliances on and plugged in regardless of time of day or hours in actual use, and at least one of them took *loooong* showers.

The family's laundry room was typical for a family of six, with piles of dirty clothes next to piles of clean, waiting to be folded. I have no doubt, though, that in this busy family, loads were rarely run half-full. But can a busy family be encouraged to line-dry their clothes and swap out the products they use to spot-treat and brighten whites? It made me think back to laundry days in my childhood, in a house also busy with four active kids. I remember that we ran the dryer when we needed to, but we also hung a lot of our clothes and linens on the line outside or over racks inside in the winter.

My parents were so mindful when it came to water conservation. I think it came from my grandpa (my mom's dad), who, living out in the sticks like the rest of us, was always worried that his and my grandma's well would run dry. I've told you about him in previous chapters. He was quietly enthusiastic about protecting in every way possible the natural environment around him. And because he was also an accountant, he was deliberate and thoughtful about how he proceeded in doing so. Water conservation was one such way. He considered every gallon of water they used, careful that they wouldn't run out.

We often think of water conservation in terms of the bathroom and kitchen, but the laundry room is, in fact, one of the biggest and best areas of the home where small changes can bring about big results.

Conserving Water and Energy

Conservation is fairly easy in the laundry room because there are a number of simple steps you can take. First, only do laundry loads in the washing machine when you have enough clothes for a full load. Resist the temptation to throw a few items in just to get them out of sight. I know a number of people who do this: they come in from a walk and their sweaty clothes go straight into the wash; their baby spits up and her onesie goes straight into the wash. How about waiting a day or two until you have a true full load? You'll save a little of your own energy as well.

Ideas to Grow On

If you absolutely have to do a small load (like when your little one is screaming for her binkie), adjust the water level so the washer doesn't fill all the way.

Cold Water

Using cold water will cut down on the energy required to heat the water. Many detergents are specially formulated for cold water, and most that aren't will still do the trick. You'll also cut down on the wear and tear on your garments by keeping them out of scorching hot water.

Line-Dry

Have you ever dressed your beds with sheets fresh off an outside clothesline? I'm not sure there is much that smells better. Hanging a clothesline is simple, and the best part about it is, you don't pay a dime for the wind that blows or the sun that shines, so your clothes dry without costing you a penny in energy use. I learned this from my mom, who still loves few things more than sheets fresh from the outside clothesline.

When the sun stops shining and the wind is cold enough to make ice crystals dance on your denim, it's time to pack up the clothesline and bring it indoors. Try stringing it in your shower or corner to corner in your laundry room. Or invest in a simple clothes rack and hang as many items as your space allows. The dryer can be your backup. Even if you still use it to dry half your clothes, that's only half as much as before.

Optimizing Your Dryer

Cleaning the lint filter of your dryer before you do each new load will improve air circulation and lead to greater efficiency. And if you figure your clothes will take forty minutes to dry, set it for heat dry with a twenty-minute cool-down. There will still be enough heat in the clothes that the air will circulate through to dry and fluff.

Energy Savings for the Laundry

- Wait until you have a full load.
- Wash in cold water.
- Line-dry what you can.
- Be sure your dryer vent is clean.
- Set your dryer to a timed dry with cool-down.

Energy Star

The Energy Star program, a joint effort between the U.S. Environmental Protection Agency (EPA) and the U.S. Department of Energy, was started in 1992 as an elective labeling program to be used as an identifier of energy-efficient home and workspace products. Their ultimate goal was the promotion of these products to help reduce greenhouse gas emissions. First used on computers and computer monitors, the Energy Star label can be found today on fifty thousand product categories that are used throughout a typical home or workplace, including major appliances like washers, dryers, refrigerators, and central air-conditioning, minor appliances such as telephones, televisions, VCRs and DVDs, lighting, and office equipment. The program estimates that Americans can save 30 percent on their energy bill, or about six hundred dollars a year, by using Energy Star items.

According to the Energy Star program, the average home holds two TVs, one VCR, one DVD player, and three telephones. If we all replaced each of these items with Energy Star models, we could save over 25 billion pounds of greenhouse gas emissions, the equivalent of taking over 3 million cars off the road today.

Most standard washing machines use about forty gallons of water per load, but Energy Star models use 40 percent less energy and 55 percent less

LAURA HOWARD

Ten years ago Laura Howard was living the fast life of a Hollywood film producer. She spent her hard-earned money on shoes, dinners, and travel. Everything, in her words, was ephemeral and life flew by in a blur. Today her life is not unlike the set of a movie she may have produced back in that former life. She is a wife, a mother, and an ice cream company owner. And, to boot, she lives on a goat farm in northern California, where each day feels like a mini lifetime.

How did she get from Hollywood to the farm? Her odyssey started, actually, in a likely spot: her gut.

On a journey, more spiritual than physical, with her yoga teacher, Laura was encouraged to visualize her digestive tract as a swamp. The more polluted the swamp became, the easier it would be for airborne viruses and bacteria to take up residence. The cleaner and less "swampy," the less likely she would be to get sick. On point to de-swamp her digestive tract, Laura decided to cut out cow's milk and substitute in the non-mucus-forming milk of a goat instead.

But it was a love for ice cream that led her to abandon life as a Hollywood go-to gal and move to a farm where she could spend her days cooing to goats and sloshing their milk into her kitchen, in attempt after attempt to create decadent, lactose-free ice cream.

So why do I profile Laura here in the laundry room? It's because, with an arsenal of flavors like Strawberry Darling, Rumplemint, Black Mission Fig, and Vanilla Snowflake under her belt, water is what she's interested in defending today. And that's because one of the biggest offenders to our waterways around the country is factory farming. Thousands of animals (like cows and chickens) are crammed into warehouse-style buildings, creating one of the greatest sources of water pollution in the United States. But goats in the United States are not raised in confined animal feeding operations (CAFOs). Today most goat farms are still family-owned farms with diverse biospheres

continued

and no more than forty animals. But Laura began to fear that over time and with the increasing popularity of goat's milk cheese, ice cream, and other products, goat milk operations would begin to look more and more like dairy farms, polluting and threatening our waterways and our communities. To fight against this, Laura and her ice cream company, Laloo's, teamed up with the Waterkeeper Alliance, an organization committed to preserving and protecting water from polluters.

To me Laura exemplifies two things. She lived her first dream, and when she realized it was no longer her dream nor meant to be her life's work, she moved on and created the second phase of her life. And it's in this that she has been led to protect one of our planet's most precious resources—clean water. Today her hope is for goats to be a beacon of sustainability. Why not? Stranger things have happened! ■

water, which will save you about fifty dollars a year, or over five hundred dollars over the life of the machine. And while you're saving yourself five hundred dollars you're also saving seven thousand gallons, enough to provide a lifetime of drinking water for six people.

Energy Star washers can typically handle twenty pounds of laundry per load instead of the ten to fifteen pounds a conventional washer can handle, so you're saving yourself time as well.

Greener Cleaning

Doing laundry is just the tip of the iceberg when it comes to cleaning a home. How about toilets and tubs, counters and floors? Because I, like a lot of people, keep my cleaning products tucked out of sight in the laundry room, I think this is a fitting chapter for a discussion on greener cleaning.

I'll admit it, I too like a clean home. I like bathrooms that smell good, floors free of dog hair and bread crumbs, and because I'm a fool for clean surfaces, I'm constantly straightening and wiping down countertops. But nearly all of the cleaning that is done in my home is done without the use of any chemical products. I wipe counters with little more than water and a rag, maybe some vinegar-water when I'm really getting down to it. And in my bucket of cleaning products, I have a small array of multipurpose, window and glass, toilet bowl, and specialty cleaners that are all natural and eco-friendly.

The average person who is beginning to make lifestyle changes typically starts in the kitchen. By now you're probably feeling pretty good about the foods you're eating, how you've learned to read labels and avoid certain ingredient pitfalls. And that's great. And maybe you've made some serious strides in the bathroom. Now I want you to think about all the other *products* you use around your house.

Cutting Back

These days you can easily fill your cleaning closet with a separate product for nearly every job. A trip down the cleaning aisle finds promises on hundreds of different sparkling packages: toilet bowl cleaners, disposable brush pads, daily shower sprays, soap scum cleaners, cleansers with scrubbing bubbles, bright-whites laundry detergent, dark-color detergent, spot removers and fabric softeners, wood floor washes, disposable dry floor pads, disposable wet floor pads, and the list goes on. Each of those products means another bottle or box that will land in the dump, or in the best-case scenario, go to recycling. And it means that a lot of green was wasted from your wallet.

Instead of falling prey to the advertising claims, select a few multipurpose products and stick with those. An all-purpose countertop spray will work as well in the kitchen as it will in the bathroom. A shared scouring agent can be used in those two rooms as well. Most laundry detergents can work as a spot remover when used directly on the garment, and your toilet doesn't need disposable brush pads—it can be cleaned with the same scrub brush week after week. Look for ways to cut back on the number of products you buy to save the earth and your pocketbook.

Antibacterial Overload

When you consider that antibacterial cleaning products are under regulation by the EPA because their active ingredients are classified as pesticides, you realize what a harsh product these "mild" soaps really are. The ingredients in an antibacterial product are designed to kill germs, to kill living things. That's a bit harsh for my home and I hope it is for yours as well.

It may be because we rely so heavily on these "pesticides" to keep us clean that the bacteria around us are getting stronger, and our bodies are getting less and less able to fight them off on their own. Today antibacterial products make up 75 percent of the cleaning market and scientists and studies are pointing to this abundant use of antibacterial products as one of the causes for the rise in resistant microorganisms. In short, our bodies are finding it difficult to cope with the germs they come into contact with.

But these antibacterial soaps may not even be doing the job people buy them to do. A doctor performing a study out of Columbia University looked at 220 New York City families. She provided antimicrobial cleaners to some of the homes and standard cleaners to the rest and found that a year later the bacteria count and type was the same on the hands of family members, regardless of the type of cleaners they used.

While there are times when antibacterial soaps may be crucial, such as when you have a newborn at home or someone with a compromised immune system, they aren't necessary for everyday life. If you are taking precautions in the kitchen by cooking and cleaning your food thoroughly and washing your cutting boards, pots, and utensils in *hot* soapy water, then there is no need for daily disinfecting soap or spray.

Body Burden

While you've grown very cautious about the foods you put *in* your body and maybe the products you put *on* your body, have you given much thought to the environment you put your body in?

According to the EPA, people are continually being exposed to extremely high levels of carcinogenic substances in their homes. In some cases, levels are as much as seventy times higher than that outdoors. And concentrations of VOCs are consistently up to ten times higher indoors than outdoors.

VOCs Refresher

VOC stands for "volatile organic compound." These are gases emitted from solids or liquids, which can have short- or long-term adverse health effects.

VOCs are emitted from thousands of products and materials, including pesticides, cleaning supplies, paints and lacquers, glues and adhesives, photographic solutions, and so on.

So while there is no doubt that cleaning products perform a host of helpful tasks, their invisible chemical agents can irritate your airways, lungs, eyes, and skin, and the worst have the potential to burn internal organs or lead to chronic illnesses. For example, the fragrances in fabric softeners can cause cold-like symptoms including sneezing, stuffy noses, and headaches, but they have also been linked to reproductive abnormalities. Air fresheners and some toilet cleaners contain a chemical that has been linked to liver and nerve damage.

And then there's cancer. In 1995 the National Toxicology Program tested four hundred of the eighty thousand different chemical compounds currently in use for carcinogenicity. Based on results, researchers estimated that some-where between four and eight thousand chemicals currently in use are likely to trigger cancer. Another study found that women who work in the home have a 55 percent higher risk of developing cancer or chronic respiratory dis-ease than those who work outside of the home. But the world outside our doors suffers too. For example, phosphates, lurking in many dishwasher deter-gents, cause excessive algae growth in rivers and streams, which deprives fish of oxygen. So not only are we hurting our own bodies, we're hurting other species and natural creatures too.

Cleaning Product Ingredients to Avoid

Obviously, not all cleaning products or ingredients are bad. Borax is a per-fect example. This simple, safe, and effective alternative to harsh chlorine bleach and ammonia was a favorite of twentieth-century housewives. It's safe to use to kill mold and bacteria as well as household pests.

However, there *are* a number of ingredients in common cleaning products that you should be on the lookout for, avoiding whenever possible. As with the list of ingredients in the nursery, avoid the temptation to be over-whelmed by the list below. You'll see that right below it I list a number of perfectly safe and extremely easy-to-find cleaning ingredients. But first, it's important that you understand why avoiding these ingredients is a good step to take.

Ingredients to Avoid

Alkyl phenoxy ethanols (APEs) are a suspected hormone disruptor. APEs are common in detergents, disinfectants, and all-purpose cleaners.

Ammonia is poisonous if swallowed and can be extremely irritating to respiratory passages. It is a common laundry room staple.

Butyl cellosolve is a liver and kidney toxin and a lung and tissue irritant. It is also poisonous if swallowed. Butyl cellosolve (also called **butyl glycol** or

ethylene glycol monobutyl) is found in all-purpose cleaners, window cleaners, and scouring powders.

Chlorine bleach (also called **sodium hypochlorite**) is a severe irritant, primarily attacking the eyes and lungs. Sodium hypochlorite creates organochlorines, a suspected carcinogen that also works as a reproductive, neurological, and immune system toxin.

Crystalline silica is a known carcinogen that can be found in scouring powders and all-purpose cleaners.

Dichloromethane (**DCM** or **methylene chloride**) is a chemical liquid solvent that is a known carcinogen, liver and kidney toxin, and cardiac trigger. DCM is found in degreasing agents.

Diethanolamine (**DEA**) combines with the preservative nitrosome to create carcinogenic nitrosamines that can penetrate your skin. DEA is in many liquid dish soaps, detergents, and all-purpose cleaners.

Dioxane is a carcinogen and immunosuppressant, an ingredient that suppresses the immune system. Dioxane is found in laundry detergents, liquid dish soaps, and window cleaners.

Ethylene glycol is a neurotoxin that is found in many all-purpose cleaners.

Formaldehyde is a known carcinogen found in many materials around our homes, including the adhesive used in most pressed-wood furniture. In cleaning products it is found most commonly in germicides as well as disinfectants and deodorizers.

Glycol ethers are a group of solvents that are known reproductive toxins and liver and kidney toxins. This solvent group is often in window and all-purpose spray cleaners and scouring powders.

Nitrobenzene is a blood poison considered to be highly toxic and is often in floor polishes.

Para-dichlorobenzene (p-dichlorobenzene or **p-DCB)** is a neurotoxin and known carcinogen that also causes disruption to the endocrine (hormone) system. It's used primarily as a moth repellent.

Phosphates are highly caustic and can be deadly if swallowed. But phosphates hurt more than just us. When they go down the drain, they contribute to algae bloom in our lakes, rivers, and streams, which can decimate fish populations. Phosphates have been removed from laundry detergents; unfortunately, they're still prized—and may be included—in dishwasher detergents for their ability to eliminate spots.

Sodium hydroxide is highly irritating to the eyes, nose, and throat and can burn skin tissue on contact. Sodium hydroxide is often in metal and oven cleaners.

Sodium lauryl/laureth sulfate is a skin irritant that can lead to dermatitis. It is a common sudsing agent found in many soaps and detergents.

Synthetic fragrances are especially bad because of the toxic ingredient phthalate that they contain. Phthalates have been linked to cancer, reproductive abnormalities, and asthma.

Knowing all of this, it's almost not surprising to note a study by the *New Scientist* in 1999 that found that moms in homes where aerosol sprays and air fresheners were used were 25 percent more likely to suffer from headaches and 19 percent more likely to suffer from depression. Babies less than six months old in the same environment had 30 percent more ear infections and 22 percent higher rates of diarrhea. Toxic chemicals can create toxic results. It's much better to steer clear of these harsh products and favor natural alternatives instead.

Greener Cleaners

Enough of the scary stuff. There is a way out of this mess and it involves a much less expensive, family-friendly, healthy solution. In fact, all you need for a fresh-smelling, clean home are a few simple kitchen staples.

Green-Cleaning Tool Kit	
Vinegar—distilled white	Borax
Baking soda	Hydrogen peroxide
Lemon juice	Tea tree oil
Soap	Essential oils
Olive oil	Spices

Vinegar—Distilled White

This kitchen staple is a workhorse! Distilled white vinegar helps kill bacteria, mold, and viruses and can be used for disinfecting, deodorizing, and cutting grease and wax build-up, as well as removing stains on carpet, countertops, pots and pans, and coffeepots. Be sure to use distilled white vinegar to avoid a lingering aroma; the smell will disappear almost immediately.

You'll find some nondistilled apple cider vinegars at the store, and while those are great for your health, they're not the best for your cleaning needs.

• For an all-purpose cleaner, fill an empty spray bottle with equal parts water and white vinegar. This can be kept on hand for all-purpose cleaning around the home. Use on countertops, glass surfaces, chrome fixtures, and tile.

• To freshen a toilet bowl, pour two or three cups of white vinegar into the toilet bowl, let it sit for a few hours, then scrub and flush.

• For windows, fill a spray bottle with water and a quarter cup of white vinegar. Use newspapers in place of paper towels for a streak-free finish. You can still toss them in the recycling bin when you're through.

• Wood floors will avoid the streaky look when you add about a quarter cup of white vinegar to your pail of water. Be sure to wring your mop out well so as not to over-wet the floor.

• Add a quarter cup of white vinegar to your washing machine's rinse cycle. This will help to rinse out the detergent completely and leave your clothes feeling soft and free of static cling.

Baking Soda

This common baking ingredient is effective at removing stains and absorbing odors in the kitchen and around the home. It is also a mild scouring tool for pots and pans and kitchen surfaces.

• Add a quarter cup of baking soda to the wash cycle of your laundry machine to soften fabrics naturally, eliminating the need for chemical, and often highly fragranced, fabric softeners.

• Mix a small amount of baking soda with liquid castile soap to get your countertops, sinks, and tubs shiny. For a "fresh smell," try adding a few drops of rosemary, orange, or lavender essential oil.

• If your carpet is holding on to pet or other odors, sprinkle it with baking soda before you vacuum.

• To clean your oven, mix together three parts baking soda with one part salt and one part water. Spread the mixture across the oven surface and allow it to sit for up to eight hours. Scrape and wipe clean.

• For a clogged drain, pour a half cup of baking soda down the drain, followed by a half cup of white vinegar. Allow the mixture to fizz, then flush with hot water.

• To clean your toilet, pour one part baking soda and four parts white vinegar into the toilet basin. Let it sit fifteen to thirty minutes before scrubbing and flushing through.

Lemon Juice

Lemon juice cuts through grease naturally, so it works well for kitchen cleaning especially.

• For a healthful alternative to common aerosol air fresheners, combine one-half quart of hot water with equal parts baking soda and lemon juice (about a teaspoon each).

• To brighten whites in the wash, add a small amount of lemon juice to your machine's rinse cycle.

• Mix together a mild liquid soap and lemon juice for an excellent dish soap. (This should not be used on silver.)

• A spray bottle filled with water and a quarter cup of lemon juice will get greasy windows and mirrors clean.

Soap

Find a soap—in liquid, solid, or powder form—that is biodegradable, free of dyes, and non-petroleum-based. Castile or other plant-based soaps are a great choice.

• Cleaning your wood floors is best done only occasionally, with warm water and a drop of mild soap. Be sure your rag is only damp. Wipe or scrub, use another rag to rinse, then a dry rag to buff your surface clean.

Olive Oil

Olive oil is not only delicious, it is great for moisturizing and conditioning.

• Mix together two parts olive oil to one part lemon juice for a natural furniture polish.

• To brighten brass surfaces and keep them from tarnishing, rub with a cloth dampened with olive oil after cleaning.

• Rub olive oil onto stainless steel surfaces to remove streaks and prints.

• Mix together a quarter cup of olive oil with a few drops of lemon juice for a natural shoe polish. Simply dip your rag, wipe on, and then buff off.

Borax

Borax is a powder that has been used for decades in laundry rooms. It is effective at cleaning, softening water, deodorizing, and disinfecting.

• For a strong disinfectant, create a mixture of four tablespoons white vinegar and two teaspoons of borax to three cups of hot water. A few drops of liquid soap can be added in as well.

• To spot-treat your carpets, mix together equal parts of borax, salt, and white vinegar. Apply the paste to the stains and allow to dry, then vacuum up the paste.

• Dissolve borax in a sink full of hot water to clean your heirloom and fine china.

• To deter rodents, sprinkle borax at their point of entry. Be sure to keep small children away, as borax can be harmful if swallowed.

Hydrogen Peroxide

This is gentler than chlorine bleach and can be used for sterilizing and disinfecting, both in your home and on your body.

• To treat moldy tile grout on bathroom walls, fill a spray bottle with one-half cup hydrogen peroxide and one cup water. Spray onto moldy areas, let sit for an hour, then rinse off.

• Keep a spray bottle of hydrogen peroxide on hand and another filled with white vinegar (don't mix the two in one bottle). For a disinfecting spray for vegetables and surfaces, spritz with one, then the other, then wipe clean. This is great for spraying apples, tomatoes, and other produce items, as well as wooden cutting boards.

- Hydrogen peroxide can be used as an effective, inexpensive mouthwash.

Tea Tree Oil

This little oil is one of my favorite things. It is a natural fungicide and germicide, as well as being naturally antibacterial and antiseptic. It is great for home and personal care. You'll often find tea tree oil in soaps because it helps fight the fungi and bacteria that cause athlete's foot and acne.

- To treat household areas with mold and mildew, mix five to ten drops of tea tree oil and a cup of water in a spray bottle.

- Help shower doors and tile stay cleaner by wiping them with a mixture of tea tree oil and water.

- To deter rodents, wipe pantry doors and cupboards with a towel damp with tea tree oil. You can also leave a few drops of the oil at the rodents' points of entry.

- To freshen wash and repel moths from your clothes, add two teaspoons of tea tree oil to your washing machine.

- Dab a few drops of tea tree oil onto a tissue, then place that in your vacuum cleaner's bag for a fresh scent and to help kill dust mites as you clean.

- For a soothing bath, add twenty to twenty-five drops of pure tea tree oil to your hot water.

Essential Oils

There are so many oils and so many uses for them. Not only are essential oils great for adding fragrance, they perform other tasks as well.

Lavender, orange, rosemary, and clove are wonderful scents for your home. You can combine oils to create citrus, floral, or spicy combinations.

• For an air-purifying spray, mix essential oils of eucalyptus, lemon, and thyme with water in a spray bottle, then spritz your germ-filled rooms.

• To defog a mirror, rub it with eucalyptus oil.

• Eucalyptus oil and steel wool can be used to treat stained surfaces. Skip the steel wool if the surface shouldn't be scratched. Eucalyptus oil on a rag will remove stains and sticky residues.

> ### Disposing of Old Products
>
> It's generally okay to pour old products that you no longer want to use down the drain. Just don't pour anything containing bleach and ammonia together because the mixture creates toxic fumes.
>
> Contact your sanitation department for heavier-duty product disposal.

Spices

You probably have an abundance of dried spices in your cupboard. Put them to use deterring rodents and keeping rooms smelling fresh.

• Mix together equal parts of dried cloves, rosemary, and thyme and place in small cloth pouches or tea bags. Hang these in closets or fold in with out-of-season clothing to deter moths and rodents. Dried lemon peels will also do the trick.

• For a natural air freshener, simmer cloves and cinnamon in water. Orange juice or a few drops of orange essential oil is a nice addition as well.

The best part about cleaning with common household items like vinegar, baking soda, and lemon juice is that it saves you money. A spray bottle filled with vinegar and water will cost you pennies, compared to the two or three dollars you might pay for a store-bought all-purpose cleaner.

In the Office

To Office or Not

In my house today our walk-up attic has been converted into an office. The room has a door leading out onto the roof and two little quarter-round windows. My husband and I each have desks, and some of my favorite moments are when he and I are each at work at our desks, backs to one another, and I'm trying so hard not to throw paper airplanes or spit spitballs at him.

In my house growing up, we had an office that later became a bedroom. But I also remember distinctly the day when my parents brought home a small, unfinished secretary desk with three drawers and a fold-down front that hid small cubbies for bills and calendars and envelopes. This became my mom's desk in the kitchen. I can still hear the cries of "Mom, where are the scissors?" "In my desk in the kiiiiiiiitchennnnnn," she would call back. This desk was my mom's workspace, from which she organized our family's daily activities.

No matter what kind of "office" you have, it is likely an area where you use paper, pencils, ink, and other resources, where you support companies and vote with your dollars (by making purchases from one particular company or another), and do a number of other office-like activities. What I'm saying is I don't much care whether or not you have a room with four walls and a ceiling that you call the office, because the tips we'll walk through in this chapter will come into play regardless.

Mail Makeover

The one thing you probably *do* do in your office, whether it's a desk in your kitchen or a room of its own, is sort mail. We get so much mail today, don't we? Bills we wish wouldn't come but we really should learn to expect, correspondence from people and groups, magazines we've subscribed to, and *other stuff*. It's the *other stuff* that I'm really worried about: catalogs, circulars, solicitations, and envelopes full of coupons you'll never use. So what is the right thing to do with all of this paper stuff?

Recycle

I am a neurotic recycler, especially when it comes to opening the mail. All unwanted catalogs and circulars go straight into the recycling bin. And sometimes this paper waste comes back out. If I'm shipping a box or have something that needs some filler, I'll use wadded or shredded pages from the recycling bin for that.

While all of this (putting it in the bin and taking it out for reuse) is considered recycling, you can go a step further. When I open my bills, I save aside the return envelope and my statement and toss everything else into the recycling bin; the little advertisements they tuck inside and the outer envelope, plastic window and all. Birthday cards, baby announcements, alumni recruitment letters, all of this, after careful consideration and the appropriate amount of respect, go into the recycling bin. For those items that I wouldn't want to fall into the wrong hands, I have a shredder. Credit card solicitations and such go straight to the shredder, and the shredded paper then goes to recycling. Not only does this keep a significant amount of waste out of the trash can, it keeps clutter from building up in my home.

Junk mail alone accounts for 30 percent of all mail delivered in the world, and nearly half of it never gets opened, heading, instead, straight into the dump. Recycling that junk mail is certainly a better option, but getting your name off the junk mail lists is the best thing to do. Sites like *donotmail.org* can help.

Ideas to Grow On

Use shredded or wadded catalog pages and newspapers for packing
material or instead of paper towels to clean windows.

Catalog Cutback

Every year, 20 billion catalogs are shipped out. That's sixty-seven per man, woman, and child in the United States. Sears produced the first catalog ever back in the 1880s. Today they print approximately 425 million catalogs a year, most of which contain zero percent recycled content. But as with junk mail, recycling these catalogs isn't the greenest step you can take. Initiating a major cutback in the amount you receive is the best thing you can do. There are a few websites today designed to help you decrease the number of catalogs you'll receive. *Catalogchoice.org* and *greendimes.com* are just two.

You can also recommend that the catalogs or magazines you do receive be printed on recycled paper. After a significant amount of pressure was placed on them, Victoria's Secret and other catalog heavies like Dell and Williams-Sonoma cleaned up their act, now printing on partially-recycled-content paper. If the entire U.S. catalog industry started using recycled content paper, we would save enough wood to build a six-foot-tall fence that would stretch coast-to-coast across the country seven times.

Online Bill Payment

Paying bills online is another great way to cut back on your paper mail as well as on the amount of petroleum needed by the postal service to ship those envelopes back and forth. If every U.S. home viewed and paid bills online, we would cut solid waste by over 1.5 billion pounds and save over 2 million tons of harmful greenhouse gas emissions a year. Simply enroll through your bank or your individual billing companies, or use well-designed and secure computer software to start.

Greener Supplies

No matter what kind of work happens in your office, you're almost surely using paper. It's one of the most widely used materials in the world. In fact, since the mid-1970s, paper use across the globe has doubled, with the average American using over 650 pounds of paper a year. Paper production is responsible for a fifth of the world's total wood harvest, with each ton of paper requiring almost three times its weight in trees.

Recycled and Recyclable Materials

But we don't have to cut down forests to do our work. Recycled paper is made from materials that have already been around the block a time or two, and the making of it creates almost 75 percent less air pollution and 35 percent less water pollution than a standard "virgin" ream.

Beyond paper there are a number of office supplies made from recycled materials from which you can choose: pencils made from retired currency, clipboards from old computer parts, boxes from reclaimed cardboard, and so on.

Ink cartridges remain an item we go through at an exuberant rate, particularly if we're printing photos at home. Granted, we need the ink like we need the paper, but there are better ways to go about replacing your empty ink cartridges. Rather than replacing the entire cartridge, simply replace the ink used therein. I've watched my dad, a busy businessman but never too proud or too out of touch with the needs of our environment, refill the ink cartridges in his home office. Refilling cartridges takes only a little extra effort over buying a new one, and the materials you need to do so are available through any major office supply store.

Recycling E-waste

"E-waste" generally refers to discarded computers and other consumer electronics. It's one of the fastest-growing segments of our waste stream, as

less than 10 percent of out-of-use or discarded computers are properly recycled. Most e-waste is either improperly stored or tossed, with a great portion
ending up in developing countries where the electronics are dumped and
dismantled for parts, allowing the harmful toxins contained within the electronics, like lead, mercury, and fire retardants, to leach into the soil and
water. But when properly recycled, a variety of materials, including metals,
can be recovered and reused from these electronics, reducing the need to produce or mine for new metals.

Technology is constantly advancing but your gadgets don't necessarily
need to. Consider how much you really need that newest cell phone or computer before you make the purchase. And when you do, think hard about
what to do with your old one. Cell phones, computers and monitors, telephones, toner cartridges, and other office machines can all be recycled.
Earth911.org can help you find an e-waste recycling center close to you. Or
consider selling your older model on eBay or Craigslist or donating it to a
local church, community center, or other not-for-profit.

Paper

Despite the promise of a "paperless revolution," paper remains such a big
part of our lives that we should do all we can to cut down on our consumption of it. So how can we do so?

Print Double-Sided
Remember back in middle or high school when you used to get handouts
that were printed on both sides? You knew that the teacher had gone
through extra trouble to photocopy it on one side, then painstakingly load
the paper back into the copier and copy the second page on the back side of
the paper. You could usually tell this is what she had done because the back
side was upside down or somehow inverted from the front. Whether she was
doing it to save the school system's money or because she had greater plans
for our nation's forests in mind, we'll likely never know, but I for one am glad
she did.

It's not hard to follow in her footsteps. If your printer has a manual setting, set it to duplex or double-side printing. If not, simply set it to print even pages, then collect those, reload them, and tell it to now print the odd pages. You'll have double-sided printouts.

Check Before You Print

Before you print, do a quick check of your document to decide whether you really need to print all of the pages it is proposing. "Print preview" is the option you'll be looking for. Also, lessen the margins so you can fit more words on a page, decrease the font size or line spacing, and make sure you aren't printing any extraneous pages with only a line or two on them. Find a way to fit those lines onto a former page.

Scrap Paper

We've all hit Print too soon, though, and then realized we needed to reprint after a few more edits. Rather than chucking those wasted pages into the garbage or recycling can, stack them to the side of your printer and use them the next time you are printing a draft or something just for your own review. Or cut the pages into quarters or eighths to make scrap paper for grocery lists or notes in your kids' lunch boxes.

A friend recently told me she hasn't bought paper in a year because she's been collecting all the discarded paper from her office and bringing it home.

Ideas to Grow On

Make scrap paper for lists and notes out of unused office paper—misprints, already read documents, and anything else.

Avoid the Phantom Draw

Picture, if you will, the octopus of cords under your desk or, if your desk isn't as busy as some, the octopus of cords behind your main TV, the one with the DVD player, gaming system, and cable box attached to it. All of these appliances—computers, printers, TVs, stereos, microwaves—are drawing electricity from your home's source *all* of the time, day and night, whether they're actively in use or not. This is called "phantom draw" or "vampire power" because power is being sucked by your appliances in the middle of the day or night, when you're least aware it's happening. Each year vampire energy costs U.S. consumers to the tune of $3 billion.

Unplugging appliances when they're not in use will prevent this from happening. So that you don't have to go around constantly unplugging and plugging back in, you can connect multiple electronics all through one power strip, and simply shut off the power strip at night or when you leave during the day to cut the electricity that flows to and from the devices. This works especially well at desks, home entertainment systems, and other busy electronic areas in the house.

Avoid the Phantom Draw

- Invest in a few smart power strips for busy electrical areas of your home.
- Optimize the standby mode for short periods away.
- Shut down computers and TVs when you're not around them.
- Unplug chargers and other electronics when they're not in use.

A "Smart Strip" power strip does half this work for you, though. Banking on the likelihood of you not wanting to crawl behind your desk or TV before and after sitting at it, innovators have created a smart power strip that monitors the electricity use of each device plugged into it and automatically shuts off the power to the ones that have been idle for a certain period of time. Look for smart power strips online or at home improvement centers.

Setting your computer to sleep or standby mode is a good option if you're walking away from it for more than a minute or two, but anything longer than an hour and you should just shut it down. Most electronics "standing by" use about 40 percent of their full operating power, and each year standby electronics waste the equivalent of twenty-six power plants' worth of electricity. Remember to simply turn them off when you're going to be away for a bit.

Cell phone chargers are quite possibly the worst offender. Think about it. When you got your cell phone, you probably plugged the charger into the wall in your kitchen, your office, or your bedroom, and it's been there ever since. When you tuck yourself in at night, you plug your phone into it to charge. When you get up in the morning, you unplug your phone and take it with you, but you leave the charger behind, still plugged into the wall. Have you ever felt your charger after it's been sitting there, dangling like an umbilical cord from the wall all day? It's warm. That's because only 5 percent of the power used by a cell phone charger is used to actually charge the phone. The remaining 95 percent of the energy your phone charger pulls is wasted energy, when it's left plugged into the wall. Unplug to save your home en-

---

Phantom Energy: The Biggest Wasters (Annually)

- Rechargeable toothbrush: wastes 12.3 kilowatt hours, costing you $1.35

- LCD computer monitor: wastes 22.8 kilowatt hours, costing you $2.51

- Cordless phone base: wastes 28.9 kilowatt hours, costing you $3.18

- Convection microwave: wastes 35 kilowatt hours, costing you $3.85

- Laptop: wastes 144.5 kilowatt hours, costing you $15.90

- Computer: wastes 311 kilowatt hours, costing you $34.21

- Plasma TV (in active standby mode): wastes 1,452.4 kilowatt hours, costing you $159.76

ergy and avoid the "phantom draw." While you won't see significant dollar savings on the smaller items, you're doing your part, in the least painful way, in lowering energy consumption.

Discover Your Home's Footprint

Much of what happens in the office involves organizing and planning for your home's finances and potential efficiencies, both economical and environmental. The first step in understanding how efficiently your home is operating is to discover your individual footprint. Your footprint (called such because it indicates the size of the imprint your lifestyle is leaving on the planet) takes into account your electricity consumption, your car and other travel miles, the food you eat and where it's coming from, and all of your other big and little habits. All of these measurements demonstrate how much of our planet's resources you're using, what your carbon dioxide emissions are, and how you stack up to other families your size. As you begin to make many of the changes I've suggested in this book, you'll find that your carbon footprint will begin to get smaller and smaller.

Calculating your footprint can be done at *carbonfootprint.com*, *terrapass .com*, and other sites. As soon as you've figured out where your family stands, you're ready to take steps to reduce your footprint, by eating locally, conserving electricity, driving less, switching to non-toxic household bedding, furniture, and cleansers, and bringing nature into your home.

A very constructive step can involve investing in "carbon offsets" to counter the effects of your family's regular energy use, including your daily commute, occasional airplane flight, heating your house, and basically most any activity that you can imagine. The company that sells you the offsets invests your dollars in wind farms, solar arrays, and methane-capture facilities, as well as innovative research and development. (Often the groups responsible for creating clean energies and projects to reduce greenhouse gas emissions have a lack of funding.)

While reducing your footprint is the best thing you can do, not many families can live footprint free. You'll probably still have to fly from time to time,

MARK RETZLOFF

Mark Retzloff began his career in the organic food industry in retail. He was a business partner of my dad's in the early days of Eden Foods, then went on to found the natural food stores Rainbow Groceries and Alfalfa's Markets in Colorado in the 1970s. He grew Alfalfa's into a successful regional chain before retiring from there in 1990 and spending a year in Washington, DC, as chairman of the Organic Food Alliance, working to get the Organic Food Production Act passed.

But it was during his time at Alfalfa's that Mark noticed a gap in organic food offerings—dairy. Having finished his work on Capitol Hill, Mark cofounded the first, and from then on the largest, company selling organic milk, Horizon Organic. Twelve years later, two years after retiring from Horizon, Mark founded Aurora Organic Dairy to provide private label organic milk to supermarkets. Aurora became one of the fastest growing organic companies ever. In four short years it grew from zero to $130 million in sales.

As if his business plate wasn't already full enough, for nearly a decade Mark has consistently invested in early-stage and growth-stage businesses in the organic and LOHAS (an acronym that stands for Lifestyles of Health and Sustainability) categories, including alternative energy, organic and natural food, and lifestyle companies. He helped start a venture capital company called Greenmont Capital Partners, investing millions in companies such as these.

Mark's credo throughout his business career has been to work with people who share the same values and beliefs as him. And when you take a close look at Mark's personal life, closer than just a look at his portfolio and his business achievements, those values aren't hard to see.

For the last twenty-eight years he and his wife, Terri, and their three children have lived in a home just nine miles outside of Boulder, Colorado, nestled up on the plains, next to the foothills of the

Rockies. It is there, on their seventy-one acres, that they practice exactly what they preach. One hundred percent of the electricity they use is solar powered. Most of their house and the rest of the buildings are heated through solar heat. Scattered across their private patch of land are a secluded yoga studio that he and Terri both practice in, barns, chicken coops, compost piles, a greenhouse, and a quarter-acre garden. Mark estimates that 75 to 85 percent of the vegetables they eat throughout the year come from this quarter-acre garden. Their eggs all come from the chickens on the land and, as their electricity use would indicate, nearly all of their energy comes from the sun's rays.

While Mark has certainly made an impact on the business of organics, he works daily to *reduce* his impact on a personal consumption and environmental destruction level. As a result, low-impact living is not only his goal, it's his achievement. Mark doesn't call himself a fanatic; in fact, he's happy to announce that they still eat out and travel and such. But, above all else, conscious sustainability is the most important thing for him and his family—to leave the world a better place for the next generation. ■

still drive to work and to the store, still heat your home and power your microwave and TV. So once you determine your footprint and reduce the size of it as much as possible, investing in carbon offsets to make up for your impact is the most responsible thing to do. It doesn't undo our damage, but it helps to counterbalance it.

Socially Responsible Investing

Socially responsible investing (SRI) has become something of a buzzword. It accounts for almost three trillion out of twenty-five trillion invested dollars in the United States. The idea is to discontinue the investment stream from going toward businesses and institutions that pollute or otherwise damage the environment, that use unfair labor practices, or that employ practices that are damaging to life quality. Instead consumers invest in socially responsible and socially just companies and not-for-profits.

One of my favorite ways is through what is called *microfinance*, which allows you to make a loan to an actual individual (often in desperate or third-world areas) who will use the money to start or continue a business. Many microfinance recipients maintain cottage industries like sewing or basket making, or they run food stands in city markets, small farms, or other methods of production and revenue generation. A large contingent of microfinance clients is made up of women who have been abandoned or widowed and whose business is their only source of income.

A year ago my family was deciding what to do for our Christmas gifts to one another. We decided long ago that we all have enough *stuff*, so we no longer buy gifts for each other, instead choosing to make a donation to a worthy organization. We opted this past year for a microfinance model through FINCA (the Foundation for International Community Assistance). Instead of loaning our money, we donated enough money so that a brand new bank could be established in Malawi, Africa, to loan money to members of that community. Because of the small investment my family made, an endless number of needy loan recipients will be able to begin or continue their industry. As each individual repays his or her loan, the money goes back into the village bank and is loaned out again to the next individual. The village banks, like the one my family's money formed, make loans to individuals who have no collateral and would not typically be candidates for credit, lending them the money necessary to build businesses, create incomes, and increase their families' well-being, by allowing them to purchase basic necessities and nutritious foods and send their kids to school.

It is a powerful thing to know that your money, whether carefully saved or scrap change, is able to help an individual get on his or her feet and live a healthy, productive life. If you have a little extra, as you probably do, share it with someone who needs it. This is sustainability at its finest.

Ideas to Grow On

If you're short on money but long on time, volunteer. Find a local group doing riverbed or parks cleanup. Volunteer at your town's recycling drop-off center. Make volunteering a family activity.

Cut Your Commute

Worker bees in America spend nearly fifty hours per year driving back and forth to work in rush-hour traffic, using up over 3.5 billion precious hours and 23 billion gallons of gas. In fact, transportation alone accounts for 30 percent of all U.S. carbon dioxide emissions. What can you do? Take public transportation, at least a few days a week. You'll be amazed, not only at how much fuel you'll save, but how much work you can get done on an hour-long train ride!

Moving closer to work probably isn't an option for most people, but bringing your job to you by working at home one or two days each week may be in the cards, at least for some. This alone can save a considerable amount of fuel and save the environment from harmful carbon dioxide emissions.

Travel Planning

What about when your commute involves a trip to another state, for business or pleasure? Can you still travel and live responsibly even when you're headed out of state? Of course, it just takes a little advance planning and maybe a change of pace.

Planes, Trains, and Automobiles

First off is how to get there. Airplanes emit the most carbon dioxide per traveler, followed by cars, then trains, then buses. In fact, air travel releases three times more CO_2 emissions than trains, and is responsible for more than

3 percent of all U.S. global-warming gases. One flight from Los Angeles to New York or vice versa emits almost a thousand pounds of CO_2 per passenger.

I d e a s   t o   G r o w   O n

Fly direct. Because a large portion of the harmful greenhouse gas emissions happens during takeoff and landing, you'll be cutting down on your CO_2 load.

If you must fly, consider offsetting your carbon emissions. To make up for the CO_2 emissions from your flight, you can purchase an "offset" for that particular flight path. The offset cost of a one-way flight from Los Angeles to New York, for example, might be between five and ten dollars, and the money is invested on your behalf in those green energies that can help to reverse some of the damage the plane has done.

Greener Stays

Once you've made it to your destination, you have a number of choices in how and where to stay. A green (and often economical) choice is to rent an apartment rather than stay in a hotel. With the use of a kitchen, you're able to cook your own meals and avoid unhealthy restaurant food and un-eco takeout. Plus you avoid all of the excessive resource use that is common in hotels.

If, however, you are going to be staying in a hotel, there are things you can do to make your stay a little greener. First, bring your own shampoo, conditioner, and body lotion. This way you'll have no need for the little disposable-sized ones that come with your room. These waste a lot of plastic, especially when they're replenished daily.

Next, think about how you live at home. Do you really wash your sheets and towels every day? Do you vacuum your bedroom floor daily? Do you get new soap and shampoo each day? So why do you need it when you're on the road? The best way to avoid this is to make use of the Do Not Disturb sign. Because I certainly don't need housekeeping in my room wasting electricity to vacuum, water to launder sheets and towels, or plastic for new toiletries, I hang the Do Not Disturb sign on the outside of my door as soon as I arrive, and I leave it there until I depart. Sometimes a call down to the front desk to let them know why the tag is there is a good idea. You don't want them to worry if they can't get in for more than a few days.

Finally, leaving your hotel room for the day is just like leaving your house for the day. Take a look around the room and turn off all lights, set the thermostat so it doesn't run while you're gone, and make sure your TV and computer are turned off. Once you're sure your room isn't going to be an energy hog while you're away, head out the door and enjoy the day!

Green Your Hotel Stay

• Bring your own shampoo, lotion, and other toiletries.

• Hang the Do Not Disturb sign to avoid housekeeping waste in your room.

• Power down when you venture out.

Green Endings

This may seem like a strange topic on which to end a chapter, but it's important. And since the home office is likely where you'll do any estate planning or preparation for what happens when you pass on, I think it's actually quite fitting.

A while ago I did a segment for an episode of *Get Fresh with Sara Snow* on green funerals. When I first proposed the segment, I thought it would be quickly dismissed as too creepy or too strange. But somehow I got one of my producers excited about it and we went for it. Not long before, we had buried my grandfather in a green funeral of sorts. Here was a man who had been a lifelong environmentalist, a grandpa, a dad, a brother, a son, and a husband of sixty years. He loved us all, he loved his God, and he loved this earth. And he absolutely did not want his body taking up unnecessary space in a concrete box or polished wood coffin after he was gone. But he had a very specific idea of what he did want after he passed. In the summer of 2004 we had my grandfather's body cremated and then held a small family memorial service for him out by the organic gardens at his and my grandma's house. Our burial for him was unconventional by anyone's standards. We each took turns, one by one, turning small handfuls of his ashes into his compost pile. In so doing, we were releasing him back to the earth and soil where he belonged. My mom still has a handmade urn with his ashes in it, and each year she adds a little more to her compost heap. It's beautiful. He's continuing to help grow the foods that we all eat. And he lives on.

A typical green funeral maintains three principles: no embalming fluids, no concrete vaults, and burial in a biodegradable casket. The argument for all of this is simple. Each year in the United States we bury over eight hundred thousand gallons of embalming fluid (though the fluid is not required by most states), over a hundred tons of steel, almost three thousand tons of copper and bronze, over a million and a half tons of concrete, and more than 30 million board feet of wood. Nearly 90 percent of all coffins today are made from particleboard or chipboard, with glues that contain formaldehyde, a toxin that leaches into the soil and water as it decays.

On top of that, conventional cemeteries use countless amounts of pesticides, fertilizers, and fuel to keep green spaces pristine. And undeveloped land is flattened and mowed to make room for more burial spaces, displacing birds and other forest creatures, as well as carbon-capturing trees.

A green funeral is the antithesis of this. Bodies are left unembalmed and are buried in shrouds, woven bamboo caskets, or simple wooden boxes that are made of untreated wood or cardboard, with no glues, metals, or lacquers. Shrouds are made of linen or organic cotton or a favorite family blanket or quilt. Vaults are never used. The idea is that the body and the covering will return to the earth without polluting the surrounding soil and water. For centuries, as organisms have lived and died, they have returned to the earth by way of the natural microbial activity in the soil, creating no waste.

In a natural funeral, the burial still must take place within designed cemetery grounds (you can't bury a loved one in your backyard like in olden days), but the setting is immensely different from a typical cemetery. Green cemeteries look more like natural preserves or forests than anything else. They serve as habitats for woodland creatures and birds and flora. Often the burial land includes lakes and streams. Gravesites are marked with native trees, wildflowers, shrubs, or rocks, rather than large headstones. Many newer green burial sites are also marked with a computer chip that is trackable with a GPS device so that the location of the gravesite can be archived and easily found again once the tree has grown or the wildflowers have spread.

Dealing with death is never easy, but it is, sadly, inevitable. I understand the sense of tradition and responsibility that some people feel, but I also understand the need to preserve our land and to allow someone to be celebrated and memorialized with the same eco convictions with which he or she lived. If you're taking so much care to tread lightly and live responsibly now, you certainly don't want that to be undone in your final moments.

Outdoors

Beyond Your Four Walls

The changes you've begun making in your home are worthy of applause. So go ahead and take a bow. But once you start eliminating toxins from the environment inside your home, it's hard not to begin to look beyond. There are hordes of people out there who eat organic foods, recycle all they can, and even use eco-friendly cleaning supplies. But head *out*side their front door and the yard and garage tell a different story. They still rely on chemical-heavy fertilizers to produce a bright green lawn and jaunt around town in gas-guzzling vehicles. You may be one of those people. And here's what I say to that: fantastic! Now we just figured out where you can go one step further.

For a lot of people it's a matter of keeping up with the Joneses. We put so much stock in our yards and our cars, often forgetting the extreme environmental impact that each can have. When I got married, my husband and I had a little bit of lifestyle blending to do. He understood who he was marrying, don't get me wrong, and he was on board with about 99 percent of the changes I was suggesting to him, but for a while there were two areas of hesitation—the yard and his car.

The yard took a little time, but he now maintains healthy grass with natural fertilizers and grows certain plants to attract birds, bees, and other beneficial insects, rather than doing his best to get rid of them. But the car, that took some doing. The man was a car guy. He drove fancy sedans and liked to swap them out for newer varieties every few years. One day, though, I was home working when he walked in the door and announced that he had a surprise for me. I knew that he had been looking at new cars, and while I had made a few *suggestions* on what he might buy, I was, as usual, careful not to push too hard. Ryan is the prime example of someone who, when something is forced upon them, will consider every reason to go in the opposite direction instead. But because he is a smart man who also loves me, my family, our ideals, and his other mother (Mother Earth), he made the better choice all on his own. As he walked me outside, hands over my eyes, he explained that he had been to a couple of car dealerships that day and though he was strongly considering a new-model luxury sedan, he had changed his mind at the last minute and driven home in a new hybrid (gas-electric) instead. Few things have pleased me as much as that did. For me it meant a lot of things: that he really loves me, that he understands his impact on our environment, and that he wants to be a billboard for eco-friendly choices and living. Since then a whole slew of Ryan's friends and colleagues have traded in their cars for hybrids.

Greening Your Ride

But buying a brand new hybrid is not the best option for everyone. Because of financial constraints it may not even be an option at all. And truly, if everyone decided to dump his or her old car for a hybrid instead, the amount of waste that we'd incur would far outweigh the fuel we would save.

That said, the sale of hybrid cars is on the rise. Although they still account only for 3 percent of total U.S. car sales, the number sold in the first four months of 2008 was 25 percent greater than in the same period the previous year. Hybrid vehicles run on a combination of gas and electric power. They produce fewer greenhouse gas emissions and get typically one-third better fuel efficiency than comparable gas model vehicles, making prices at the pump today almost bearable.

Outdoors   195

Of course, the ultimate driving machine just may end up being hydrogen powered, vegetable oil fueled, fully electric, or some other car of the future. Every day more and more research is being done into alternative fuel and energy sources for vehicles. While the technology exists for electric, hydrogen, and many others, you can imagine what it will take to transform our countryside so that there are other types of fueling stations where once we pumped gas. A good amount of work still needs to be done, but the exciting news is that it *is* being done.

Regardless of what kind of car you drive today, there are a number of steps you can take to make your vehicle more fuel efficient. And that's good news considering that American families spend about nineteen cents of every dollar earned on transportation, more than on food and health care combined. Add to the equation the sobering statistic that over 40 percent of our country's air pollution is from on-road vehicles, and we've got even more reasons to drive efficiently.

So here's how.

The Top Ten Tips for Greening Your Car

1. Chill out.
2. Check your tires.
3. Tune up.
4. Lighten up.
5. Pick your pump.

6. Shut it off.
7. Commute consciously.
8. Embrace public transit.
9. Drive less.
10. Offset.

Chill Out

First things first: when you hit the road, let's make sure you're driving as sensibly as possible. Road rage, or even just aggressive driving, might be your and your gas tank's worst enemy. Speeding, rapid accelerations, and sudden braking can lower your gas mileage by as much as 33 percent on the highway and 5 percent in town.

Typically, any speed above sixty miles per hour leads to decreased fuel efficiency. Every five miles per hour over sixty is like paying an extra thirty cents per gallon for gas. On long highway trips, that adds up quickly. In fact, chilling out and avoiding aggressive behavior on the roads can save you 125 gallons of gas and nearly five hundred dollars a year. That's enough to buy plenty of stress balls as an alternate method of releasing pent-up aggression.

As a basic guideline, you want to keep your engine speed between twelve hundred and three thousand rpms, and upshift between two thousand and twenty-five hundred.

Check Your Tires

Your car has a recommended tire PSI, which stands for "pounds per square inch." By keeping your tires properly inflated, you can improve your fuel efficiency by at least 3 percent. In fact, if everyone in America would drive around on properly inflated tires, we'd save around 2 billion gallons of gas a year.

Tune Up

I had always been of the mind that when the guy suggests a new air filter during an oil change, he's just trying to nickel-and-dime me. That was until I learned that a clean air filter could improve my or any car's gas mileage by 10 percent. Simply keeping your car in shape (checking your air filter, spark plugs, sensors, hoses, and belts) can save you over 150 gallons of gas or six hundred dollars a year.

Lighten Up

Every extra one hundred pounds in your vehicle can reduce your miles per gallon by as much as 2 percent, which is the equivalent of an extra eight cents per gallon. While I'm not suggesting you throw passengers out the window, you might consider storing that cooler, golf bag, extra stroller, and whatever else you've been lugging around.

Ideas to Grow On

Take a good assessment of everything in your car. Extra strollers, bags, even shoes just take up space and create extra weight in your car. By downsizing on your gear, you'll save fuel and you may even discover that you can get by with a more compact vehicle.

Pick Your Pump

Picking your pumping time and temperature is actually very important. Refueling when the air is cooler, like in the early morning or late evening, allows for less evaporative emissions. Also avoid the temptation to top off your tank. Trust that the auto shutoff knows best.

Shut It Off

Think of it this way: when you are idling, your car is getting zero miles per gallon. If you need to sit in the carpool line at your child's school or in the driveway or waiting for a teller at the bank drive-up, you're better off turning your car off if you're going to idle for any time longer than thirty seconds.

Commute Consciously

By driving to and from work at non-rush-hour times, you'll consume less fuel, release less greenhouse gas emissions, and save yourself precious time. If

your boss will allow it, work on flex hours so you can come in and leave a little earlier or later than the rest of the traffic, or even work from home one
day of the week.

Try carpooling with others from your office or children's school. The ultimate goal is for each of you to simply drive fewer miles, especially during
prime hours, per day.

Embrace Public Transit

Public transport is on the rise once again. Almost 85 million more public
transit trips were taken in the first quarter of 2008 than the year prior. And
this resulted in vehicle miles on our roads declining by over 2 percent.

While you may not live in a public-transit-friendly city, it's interesting to
know which are the most efficient options, if you're ever given the opportunity
to take one or another. The most efficient, in terms of CO_2 emissions, is light rail
(streetcars and trolleys), then buses, then heavy rail (subways and elevated
trains). But even subways are enormously better than driving your one body in
your own car. Any way you slice it, public transit saves nearly a billion and a half
gallons of gas and about 14 million tons of carbon dioxide emissions per year.

Drive Less

If all else fails, simply do whatever you can to drive fewer miles. Cars release somewhere close to a pound of CO_2 for every mile driven, so avoid
driving twenty miles a week and you'll eliminate about a thousand pounds
of CO_2 emissions over the course of a year. By skipping your daily commute
one day a week, you could reduce your greenhouse gas emissions by about
four hundred pounds per year.

Offset

No matter what car you're driving, how many miles it travels, or what sort
of fuel efficiency you're getting, CO_2 offsets are a sensible way to counter-

balance the amount of pollution your car generates while investing in clean energies and carbon-capturing projects like wind farms and biomass generation. There are a number of websites that will calculate the amount of CO_2 emissions you're responsible for; just have on hand your car's make, model, year, and annual mileage. A 2007 Toyota Prius driven twelve thousand miles a year, for example, emits a little over four thousand pounds of CO_2, while a 2007 Hummer H3 emits just under fourteen thousand pounds. The Hummer emits more than three times as much CO_2 for the same amount of miles. (This statistic probably doesn't surprise you, though.) Offsets are not a license to drive recklessly all over the country, but they are a way of recognizing the effect your consumption is having and investing responsibly to try to balance the damage.

Do what you can to conserve fuel in as many of these ways as possible, and you could save as much as two dollars per gallon. At four dollars a gallon, that's a savings of half your annual fuel cost. For most people, that amounts to between one and two thousand dollars over the course of a year.

Recycling

Every single day the average American throws away seven and a half pounds of garbage. With over 300 million Americans, that amounts to more than 2 billion pounds of garbage produced every single day, the majority of which goes to landfills.

By recycling, we're saving space in landfills, using less energy and fewer natural resources, and saving our soil and water from unnecessary pollution. In addition to all of that, we are returning borrowed materials so they can be made into new items. This too saves our environment. For example, making glass from recycled glass releases 20 percent less related air pollution and 50 percent less water pollution.

Recycling saves resources and money. In 2004, the Dallas District of the U.S. Postal Service collected recyclable office paper, cardboard, and such from buildings and facilities along their regular routes. They also collected all of the district's undeliverable mail and, using existing trucks on existing routes, they transported this to a recycling facility. In so doing, they saved the district $250,000 in trash-hauling costs and generated an additional $300,000 in revenue.

Today the United States recycles approximately 32 percent of its waste. Specifically, 52 percent of all paper, 45 percent of all aluminum beverage cans, and 31 percent of plastic soda bottles are recycled. Additionally, 67 percent of all major appliances and 63 percent of all steel packaging are now recycled. Fifteen years ago we were only recycling half that amount. Perhaps that is because recycling is getting easier. Twenty years ago there was only one curbside recycling system in the country, but by 2006 there were over eight thousand.

Read the Signs

 This means a product **can be recycled.**

 This means a product is **made from recycled materials.**

You might find it beneficial to have a recycling collection center inside your house as well as in a shed or garage. I have a small collection basket in my kitchen, another set of bins in my laundry room downstairs, and a recyclables can next to the garbage can in my office. All of these are dumped into the large, curbside pick-up bins in my garage. And from here I take the majority of my recyclables to the curb for my curbside pick-up. The rest (cardboard and certain plastics) have to be dropped off elsewhere.

The four common recycling methods include curbside pick-up, drop-off centers, buy-back centers, and deposit and refund programs. From each of these, the recyclables are sent to a facility where they are then sorted and sold as raw materials. Once cleaned, melted, shredded, or whatever is necessary, the recycled materials are then used in the manufacturing of any number of products, from laundry detergent bottles and newspapers to roadways and park benches.

Setting Up a Center

First find out if recycling is required by your local ordinance. Many municipalities have mandated recycling of newspapers, cardboard, bottles, egg cartons, batteries, and more. The website *www.earth911.org* offers a recycling locator that allows you to find recycling programs (mandatory or voluntary) in your area simply by plugging in your zip code. If recycling isn't mandatory in your area, or if you want to go even further than the requirements, check *earth911.org* or your local government's website (they all have them now, and, depending on how much effort your municipality has invested in its development, the website may be a great resource for many sorts of activities and "green" programs).

As of just a couple of years ago, there were over eight thousand curbside pick-up recycling programs in the country. By using *earth911.org* or calling your local waste management company, you should be able to determine if you have such a program in your neighborhood. Often you'll have to pay for the pick-up service, but, for example, my monthly cost is the equivalent of one Starbucks trip. If you don't have a recycling pick-up or decide you'd rather not pay for the service, you'll simply need to transport your recyclables to a drop-off location. These are often located in parks or large public parking lots. Most drop-off centers require that you sort your recyclables, so a drive-by of your local center is advised before you begin your at-home collection.

You may decide to start off by only recycling paper and plastic soda bottles or soda cans. Or you may decide to recycle everything you possibly can. It doesn't matter what you start with, just that you start.

Next, decide where and how you'll collect these items. You can do as I do and have collection bins all throughout your home, or just have one centralized site where people can drop their recyclables. There are slick store-bought recycling centers, but cardboard boxes, plastic tubs, or old garbage cans work just as well.

Ideas to Grow On

If you'd rather not invest in new bins for your recycling, find a few (the number will depend on whether you need to sort your recyclables and how many categories of recyclables you'll have) old garbage cans, buckets, or boxes.

Using chalkboard paint, paint a large square on the front of your container. Once dried, label the container according to what recyclable should go in it and any other instructions for your recycling participants.

You'll need only as many bins as categories of recyclables that you'll have. If your recycling program or facility doesn't require that you sort your recyclables, then one or two may be sufficient. Whatever container you use should be washable, as it's likely to get wet and sticky. For this reason cardboard boxes aren't the best option, unless you plan to recycle yours and swap them out for new ones once they get too soggy for further use.

Again, depending on your program, there may be certain guidelines you're required to follow. I am required to break down my cardboard boxes before I can drop them off. Most ask that you bundle your newspapers, remove caps from washed glass and plastic bottles, and flatten tin cans. Many programs print illustrated posters that you can hang near your recycling center. Alternately, print off a list of instructions and post it for all your helpers to reference. I also recommend posting a sign near your kitchen garbage, reminding family members to think before they toss.

The final step in setting up a recycling center is to recruit some help. This shouldn't be a job you champion on your own. The whole family will need to be on board to successfully change your disposal habits. Sorting recyclables is a great job for small children, while bundling newspapers is an excellent task for a teenage child.

If you live in a community area, like an apartment building or a co-op, where recycling isn't already mandatory, recruit neighbors to recycle with you. Try to get permission to set up a large recyclables collection zone in the parking lot. If you're doing this, printing the rules is especially important.

> **Setting Up a Recycling Center**
>
> - Find your mandatory or voluntary recycling program.
> - Decide what you'll recycle.
> - Create a collection zone.
> - Post labels and/or rules.
> - Recruit helpers.

Perhaps one of your older children or your spouse or roommate could help you calculate the amount of trash versus recycling that you have when you start and each consecutive month after that. Start off by weighing your trash bags on garbage day. Then continue weighing those as well as your bags or containers of recycling. Create a chart that shows how much less you're sending to the dump and how much more you're sending to recycling as time goes on.

What to Recycle

The main recyclables include aluminum cans, glass bottles, paper (including magazines and newspapers), plastic, and steel or tin cans. Depending on

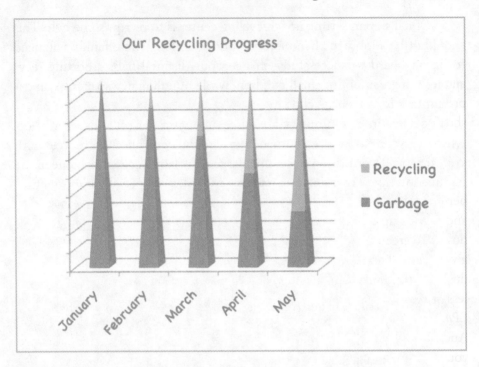

your recycling facility, you may have to sort these items according to their category. The company responsible for my recycling pick-up allows me to throw all of my recyclables together in one bin, with the exception of certain plastics and corrugated cardboard, and other large and unusual items. These I have to take and drop off at a separate facility.

Aluminum

The aluminum can is the most-often-recycled item in the United States and for good reason. It can be used indefinitely, making it an extremely valuable material, and there are an abundance of them in play every day. The average person disposes of (either in the dump or through recycling) twenty-five thousand cans in their lifetime; recycling just one of those cans saves enough energy to power a TV for three hours. Amazingly, it takes the same amount of energy to make one aluminum can from virgin ore as twenty aluminum cans from recycled aluminum. And it takes only sixty days for a can to be recycled, cleaned, melted, shaped, and turned into a new can, then filled, shipped, priced, and put back on the shelves. Aluminum siding, gutters, window frames, and car parts can also be recycled. Thankfully, 50 percent of all aluminum cans produced are recycled, so it's clearly an easily recycled material and one that should definitely be on your starter list.

Glass Bottles

The amazing thing about glass is that it can be recycled an indefinite number of times without losing quality or purity. But don't recycle a glass bottle and it ends up in a landfill, where it can take up to a million years to break down. To create new glass, sand and other ingredients are heated to 2,600 degrees Fahrenheit. The process consumes a lot of energy and creates a good deal of pollution. Making glass out of recycled materials requires 40 percent less energy and cuts related water pollution by 50 percent. According to an EPA study, only about 25 percent of glass containers are currently recycled. And 18 percent of all glass bottles come from bars and restaurants. So once you've started recycling your glass at home, do your part to spread the word and encourage glass recycling on the part of your neighbors and neighborhood watering holes.

Paper

We take for granted how much we rely on paper products; it's what we wipe our noses with, what we get our news from, and what we scribble little notes on each day. Making new paper from recycled paper reduces related air pollution contributions by 95 percent, and recycling one three-foot stack of paper saves one tree. Today 86 percent of Americans have access to programs to recycle paper, and thankfully, most took advantage in 2006, recycling 53 percent of our nation's paper consumption. And yet every year Americans throw away enough office paper to build a twelve-foot-high wall of paper that would stretch all the way from Seattle to New York. Paper can be grouped into four main categories: newsprint, office paper, mixed paper (magazines, catalogs, pamphlets, inserts, etc.), and corrugated cardboard.

Your recycling center should be set up to take all types, but corrugated might have to go to a special bin or drop-off location.

If nothing else, start by recycling your newspapers. Every day 63 million newspapers are printed, and only about 30 percent of those are recycled. Get on board! You'll save four trees just by recycling your Sunday papers for a year.

Plastic

Plastics are integrated into more parts of our daily lives than you might realize. Americans buy around 28 billion plastic water bottles every year, and only around 20 percent of those are recycled. More than 17 million barrels of oil were used in plastic bottle production in 2006 alone, but the need for all that oil is dramatically reduced when we recycle. In 2005 the United States recycled over 3 billion pounds of post-consumer plastics. Recycling just one plastic bottle saves enough energy to light a sixty-watt bulb for six hours.

Recycling plastics can be a little confusing because there are different types. Look on the bottom of your plastic yogurt container, soda bottle, or anything else for the code: a number inside the small triangle.

Most recycling centers collect at least plastics 1 and 2, which include PETE or PET bottles and HDPE plastics. Drop-off centers for other types of plastics can be found through *www.earth911.org.*

And what's really cool is that plastic bottles can be recycled into more than just more plastic. PET bottles, the type used for soda and water, can be turned into soft fibers like fleece for clothing and carpet, as well as hard goods like lumber for decks and park benches. It takes only five soda bottles to make enough fiber to fill a ski jacket or for one extra-large T-shirt.

Steel/Tin Cans

While steel doesn't sound like a product you use or dispose of every day, according to Earth 911 it is one of the most abundantly recycled and reused. The canned soup you eat is likely in a steel "tin" container, as is your dog's

Types of Plastics

1 (PETE) (Polyethylene terephthalate): soda and water bottles, peanut butter, cooking oil, ketchup, and salad dressing containers, etc.

2 (HDPE) (High-density polyethylene): "cloudy" jugs like milk or juice jugs, butter and some yogurt tubs, bleach, laundry/dish detergent and household cleaner bottles, shampoo and conditioner bottles, some shopping and trash bags, cereal and cracker box liners, etc.

3 (V) (Polyvinyl chloride, or PVC): cling wrap, some food and liquid containers, shower curtains, pipes, plastic food wrap, loose-leaf binders, baby bottle nipples, some household cleaner and body care bottles, etc.

4 (LDPE) (Low-density polyethylene): some food, dry-cleaning, and grocery bags, squeezable bottles, furniture, carpet, etc.

5 (PP) (Polypropylene): more "rigid" food storage containers and yogurt cups, baby bottles, cups and bowls, some medicine bottles, bottle caps, drinking straws, some diapers, etc.

6 (PS) (Polystyrene): Styrofoam coffee cups, egg cartons, meat and bakery trays, carry-out food containers, plastic tableware, insulation, packing peanuts, CD jackets, etc.

7 (OTHER) (Miscellaneous, a combination or polycarbonate): Large water bottles, some food containers, clear baby bottles, linings of metal cans, nylon, bulletproof materials, DVDs, etc.

food, your canned vegetables, and that paint you used on your walls. Every year we recycle more steel in North America than aluminum, glass, paper, and plastic combined. And it's a good thing, because we're going through about 100 million steel cans a day, not to mention the steel in appliances, cars, and buildings. Today over 65 percent of the steel produced in the United States is recycled.

The Yard

When I was growing up, our "yard" consisted of large vegetable and fruit gardens, untouched forests, and a small portion that we mowed so we could play badminton, bocce, and other games. Even today my parents' yard is shrinking into greater areas of garden and wildflowers and smaller areas of cultivated grass. But growing large areas of green grass is tempting, isn't it? Especially if you live in a neighborhood where landscaping is the norm. Consider for a moment what it takes to grow large areas of green space—water, fertilizer, petroleum, and time, to say the least. The climate in some areas of this country doesn't support grass naturally at all, so if you're in an area like that—Arizona or Nevada, for example—shouldn't you consider a lawn free of turf altogether?

There are ways to maintain good-looking lawn areas and make your yard a lot greener . . . in the good sense of the word.

Non-toxic Lawn Care

I typically shy away from using scare tactics, but when it comes to dousing our lawns with chemicals, there's no way around the hard sell. A study by the National Cancer Institute, of the U.S. National Institutes of Health, found an almost seven times greater risk of leukemia in children whose parents use pesticides on their homes or gardens. Results from a U.S. Geological Survey state that about a billion pounds of pesticides are used each year and that, not surprisingly, traces of those pesticides were found in every stream tested across the country. And if you think that the chemicals you're spraying or spreading on your lawn and garden aren't weedicides, herbicides, or pesticides, you're sadly wrong.

Common Lawn Pesticides

Of the thirty lawn pesticides most commonly used, nineteen have been linked to cancer, thirteen to birth defects, twenty-one to reproductive effects, and twenty-six to liver or kidney damage.

So now let's think about what happens on your lawn: you walk through it, your kids run around and lie down on it, your dog runs over it, often stopping to dig his nose into it, and then all of you come inside, tracking whatever was on the grass into your house on your clothes and the bottoms of your shoes. In short, what you sprinkle and spray out there ends up in your family's home and bodies.

Children are especially susceptible to harsh chemical lawn products because of their physical size (the same amount of chemical does a lot more damage to a small body than a larger body), their still-developing systems, and their close proximity to the ground. So how can you have a healthy and beautiful lawn while keeping your family safe? There are five things to remember: that size matters and to bypass the chemicals, spike your grass, leave the clippings, and skip the gas.

Size Matters

If you're just moving into a new house, or have been thinking about re-landscaping, take advantage of this chance to think creatively about how you want to use your outdoor space. How big do you actually need your yard to be? Many lawns are up to eight thousand square feet when only one or two

The Top Five Tips for Natural Lawn Care

1. Size matters—make your yard only as big as it needs to be.

2. Bypass the chemicals—find eco-friendly fertilizers and deterrents.

3. Spike your grass—aerating makes turf stronger.

4. Leave the clippings—let the clippings fertilize for you.

5. Skip the gas—use a little elbow grease instead.

thousand would do the trick. The more lawn area you have, the more energy and water you have to expend to take care of it. Let the rest of your space go wild with a wildflower garden or planned landscapes of native plants.

There is a growing movement of people who are finding alternative uses for their yard, forgoing grass altogether. Many are choosing to grow vegetables, for profit or for their own table. Others are simply letting their lawns go natural, by allowing wildflowers, "weeds," or rocks and soil (in more arid climates) to fill in the space between the house and the street.

If you do have grass, be aware that the height of each blade of grass matters more than you might think. Allowing your grass to be shorter than an inch and a half can kill the root systems. Plus, the shorter your grass, the more the sunlight can get to the soil to dry it out quickly and help sprout weeds. The ideal, most drought-resistant blade of grass is at least three inches long. You should be able to set the blade on your mower to the exact height you'd like.

If you have a large yard with an acre or more of grass, try to leave it to its own, natural devices. See what grows if you don't mow and you'll likely be pleased with the variety of flowers and colors that naturally pop up throughout the season. Keep an eye out for overly aggressive plants but let all native plants (cultivated or not) go.

Bypass the Chemicals

If it has the suffix "cide" at the end of it, which comes from the Latin word meaning "to kill," then you don't want it. Aside from killing many more insects and organisms than those it was intended to (and impairing our body's internal systems), chemical fertilizers and pesticides can create a surplus of nitrogen, phosphorus, and potassium in your yard. And while this might help them do what they're supposed to—make your lawn greener—it also damages the soil and makes it *more* susceptible to insects and disease.

Organic fertilizers, on the other hand, feed the grass and soil and create a safe haven for beneficial insects, earthworms, and other microorganisms. Look for plant-based vinegars and corn gluten to prevent weeds. Corn gluten, which is 10 percent nitrogen, is especially effective as a crabgrass preventative. Apply twenty pounds of corn gluten per thousand square feet of lawn space in the spring and again in the fall. And let the clover grow. This plant grabs free nitrogen from the air and fixes it into your lawn's soil, helping it to grow.

Spike Your Grass

Don those golf, baseball, or soccer spikes from time to time (or, better, use a spiked garden tool or thatcher) and tread your way across your turf. This allows oxygen to creep down into your soil so that good insects, earthworms, and microorganisms can go to work.

Leave the Clippings

Invest in a mulching mower that shreds grass and sprinkles it across your lawn as you mow. Or simply rake the grass clippings once you've mowed so that they evenly cover your lawn. You don't want the layer of clippings to be too heavy in any one area, as this can starve the grass underneath. If clippings are heavy, it's best to rake and turn them from time to time. The clippings will decompose and feed nitrogen into your lawn's soil.

Skip the Gas

Whether a mower, a trimmer, a blower, or a chainsaw, gas-powered land-scape machinery is responsible for at least 5 percent of our country's urban air pollution. If you're really going full-throttle, opt for hand-powered trimmers and blade mowers instead. You'll save money and save the air you breathe.

Water Conservation

At least 30 percent of water consumption by most suburban homes is used outdoors, to water lawns, landscaping, and gardens. Probably half of that is wasted, as water falls on waterlogged ground and runs off. But a good deal of it just evaporates into the air as it is projected from the sprinkler head or hose nozzle. One way to avoid this is to install a drip irrigation system, which is no more than a hose with a number of small holes in it through which the water is slowly released. Because the hose lies directly on the ground or beneath a layer of mulch, the water isn't susceptible to evaporation or runoff. Drip systems use as much as 50 percent less water than conventional in-ground sprinkler systems and can save you more than a thousand dollars over the life of the system. And they're fairly easy to install on your own. You can find all of the necessary components at your nearest home improvement store.

If you already have a standard irrigation system installed, stick with that. It is still much more efficient than watering by sprinkler. And there are a few other things you can do to optimize your water use. Watering your lawn early in the morning, before ten a.m., is best so that the water doesn't evaporate during midday's high temperatures. And the length of your grass can help as well. Tall grass means long roots, which means less water is needed.

If you do have an irrigation system, be sure to turn it off when you're expecting rain. There is no sense in wasting water and overburdening already hardworking sewage and drainage systems. Better yet, install an evapotranspiration controller, or "smart" controller, to do the work for you. It senses the temperature and precipitation level to determine if and when to run the sprinklers.

Using mulch prevents evaporation around your trees and shrubs. And because trees have deep root systems, they can be watered less often for longer periods of time. Many cities impose water restrictions during especially hot and dry months. So what do you do to water your flowers? Use the water from your basement's dehumidifier or the water that is otherwise wasted down the drain while you wait for your shower to heat up. Simply keep a bucket handy next to the shower to capture this water and use it to keep your flowers blooming.

Ideas to Grow On

Keep a soup or tuna fish can in your yard. When it fills up an inch, you've watered enough. And if it rains at night, check the can in the morning. If it has filled an inch, you've done your watering for the day. You can also use otherwise wasted water from your sinks, showers, and tubs for outdoor watering.

Of course, the best option of all is to skip lawn watering altogether. If you live in an arid or semi-arid area, consider a lawn free of green grass, filled with native plants and rocks instead. Watering lawns puts a huge drain on our water tables and could someday result in pipelines being built simply for the sake of (home) vanity. With areas scrounging for water simply for cooking, drinking, and bathing, it seems quite selfish to waste such copious amounts on a lawn, doesn't it?

Rainwater Harvesting

Rainwater is certainly one of the most-often-wasted lawn accessories. By attaching a rain barrel to a gutter downspout, any home can be on its way to an inexpensive method of reducing runoff, preventing erosion, and capturing clean water for use on the lawn, flowerpots, even the car.

Collecting rainwater is an age-old practice dating back thousands of years. When I was growing up, my grandparents used an old horse feed trough as a rain barrel and would scoop out buckets and watering cans full of water to use on the garden. Theirs, as do most today, had a spout on it with a hose attached that they could stretch all the way to the garden. As long as there was sufficient water in the barrel, the pressure would keep the water flowing down through the hose.

There are many types of rain barrels, varying from found or "recycled" barrels to plastic containers made specifically for the task. A rain barrel needs to have two things, a place for the water to go in at the top and a spigot or valve for hose attachment where the water will come out at the bottom. If the spigot or valve is located at the very bottom, you'll need to have your barrel up on concrete blocks or bricks so you are never asking the water to travel uphill to exit the hose.

It's best for your barrel to have an overflow valve near the top as well. If this is threaded for hose hookup, direct the hose so that it ends in a flowerbed or nearby landscaping. If the barrel gets too full, the water will automatically be diverted to good use in your favorite bed.

You'll want to install the rain barrel close to one of your home's downspouts. You may need to unscrew the downspout from the side of your house, then cut it off just higher than the height of your barrel, and, if needed, attach a flexible piece to direct the water into the top of your barrel. Or you might be able to set the barrel directly under the newly trimmed downspout, eliminating the need for a flexible piece.

Because mosquitoes breed in standing water, it's best to attach mosquito netting over the top of the barrel's hole to keep mosquitoes from getting inside.

Rain barrels can save anywhere from fifty-five to seventy thousand gallons of water a year. Look to purchase one online, in home improvement and gardening centers, or from your city. Many cities sell rain barrels at a discount to encourage their use, thereby saving city water and city sewers from extra rainwater runoff.

Growing a Garden

For as long as I can remember, I've had my hands, during the warmer months, in the soil of a garden. I've gardened for the food it produces, for the beauty it creates, and for the birds it brings and the insects it repels and attracts. But I still think one of the best reasons for gardening is the connection it affords you, and especially small children, to the soil and the origin of foods.

Ideas to Grow On

Grow a salad bowl. Take a large container, about three feet across, and plant a variety of lettuces, some chives or other herbs, and a dwarf cherry tomato plant. Harvest and enjoy!

Edible Plants

When it comes to fruit and vegetable gardening, what you plant is completely up to you. You should do some research into what grows best in your area, but the primary decision should be based on what you're most likely to eat and use, because those will be the things you'll most happily tend to. Even with very little space you can grow a great number of herbs. Basil, oregano, chives, parsley, sage, and rosemary are some good starter herbs. Some are perennials, so they'll come back year after year, and others aren't. Either way, I recommend digging up and potting your herbs as the weather turns cooler so you can continue to cook with them through winter months.

Vegetables take a little more space but a simple lettuce patch works in a small bed or even a large container. Plant a variety of greens for a colorful and nutritious salad mix: arugula, romaine, endive, and green or red leaf.

Vegetable Garden Harvesting

- **Early:** Asparagus, lettuces, radishes, rhubarb
- **Midsummer:** Beets, cabbage, cauliflower, corn, peas, tomatoes
- **Late:** Carrots, parsnips, potatoes, squash

Tomatoes can also be grown in containers, so they're a perfect vegetable to try if you don't have much space. If space is not what you're short on, then start with a patch of a few vegetable varieties. Don't overdo it the first year. You are beginning something you can build upon year after year.

Insect-Friendly and Repelling Plants

Worms and spiders might make you squirm, but there are so many good bugs out there and plants that will help attract them to your garden. Ladybug larvae eat pests and can be attracted with marigolds, dandelions, fennel, and dill. Hoverflies also help rid your garden of pests. Attract hoverflies with parsley, spearmint, gloriosa daisy, Queen Anne's lace, and English lavender. Lacewings feed on aphids, and love cosmos, angelica, prairie sunflower, and herbs such as dill, coriander, and fennel.

Butterflies and bees are necessary for your garden because they help with pollination. Encourage them to attend soirees in your patch by planting goldenrod, lilacs, bee balm, and other attractive plants. You can get a list of butterfly-loving plants that are right for your area's climate from the North American Butterfly Association at *www.naba.org*.

KATRINA FREY

Katrina Frey spent the early part of her adult life studying organic farming under Alan Chadwick, an influential English horticulturist and proponent of organic gardening, famous in and around California in the 1970s. Prior to her time with Alan, Katrina spent her childhood in Vermont, surrounded by family members who loved nothing more than dirt beneath their nails and gardens around their hands. But it wasn't until she married her husband Jonathan and discovered his family's northern California "organic by neglect" vineyard that she realized she wanted her *own* life's work to be working the soil.

In 1980, with Jonathan and his brother, Katrina founded Frey Vineyards, in Redwood Valley, California. Frey, established on the family ranch, was the first organic winery in the United States. Today four generations of Frey family members work the soil, led by Beba, the eighty-some-year-old matriarch of the family. The Frey ranch is home or workplace to fifty people, forty dogs, and countless other animals. Younger members come back from college and time spent abroad with fresh ideas and new insight, vision, and energy. Great-grandchildren are born, infusing the atmosphere with a renewed sense of purpose, strength, and hope.

Their goal is to not only create a healthy beverage, but to protect the soil as a means of reversing global warming. When soil is farmed organically or biodynamically, carbon is captured in the soil instead of being released into the atmosphere, and Katrina is convinced that this is one of the most potent ways of reversing climate change and protecting the planet. So, after raising children on the ranch and shepherding a growing and pioneering winery, Katrina has started to let her passion wander beyond the ranch boundaries. A short while ago Katrina focused her energy on Mendocino County as she helped set it

continued

on course to become the first GMO-free (free of any genetically modified crops or animals) zone in the United States in 2003. Today 40 percent of the vineyard land in Mendocino County is organic. And Katrina deserves more than a nod for that.

Thirty years ago Katrina was a young woman experimenting with new methods of organic farming. Today she not only helps manage the oldest and largest U.S. organic winery, in her quiet, soft-spoken manner she is an outspoken advocate for organic and biodynamic farming, for land preservation, and for families living and working as families once did. She found her dream and stayed put to build it layer upon layer. ■

Of course, I've never met anyone who likes mosquitoes around their garden, their lawn, or their patio. Position mosquito-repelling plants so you can relax outdoors without the temptation of spraying chemical-laden repellents. In studies, catnip has been found to be ten times more effective at repelling mosquitoes than the common bug spray ingredient DEET. Other plants that work to repel mosquitoes include geraniums, lemon thyme, marigolds, and rosemary.

Composting

A vegetable is a terrible thing to waste, unless it is being turned into what many call "gardener's gold." A compost bin is not only a handy, earth-friendly landfill for your kitchen scraps, it can go a long way toward enriching your garden's soil by improving its texture, water retention, and aeration. Even better still, compost, unlike most fertilizers, is free.

Ideas to Grow On

Composting can reduce yard waste by as much as 75 percent, and like recycling, it's a fun chore to involve the kids in. Start a compost pile and get the whole family involved.

What You'll Need

It doesn't take much to start a compost bin, and, if well managed, it shouldn't ever smell or attract rodents. We have two compost bins behind my house. And ours is a house in the city, with nearby neighbors who have never complained about it.

The Environmental Protection Agency estimates that 23 percent of U.S. municipal waste comes from yard and food waste. I send both to my compost instead. Between composting and recycling, you'll quickly find you hardly have need of a garbage can anymore.

Composting can happen indoors in bins with worms (called vermiculture) or outdoors. Traditional outdoor composting is what I'll explain here.

Compost—What You'll Need

- An outdoor container—a bin or a tumbler

- An indoor collector—any bowl or bucket with a lid

- Heat—compost forms best between 120 and 160 degrees Fahrenheit

- Air—circulating air through the pile helps it break down

- Moisture—like a damp sponge; no more, no less

- Activators—optional to help quicken the decomposition

An Outdoor Container

The first thing you will need to start a compost pile is a large bin or tumbler. I find that compost tumblers (which look like a barrel on a stand) work very well because you simply flip them on their hinges to aerate them. Bins are extremely common and don't have to be fancy or store-bought. They can have four walls, three, or even be an open heap; just be prepared to stir and turn your pile with a shovel or pitchfork.

An Indoor Collector

Next you'll need an indoor collection container. I use a small bucket that I keep under my kitchen sink. Again, this doesn't have to be fancy, but I advise something with a lid and preferably a handle. This will allow you to collect your banana peels, eggshells, apple cores, and other kitchen scraps all day, every day, without constant trips to your outdoor bin. The stuff in this indoor container will begin to break down but won't likely be the right balance of carbon to nitrogen and therefore will smell. It's important to dump this in your larger bin, along with some leaves, shredded newspaper, or other carbons, as soon as it starts to fill up, or about once every few days.

Heat

Your compost will decompose the fastest when it's between 120 and 160 degrees Fahrenheit. Heat will naturally occur as the organic matter starts to break down, but the best way to obtain heat is to keep your compost pile in partial sun.

Air

For your pile to properly compost and avoid smelling, it is important that it stays properly aerated. Tumblers make this job easy but a shovel or pitchfork will do the trick as well.

Moisture

As you add more materials, particularly greens and nitrogens, your pile will create moisture. It's important that the moisture stays evenly distributed throughout. The organic matter in your pile should be like a damp sponge, not wet enough that you can wring moisture out, but no drier either. Turning or tumbling your pile daily or at least a few times a week will help with this.

Activators

Additives and other accelerators are optional. Alfalfa, cottonseed, or blood meal will help jump-start your pile. Wood ashes will help balance out an acidic pile, and algae, seaweed, or lake weed will get things moving as well.

What to Compost

You need a proper balance of brown stuff and green stuff, called the carbon and nitrogen balance. The perfect carbon-to-nitrogen ratio is about twenty-five parts carbon to one part nitrogen. If you have too much nitrogen, the pile might stink, and if you have too much carbon, it will slow decomposition. When you look at your pile in general, you should have much more browns than greens.

- **Carbons** (browns): wood ashes, shredded cardboard and newspapers, straw, sawdust, peanut shells, cornstalks, leaves, pine needles, wood chips

- **Nitrogens** (greens): fruit and vegetable scraps, coffee grounds, garden and grass clippings, seaweed, manure, hay, alfalfa, clover and pulled weeds

Wood chips, sawdust, and shredded cardboard or newspaper are all highly carbon, so if your pile starts to stink, add more of these.

What Not to Compost

There are a number of things that should never go in a compost bin.

- **Meat products** like beef or chicken leftovers, fish, bones

- **Fats** such as peanut butter, oils, or lard

- **Dairy products** like yogurt, butter, milk, or sour cream

- **Colored papers** like magazines and construction paper

- **Pet droppings.** Though it seems silly to say, many people ask.

- **Coal or charcoal ash.** Wood ash is fine, but the other kinds are not.

- **Chemicals.** Even yard trimmings that have been treated with chemicals should never go in the pile if you're planning to use the compost in your gardens.

Once you start your pile, it will take anywhere from a month or two to a full season before you have compost that can be used around your lawn. This compost is nutrient-rich free fertilizer that can be used in your flowerpots, your vegetable gardens, or around trees and shrubs. The best part is that all of that kitchen and yard waste is being put to use, instead of being sent to the dump sealed in plastic bags.

Green Pet

If your dog is anything like mine, he or she probably lives inside more than outside. Regardless, the "outdoors" chapter seemed like an appropriate place to talk about how you can keep Fido from being left in the cold when it comes to greener living.

There are a number of organic and natural foods and treats available for dogs, cats, and other domestic creatures. Not to mention biodegradable poop bags, organic cotton chew toys, and hemp fashion.

First, let's eliminate one of the biggest dangers to your pet: pesticides. One summer only a few years ago, half of all cases reported through the ASPCA's (American Society for the Prevention of Cruelty to Animals) Animal Poison Control Center were at least partially due to pesticide poisoning. Use natural fertilizers and deterrents instead of chemical pesticides on your lawn to help keep Fido healthy and safe.

Proper Nutrition

Proper nutrition is important for your cat, dog, or other companion animal, just like it is for you and me. So beware if you're discount shopping for your pet's food, as most conventional pet foods are made up of unhealthy ingredients, including animal by-products—waste material from the beef and poultry industry. If your can of cat or dog food says FDA-certified food-grade meat, you're probably safe. Otherwise you can assume that the meat is 4-D classified, meaning it was "dead, dying, diseased, or disabled" upon admission to the slaughterhouse.

On the other hand, organic pet foods are made up of USDA organic meats and other minimally processed, non-GMO ingredients. Certified organic pet foods must meet the same USDA standards that we're already familiar with: hormone-, antibiotic-, and pesticide-free ingredients without the addition of artificial or unacceptably processed fillers. If you see a product labeled "natural," do what you would with a package of food for yourself: pick it up and read the back so you can decide for yourself if it is truly natural enough.

Better Pooper Scoopers

Conventional cat litter is laden with a "clumping" agent that can swell internally and poison your cat if ingested. On top of that, the litter has sediment

Top Five Tips for Greening Your Pet

1. Ensure Proper nutrition.

2. Use better pooper scoopers.

3. Buy greener cleaners.

4. Provide green toys.

5. Use responsible sourcing.

that is saturated with silica dust—a known carcinogen. Look for non-clumping litters like plant-based ones made from wheat, alfalfa, oat, or corn hulls. And for your pup, choose biodegradable poop bags (drop these straight into your trash can, not into a larger plastic liner, so they can break down in the dump) and your best friend's solids won't go to the dump smelling of environmental ignorance.

Greener Cleaners

Cleaner, greener cleaners, like shampoos and conditioners, are out there, free of those same harsh chemical ingredients you're avoiding in your own grooming regimen. Look to your natural foods store for some of the best available.

Green Toys

Safe, eco-friendly toys range from organic cotton chew bones to hemp collars and leashes. The biggest things to remember here are to avoid plastics when possible and to avoid excess at all costs. Your pet probably doesn't need a new carry bag each year or outfits for each season. In fact he or she would probably be just as happy with a rolled-up newspaper and you to throw it as with that fifteen-dollar toy that's caught *your* eye.

Responsible Sourcing

Responsible sourcing is a very uncouth way to say there are good places from which to buy your pets and there are bad ones. A friend or a shelter is a great place. Puppy mills, often accused of overbreeding, inbreeding, and poor living conditions, are not! There are seventy thousand puppies and kittens born *every day* in the United States. Plenty to go around and plenty to pour all of your green love upon.

Now It's Your Turn

A nd now it's your turn. I hope that isn't scary or daunting, but rather that you approach it feeling excited and empowered, knowing that you can make a difference—in your own health, your family's health, and in this communal effort of bettering the planet that we call home. Because it *is* a community effort.

A zillion tiny thoughtful actions every day make a *big* difference. Just like a zillion careless actions a day make a big difference.

In this chapter, you'll find some additional charts, recipes, and information. Don't let your learning stop here. Spend time online and reading other books. Experiment, join groups, and share your experiences with those around you. Share your questions and experiences with me too; you can always find me on my website, *www.sarasnow.com*.

I'm sure that you'll have many questions about where to buy particular products and which brands are most trustworthy. I've intentionally not given lists of brands and products because I don't want to come across as endorsing any in particular, and because I want you to become a smart consumer on your own. Armed with this new knowledge, enter into shopping situations (for food, nursery furniture, or anything else) in a new light, getting to know the company and the ideals behind its products before you blindly buy. Consider making or growing your own before you buy. And in all things, find ways that allow you to live with a lower impact on the earth and a greater emphasis on natural health.

More on Food

I wrote briefly in the kitchen chapter about food's amazing ability to heal or harm a body. Think of it this way: foods have personalities and energies. When you eat different foods, you take in their energies and allow them to interact with your body's internal energy and force. Living foods, foods just picked, or foods (like beans and seeds) that would sprout if taken from the pantry and given light and moisture, have greater and more beneficial energies than processed foods.

A food can help you relax, cleanse, energize, and so on. Consider what the food you are about to eat will enhance in or do to your body, before you eat it.

Cooking Techniques

The way you cook your food is also important. The best cookware is cast iron or stainless steel. Nonstick pans, though convenient, can release chemicals from the finish into your foods. If you use nonstick pans (I'll admit that I use one when I fry eggs in the morning), be sure you quit using it once it has been scratched or chipped. Steaming, stewing, and sautéing are all excellent cooking methods. Boiling is okay, too, because it allows you to avoid excess oils, but nutrients can get lost in the water. If you boil, try to use the "broth" for another purpose.

Cooking for a Family

It is very easy, but also very troublesome, to get into the habit of preparing separate foods for separate picky members of your family. Instead make mealtime a mindful time in your family. Allow your children to put their favorite foods on the menu, but help them understand that some days they get their favorites, and some days others' favorites. Kids make excellent prep cooks—they can help by washing vegetables and stirring ingredients in a bowl. Let them get involved so they'll become excited about the foods they're eating. Talk through the story of each ingredient: how the tomato came from the farmer at the market and the raisins were once grapes growing on a vine in California. Include a variety of colors and living, whole foods in each meal and encourage everyone in the family to eat at least a little of everything. If they complain, tell them to call me and I'll tell stories about the foods I was "encouraged" to eat as a child and suddenly your vegetarian spaghetti sauce won't seem so bad.

Also, take your time around the dinner table. Meals shouldn't be rushed. Not only because it helps with digestion to chew longer, sit up straighter, and allow our bodies stress-free time to digest, but because it encourages conversation. Spending time around the dinner table and doing jobs around the house can help develop a sense of shared responsibility. Hopefully, that sense will lead to a desire to share responsibility in understanding and protecting the environment as well. Learning about a sibling's school lessons can pave the way to curiosity down the road about another culture's traditions. Thinking twice before you throw food away might later cause you to pause before you toss a recyclable or stand by as a company dumps waste into the lake.

Pesticide-Free Foods

Close to forty-three thousand tests were performed by the USDA and the FDA to determine the amount of pesticides in fruits and vegetables that you buy every day. The Environmental Working Group analyzed this data and compiled this list of forty-five produce items listed in order from worst (highest pesticide load = dirtiest) to best (lowest pesticide load = cleanest).

Fresh Living Recipes

A few recipes to get you started follow. I hope to provide many more in a separate upcoming book. Make sure you use local and organic ingredients whenever possible.

Pesticides in Produce—The Full List

Rank (Worst to Best)	Fruit or Veggie	Score (Worst to Best)
1 (worst)	Peaches	100 (dirtiest)
2	Apples	96
3	Sweet Bell Peppers	86
4	Celery	85
5	Nectarines	84
6	Strawberries	83
7	Cherries	75
8	Lettuce	69
9	Grapes (imported)	68
10	Pears	65
11	Spinach	60
12	Potatoes	58
13	Carrots	57
14	Green Beans	55
15	Hot Peppers	53
16	Cucumbers	52
17	Raspberries	47
18	Plums	46
19	Oranges	46
20	Grapes (domestic)	46
21	Cauliflower	39
22	Tangerine	38
23	Mushrooms	37

Rank (Worst to Best)	Fruit or Veggie	Score (Worst to Best)
24	Cantaloupe	34
25	Lemon	31
26	Honeydew Melon	31
27	Grapefruit	31
28	Winter Squash	31
29	Tomatoes	30
30	Sweet Potatoes	30
31	Watermelon	25
32	Blueberries	24
33	Papaya	21
34	Eggplant	19
35	Broccoli	18
36	Cabbage	17
37	Bananas	16
38	Kiwi	14
39	Asparagus	11
40	Sweet Peas (frozen)	11
41	Mango	9
42	Pineapples	7
43	Sweet Corn (frozen)	2
44	Avocado	1
45 (best)	Onions	1 (cleanest)

Reprinted with permission from the Environmental Working Group, *www.foodnews.org*

Simple Suppers

Fresh Pesto

One of the most exciting things about belonging to a CSA (community-supported agriculture) is that you never know what fresh produce (or other) items you're going to get. And because sometimes they're foods you wouldn't necessarily buy at the grocery store, you're encouraged to try new foods and new recipes. One summer an overabundance of basil from my CSA helped me come up with this recipe for fresh pesto.

Toss it with a whole wheat linguini for dinner. For a little extra color, top with sliced sun-dried tomatoes. Try it for lunch, spread onto whole grain bread with sliced yellow peppers. Pesto goes very well with goat cheese, so a baguette slice topped with pesto and a dollop of goat cheese makes a delicious lunch or appetizer when guests come over. Enjoy!

3 cloves garlic
½ cup pine nuts
¼ cup extra-virgin olive oil
   (optional—cut in half with
   chicken broth)
Juice of one lemon

3 cups loosely packed fresh basil
   (stems removed)
½ cup grated Parmesan cheese
2 teaspoons coarse sea salt
Dash of pepper

In a food processor, pulse garlic, pine nuts, olive oil, and lemon juice until smooth. Add basil, Parmesan cheese, and salt and pepper. Pulse until well blended. Scrape down sides and pulse until smooth.

Southwest Polenta and Vegetables

Polenta can be made from scratch by simmering together cornmeal and water, or can be found already prepared in packaged rolls that look like small logs. Here I've used polenta rounds with fresh vegetables for a quick, delicious, and healthy dish.

1 tablespoon extra-virgin
    olive oil
1 medium onion,
    coarsely chopped
4 cloves garlic, diced
1½ teaspoons salt
½ pound button (or other local)
    mushrooms
3 small zucchini (or one large),
    chopped
1 red bell pepper, chopped
2 cups corn (frozen or fresh)

1 can (14 ounces) black beans
1 can (14 ounces) diced tomatoes
    (or 3 small fresh
    tomatoes, diced)
1 teaspoon fresh thyme, chopped
½ teaspoon chili powder
1 teaspoon cumin
½ teaspoon black pepper
1 18-ounce packaged
    polenta "log"
2 cups shredded Romano cheese

In a sauté pan, lightly sauté onion and garlic with ½ teaspoon of the salt in olive oil, about 2 minutes or until barely soft.

Add the mushrooms, zucchini, and red pepper and sauté 3 minutes more.

Add corn, black beans, diced tomatoes, fresh thyme, chili powder, cumin, remaining 1 teaspoon salt, and black pepper, and simmer about 5 minutes, stirring frequently.

While the vegetables simmer, lightly oil the bottom of a casserole dish or 9- × 13-inch cake pan. Slice the polenta into ½-inch rounds and arrange across the bottom of the dish. When vegetables are cooked, but not soft, pour across the top of the polenta. Top with cheese and bake in a 350-degree oven, uncovered, for 15 minutes. Serve plain or on a bed of spinach.

Hearty Tofu Spaghetti Sauce

My mom made this sauce a lot as I was growing up. Since we were a fairly good-sized family, I think it was her way of making a jar of spaghetti sauce go a long way, both in terms of filling bellies and packing us full of fresh vegetables. We used vegetables from the garden; you can do that or seek out organically grown local veggies of your own.

1 pound whole grain pasta
2 tablespoons extra-virgin
  olive oil
1 large onion, chopped
2 garlic cloves, diced
½ teaspoon salt
½ pound button (or other local)
  mushrooms, quartered
1 pound spinach
2 medium zucchinis, chopped
½ pound organic firm tofu,
  drained and mashed to
resemble a ground beef
  consistency
1 jar organic spaghetti sauce
1 14-ounce can stewed organic
  tomatoes
1 bay leaf
1 teaspoon dried oregano
½ teaspoon sugar
Salt and pepper to taste

Cook pasta according to package directions. Once cooked to *al dente,* drain but don't rinse. In a large pot, sauté onion and garlic in olive oil and salt. Add mushrooms, spinach, and zucchini. Cover and cook about 5 minutes, stirring frequently.

Add mashed tofu, spaghetti sauce, stewed tomatoes, bay leaf, oregano, and sugar. Add salt and pepper to taste. Cover and simmer 10 minutes longer.

Serve with pasta and a salad of mixed organic greens, lightly dressed.

Broiled Salsa Fish

This recipe was created on the last day of a family vacation in Mexico, using the foods we had left in the refrigerator. It just goes to show— waste not, want not. Use what you've got and you'll probably be surprised with what will come out of it.

4 filets of sustainably caught or organically farmed fish—a firm fish like Pacific cod (long-line caught) is a great choice. U.S.-farmed tilapia is often a good choice as well.

4 tablespoons salsa verde (green salsa—either homemade or from a jar)

4 tablespoons goat cheese—soft and spreadable

2 firm organic tomatoes, sliced thinly

4 teaspoons hot sauce

Prepare a broiler pan with foil (optional) and a light layer of olive oil. Arrange fish across the pan. Top each filet with a thin layer of salsa. Spread the goat cheese on top, dropping in globs if it doesn't spread well. Top that with tomato slices and drizzle hot sauce all across the top. Broil until fish is cooked thoroughly and cheese and tomatoes start to brown.

Serve with rice and a salad of mixed greens, lightly dressed.

Market-Fresh Stir-Fry

Most Americans get plenty of protein in their everyday diets, but often fall short when it comes to whole grains and vegetables. One of the best ways to get it all into one meal is through a healthful stir-fry. Try to create a rainbow of colors in your sauté pan.

2 tablespoons oil
  (olive or canola)
3 onions, chopped
3 cloves garlic, chopped
Ginger root, freshly grated
  over the pan (about
  1 tablespoon)
4 carrots, sliced
1 package mushrooms,
  quartered

3 zucchini, sliced
1 yellow pepper, chopped
1 pound tofu or 2 medium-sized
  chicken breasts
Soy sauce to taste
Brown rice, cooked according
  to directions on the package

Gently heat oil in a large pan or wok. Add onions, garlic, and ginger. Sauté until tender. Add remaining vegetables and stir to cook evenly until slightly softened but still brightly colored.

Once the vegetables have cooked, season with soy sauce and additional ginger if desired.

In a separate pan, cook cut strips of chicken breast or tofu over low heat. (To cook tofu, cut into slices and lightly sauté in olive oil and soy sauce until full of flavor. Because it is already cooked it doesn't need to be over heat for long, just enough time to absorb the flavors.)

Add chicken or tofu into the stir-fry during the last few minutes of cooking. Serve over a bed of brown rice.

Better Breakfasts

Pumpkin Banana Bread

I love bananas in smoothies, on oatmeal, or as an afternoon snack. But I hate the sight of bananas sitting on a counter going bad. When they become a little too ripe for my liking, I immediately pull out my mixer and turn them into a banana bread. Because pumpkin is another favorite flavor of mine, here's a recipe that involves both.

1 ripe banana, mashed	½ teaspoon baking soda
1¼ cups pure canned pumpkin	½ teaspoon salt
1 egg plus 1 egg white	1 teaspoon cinnamon
¼ cup canola oil	½ teaspoon nutmeg
¼ cup honey	½ teaspoon ground ginger
2 cups whole wheat flour	½ teaspoon cardamom
½ cup sugar	½ cup chopped dried apricots
¼ cup ground flaxseed	or raisins
1 teaspoon baking powder	

Grease a standard-size loaf pan and preheat oven to 350 degrees.

Beat together banana, pumpkin, eggs, canola oil, and honey until well blended and light. In a separate bowl, mix together dry ingredients (except for the dried fruit). Slowly add to wet mixture and mix until well blended. Stir in dried fruit.

Bake for 1 hour or until knife comes out clean.

Oatmeal Fruit Bars

Looking for a healthy alternative to packaged breakfast bars, I took an oatmeal cookie recipe and adjusted it to make it a healthy breakfast or afternoon snack. I cut the sugar and fat and added natural fiber, protein, and fresh fruits. Use organic ingredients whenever possible.

2 cups whole wheat flour

½ cup ground flaxseed

1 teaspoon baking soda

1 teaspoon salt

1 teaspoon cinnamon

½ teaspoon nutmeg

½ teaspoon cardamom

½ cup (1 stick) organic butter, at room temperature

½ cup natural cane sugar

2 organic eggs

½ cup honey

¼ cup rice milk

1 teaspoon vanilla extract

1 small apple, peeled and chopped

½ cup goji berries or raisins

½ cup dates or apricots, chopped

1 cup chopped walnuts or almonds (optional)

1½ cups coconut

3 cups old-fashioned organic oats

In a medium-size bowl, stir together the flour, flaxseed, baking soda, salt, cinnamon, nutmeg, and cardamom.

In a mixing bowl, beat the butter and sugar until smooth. Add in eggs, honey, rice milk, and vanilla and beat until smooth and consistent. Slowly add in dry mixture and mix together. Stir in fruit, nuts, coconut, and oats.

Press the mixture into a cake pan. Bake in a 350-degree oven for 15–20 minutes, or until knife comes out clean.

Let cool, then cut into bars.

Energy-Sustaining Breakfast Bars

This recipe was inspired by a diet recipe for breakfast bars, one that I took and turned upside down, adding fiber, protein, antioxidants, and lots of healthy goodness. These are incredibly easy to make and to keep on hand for grab-and-go mornings.

2½ cups old-fashioned organic
   quick oats
½ cup ground flaxseed
¼ cup organic dark cocoa power
   (or slightly less)
½ cup natural peanut butter
½ cup honey

½ teaspoon spirulina
   (blue-green algae rich in
   antioxidants—found in the
   supplement section of any
   natural foods store)
½ to 1 cup *hot* water

Stir ingredients together. Form into individual-sized patties, like hamburgers. Place in wax paper bags and keep in freezer or fridge.

Healthy Fruit Smoothie

Smoothies, like this one, can be a quick afternoon snack or a hearty, healthy breakfast.

1 ripe banana
6 frozen strawberries
⅛ cup frozen blueberries
2 tablespoons flaxseed oil
1 scoop protein powder (use less
   than a scoop for kids'
   smoothies)

¼ teaspoon spirulina (blue-green
   algae rich in antioxidants—
   found in the supplement section
   of any natural foods store)
½ cup soymilk, rice milk, or
   organic cow's milk
½ cup water

Blend, pour, and enjoy.

Ginger Orange Celery Tonic

*Juicing can provide a good portion of the USDA-recommended amount
of fruits and vegetables in one easy glass, with the maximum concentration of vitamins, minerals, enzymes, and phytonutrients.*

6 Valencia oranges, sliced   4 celery stalks
1 small piece of fresh ginger root

Juice together, alternating between pieces of orange and celery.
Juice the ginger in halfway through.
Drink immediately.

Fresher Cleaning and Storage

The two topics that I get asked about more than anything else are food
and cleaning. People want to know how to shop for and prepare healthy
foods, they want to know what to store them in (and what to drink their water from), and they want to know how to keep their home clean and safe,
without unnecessary toxins.

Natural Cleaning Recipes

For a refresher on cleaning-product ingredients to avoid, refer to pages 164
to 166.

Around the Home

• For an all-purpose cleaner, fill an empty spray bottle with equal parts
distilled white vinegar and water. This can be kept on hand for countertops,
highchair trays, toys, floors, and other surfaces.

• For windows, fill a spray bottle with water and a quarter cup of white vinegar or lemon juice. A great way to recycle your newspapers is to use them in place of paper towels for a streak-free finish.

• Cleaning your wood floors is best done only occasionally, with warm water and a drop of dish soap. If your wood floors tend to streak, try adding a splash of white vinegar to your pail of water. Be sure to wring your mop out well so as not to over-wet the floor.

• To treat household areas with mold and mildew, mix a few drops of tea tree oil and a cup of water in a spray bottle.

• To deter rodents, wipe pantry doors and cupboards with a towel damp with tea tree oil. You can also leave a few drops of the oil at the rodents' points of entry.

• Mix together two parts olive oil to one part lemon juice for a natural furniture polish.

• To spot-treat your carpets, mix together equal parts of borax, salt, and white vinegar. Apply the paste to the stains and allow to dry, then vacuum up the paste.

• If your carpet is holding on to pet or other odors, sprinkle it with baking soda before you vacuum.

Kitchen

• Mix together a mild liquid soap and lemon juice for an excellent dish soap. (This should not be used on silver.)

• To clean heirloom and fine china, dissolve borax in a sink full of hot water.

• Mix a small amount of baking soda with liquid castile soap to get your countertops, sinks, and tubs shiny. For a "fresh smell," try adding a few drops of rosemary, orange, or lavender essential oil.

• Keep a spray bottle of hydrogen peroxide on hand and another filled with white vinegar (don't mix the two in one bottle). For a disinfecting spray for vegetables and surfaces, spritz with one, then the other, then wipe clean.

• Rub olive oil onto stainless steel surfaces to remove streaks and prints.

• To clean your oven, mix together three parts baking soda with one part salt and one part water. Spread the mixture across the oven surface and allow it to sit for up to eight hours. Scrape and wipe clean.

Bathroom

• To freshen a toilet bowl, pour two to three cups of white vinegar into the toilet bowl, let sit for a few hours, then scrub and flush.

• To clean your toilet, pour one part baking soda to four parts white vinegar into the toilet basin. Let it sit for fifteen to thirty minutes, then scrub and flush.

• For a clogged drain, pour a half cup of baking soda down the drain, followed by a half cup of white vinegar. Allow the mixture to fizz, then flush with hot water.

• To treat moldy tile grout on bathroom walls, fill a spray bottle with one-half cup hydrogen peroxide and one cup water. Spray onto moldy areas, let sit for an hour, then rinse off.

Laundry

• Add a quarter cup of white vinegar to your washing machine's rinse cycle. This will help to rinse out the detergent completely and leave your clothes feeling soft. It can also help reduce static cling.

• Add a quarter cup of baking soda to the wash cycle of your laundry machine to soften fabrics naturally, eliminating the need for chemical, and often highly fragranced, fabric softeners.

• To brighten whites in the wash, add a small amount of lemon juice to your machine's rinse cycle.

• Mix together a quarter cup of olive oil with a few drops of lemon juice for a natural shoe polish. Simply dip your rag, wipe on, then buff off.

• Mix together equal parts of dried cloves, rosemary, and thyme and place in small cloth pouches or tea bags. Hang these in closets or fold in with out-of-season clothing to deter moths and rodents. Dried lemon peels will also do the trick.

Plastics

Because there is so much confusing information circulating these days about plastics, here is a refresher on what each of the plastics is and which are the safest. Remember, you can identify plastics by the number (as shown below), usually found on the bottom of the container. The number also serves as your recycling code, as some centers only take certain plastics (numbers 1 and 2, for example) and not others.

Safer Plastics

♳ (Polyethylene terephthalate): soda and water bottles, peanut
PETE butter, cooking oil, ketchup, salad dressing containers, etc.

(High-density polyethylene): "cloudy" jugs like milk or juice jugs, butter and some yogurt tubs, bleach, laundry/dish detergent and household cleaner bottles, shampoo and conditioner bottles, some shopping and trash bags, cereal and cracker box liners, etc.

(Low-density polyethylene): some food, dry-cleaning, and grocery bags, squeezable bottles, furniture, carpet, etc.

(Polypropylene): more "rigid" food storage containers and yogurt cups, baby bottles, cups and bowls, some medicine bottles, bottle caps, drinking straws, some diapers, etc.

Scariest Plastics

(Polyvinyl chloride or PVC): cling wrap, some food and liquid containers, shower curtains, pipes, plastic food wrap, loose-leaf binders, baby bottle nipples, some household cleaner and body care bottles, etc.

PVC becomes especially harmful when heated or in contact with oily and fatty foods.

(Polystyrene): Styrofoam coffee cups, egg cartons, meat and bakery trays, carry-out food containers, plastic tableware, insulation, packing peanuts, CD jackets, etc.

Polystyrene becomes especially harmful when in contact with hot or acidic foods. It's especially bad for the environment because it doesn't degrade, instead piling up in landfills.

(Miscellaneous, a combination or polycarbonate): Large water bottles, some food containers, clear baby bottles, linings of metal cans, nylon, bulletproof materials, DVDs, etc.

Polycarbonate becomes especially harmful when in contact with liquids or liquid foods, as it releases bisphenol A, a hormone disruptor, into the fluid.

Thinking Toward the Future

Now it's time to think back to the changes you've already made around the home. You might be surprised at how many things you're already doing, and for each of those you deserve a pat on the back.

Then, flipping back through the book, think about the changes you want to make in the next phase of creating a greener, healthier home. To avoid the temptation to feel overwhelmed, separate these into changes for today, next month, six months from now, and next year. You can even reserve some for a much later date. You can group these into categories or list them one by one. Try to include as many ideas from as many chapters of this book and rooms of your house as possible.

These small, simple steps will not only allow you and the people in your home to live in a cleaner, healthier environment, but they will help lessen your impact on the planet, protecting it for generations to come.

Fresh Living Changes Chart
Fresh Living Changes I've Already Made

1. _____

_____

_____

_____

_____

_____

_____

2. _____

_____

_____

_____

_____

_____

3. _____

_____

_____

_____

_____

Fresh Living Changes I'll Make Today

1. _____

_____

_____

_____

_____

_____

_____

2. _____

_____

_____

_____

_____

_____

3. _____

_____

_____

_____

_____

_____

Fresh Living Changes I'll Make Next Month

1. _____

_____

_____

_____

_____

_____

_____

_____

2. _____

_____

_____

_____

_____

_____

_____

3. _____

_____

_____

_____

_____

_____

_____

Fresh Living Changes for Six Months from Now

1. _____
_____
_____
_____
_____
_____
_____

2. _____
_____
_____
_____
_____
_____
_____

3. _____
_____
_____
_____
_____
_____
_____

Fresh Living Changes for Next Year

1. _____

_____

_____

_____

_____

_____

_____

_____

2. _____

_____

_____

_____

_____

_____

_____

3. _____

_____

_____

_____

_____

_____

_____

_____

Fresh Living Changes for a Much Later Date

1. _____

_____

_____

_____

_____

_____

_____

_____

2. _____

_____

_____

_____

_____

_____

_____

_____

_____

_____

3. _____

_____

_____

_____

_____

_____

_____

_____

Bibliography

My Story

Brown, Simon G. *Modern-Day Macrobiotics*. Berkeley: North Atlantic Books, 2005.

Business Wire. *The Natural Foods Merchandiser Reports U.S. Natural Products Sales Top $56.7 Billion with 9.7 Percent Growth*. 6 June 2007. 29 July 2008 <http://www.allbusiness.com/consumer-products/food-beverage-products-organic-foods/5422499-1.html>.

Hirsch, Barry. *Natural Products Expo East Attracts Record Attendance and Booth Sales Show Poised for Move to Boston in 2008 to Accommodate Continued Growth*. Press Release. Boulder: The Fresh Ideas Group, n.d.

Kaho, Todd. *Sales of Hybrid Vehicles Surge in the Midwest*. 2008. 29 July 2008 <http://www.greencar.com/features/hot-for-hybrids/>.

Kushi, Michio. *Biography of Michio Kushi*. 2003. 2 June 2008 <http://www.michiokushi.org/bio.php>.

Organic Trade Association. "Questions and Answers about Organic." 2008. *Organic Trade Association*. 23 September 2008 <http://www.ota.com/organic/faq.html>.

In the Kitchen

American Heart Association. *Trans Fats*. 30 July 2008. 30 July 2008 <http://www.americanheart.org/presenter.jhtml?identifier=3045792>.

Benbrook, Charles, PhD. "New Insights on the Consumer Benefits of Organic Food and Farming." 27 January 2006. *The Organic Center*. 21 May 2008 <http://www.organic-center.org/reportfiles/Res_Overview_2006.pdf>.

Blue Horizon Organic. *What Is Sustainable Seafood: Questions & Answers*. 8 May 2008. 21 May 2008 <http://www.bluehorizonseafood.com/seafood_faq.html>.

Burros, Marian. "Supermarket Chains Narrow Their Sights." 6 August 2008. *New York Times*. 22 September 2008 <http://www.nytimes.com/2008/08/06/dining/06local.html>.

Center for Food Safety. "Genetically Engineered Food." *Center for Food Safety*. 23 September 2008 <http://www.centerforfoodsafety.org/geneticall7.cfm>.

Consumer Reports. *Greener Choices: Products for a Better Planet: Meat, Dairy and Eggs Buying Guide*. December 2006. 22 May 2008 <http://www.greenerchoices.org/products.cfm?product=meat&page=RightChoices>.

David, Laurie. "Climate Change: 25 Things You Can Do." From *Stop Global Warming: The Solution Is You!* by Laurie David. 2006. *Gaiam Life*. 10 June 2008 <http://life.gaiam.com/gaiam/p/Climate-Change25-Things-You-Can-Do.html>.

Demeter USA. *Demeter USA Background*. 2006. May 2008 <http://demeterusa.org/?page_id=6>.

Environmental Working Group. "Environmental Working Group's Shopper's Guide to Pesticides in Produce." *Shopper's Guide to Pesticides*. 9 January 2007 <www.foodnews.org>.

———. "Methodology." *Food News*. 1 October 2008 <http://www.foodnews.org/methodology.php>.

Fish Wise. *Fishwise Program: Get Involved*. 2008. 21 May 2008 <http://www.fishwise.org/index.php?option=com_content&task=view&id=27&Itemid=35>.

Green Peace. *The Trash Vortex*. 18 July 2008 <http://www.greenpeace.org/international/campaigns/oceans/pollution/trash-vortex>.

Hartman, Eviana. "High-Fructose Corn Syrup: Not So Sweet for the Planet." *Washington Post*. 9 March 2008.

Mayo Clinic. "Antioxidants—Preventing Diseases, Naturally." 4 September 2007. *Mayo Clinic*. 22 September 2008 <http://www.newmayoclinicdiet.com/news2007-mchi/4216.html>.

———. *Ask a Food and Nutrition Specialist*. 9 January 2008. 24 May 2008 <http://www.mayoclinic.com/health/monosodium-glutamate/AN01251>.

Meadows, Michelle. "MSG: A Common Flavor Enhancer." 6 January 2003. *FDA Consumer*. 23 September 2008 <http://www.fda.gov/FDAC/features/2003/103_msg.html>.

Mercola, Joseph, OD. "How High Fructose Corn Syrup Damages Your Body." 10 July 2007. *Organic Consumers Association*. 23 May 2008 <http://www.organicconsumers.org/articles/article_6210.cfm>.

Monterey Bay Aquarium. "Seafood Watch Pocket Guide." 2008. *Seafood Watch.* 22 July 2008 <http://www.mbayaq.org/cr/cr_seafoodwatch/content/media/MBA_SeafoodWatch_NationalGuide.pdf>.

Organic Center. *Core Truths: Serving Up the Science Behind Organic Agriculture.* Boulder: The Organic Center, 2006.

Organic Trade Association. "10 Good Reasons to Go Organic." 2008. *Organic Trade Association.* 30 July 2008 <http://www.ota.com/organic_and_you/10reasons .html>.

——. *US Organic Standards.* 2007. May 2008 <http://www.ota.com/organic/ us_standards.html>.

Pollack, Andrew. "Which Cows Do You Trust?" *New York Times.* 7 October 2006.

Smith, Jeffrey. "Spilling the Beans: Unintended GMO Health Risks." March 2008. *Organic Consumers Association.* 24 May 2008 <http://www.organicconsumers .org/articles/article_11361.cfm>.

Sustainable Agriculture Research and Education. "Transitioning to Organic Production: What Is Organic Farming?" *sare.org.* 30 July 2008 <http://www.sare .org/publications/organic/organic01.htm>.

Townsend, Mark. "Soy Allergy/Adverse Effect Rates Skyrocket—Monsanto's Roundup-Ready Soy Blamed." 12 March 1999. *Monsanto Investing News.* 23 September 2008 <http://www.ethicalinvesting.com/monsanto/news/10037 .htm>.

TransFair USA. *Fair Trade Certification—Frequently Asked Questions.* 19 March 2008. May 2008 <http://www.transfairusa.org/content/resources/faq.php>.

U.S. Food and Drug Administration. *Revealing Trans Fats.* September 2005. 24 May 2008 <http://www.fda.gov/FDAC/features/2003/503_fats.html>.

USDA and Mary V Gold. "Organic Production/Organic Food: Information Access Tools." 2007. *USDA National Agricultural Library.* 30 July 2008 <http:// www.nal.usda.gov/afsic/pubs/ofp/ofp.shtml>.

USDA Food Safety and Inspection Service. *Fact Sheets: Food Labeling: Meat and Poultry Labeling Terms.* 24 August 2006. May 2008 <http://www.fsis.usda.gov/ Fact_Sheets/Meat_&_Poultry_Labeling_Terms/index.asp>.

Vanity Fair. "Fifty Ways to Help Save the Planet." *Vanity Fair.* 17 April 2006: 9.

Warner, Jennifer. "Antioxidant Riches Found in Unexpected Foods." 17 June 2004. *Web MD.* 22 September 2008 <http://www.webmd.com/diet/guide/20061101/ antioxidants-found-unexpected-foods>.

In the Bathroom

African Well Fund. 2005. April 2008 <http://www.africanwellfund.org/waterstats .html>.

Arditti, Rita. "Cosmetics, Parabens, and Breast Cancer." 6 September 2004. *Organic Consumers Association*. 23 July 2008 <http://www.organicconsumers.org/ bodycare/breastcancer090604.cfm>.

Building Online. "Survey Reveals Many People Multitask in the Bathroom." 4 September 2008. *Where the Building Industry Is Found on the Internet*. 1 October 2008 <http://www.buildingonline.com/news/viewnews.pl?id=7452&subcategory=186>.

David, Laurie. "Climate Change: 25 Things You Can Do." From *Stop Global Warming: The Solution Is You!* by Laurie David. 2006. *Gaiam Life*. 11 June 2008 <http://life.gaiam.com/gaiam/p/Climate-Change25-Things-You-Can-Do.html>.

Department of Health and Human Services. "What Is Formaldehyde?" 21 May 2008. *Agency for Toxic Substances and Disease Registry*. 23 July 2008 <http:// www.atsdr.cdc.gov/substances/formaldehyde/>.

Eby, Myra Michelle, and Karolyn A. Gazella. *Return to Beautiful Skin*. Laguna Beach, Calif.: Basic Health Publications, 2008.

Environmental Protection Agency. *EPA Water Sense*. 28 March 2008. April 2008 <http://www.epa.gov/watersense/pubs/supply.htm>.

———. *Indoor Water Use in the United States*. 28 March 2008. 21 September 2008 <http://www.epa.gov/watersense/pubs/indoor.htm>.

———. *What Are the Environmental Benefits of Water Efficiency?* 28 August 2008. 20 September 2008 <http://www.epa.gov/watersense/water/save/env_benefits.htm>.

Environmental Working Group. "Companies That Signed the Compact for Safe Cosmetics and Were Approved as of August 13, 2008." 18 August 2008. *The Campaign for Safe Cosmetics*. 22 September 2008 <http://www.safecosmetics .org/docUploads/Compact%20Signers%20%2D%20August%2013%2C%20200 8%2Epdf>.

———. *Cosmetics with Banned and Unsafe Ingredients*. 26 September 2007. April 2008 <http://www.ewg.org/node/22610>.

———. *Skin Deep Cosmetic Safety Database*. April 2008 <http://www.cosmetics database.com/special/whatnottobuy/>.

———. *Sunscreen Summary—What Works and What's Safe*. April 2008 <http:// www.cosmeticsdatabase.com/special/sunscreens/summary.php>.

———. *Why This Matters*. April 2008 <http://www.cosmeticsdatabase.com/ research/whythismatters.php>.

The Green Guide. April 2008 <www.thegreenguide.com/products/bath/toilets>.

Greene, Alan, MD. *Raising Baby Green*. San Francisco: Jossey-Bass, 2007.

Malkan, Stacy. *Not Just a Pretty Face: The Ugly Side of the Beauty Industry*. Gabriola Island, British Columbia: New Society Publishers, 2007.

Mosiman, Dean. "Proposal: Reduce Water Use with a High-Efficiency Toilet, Get a $100 Rebate." *Wisconsin State Journal*. 18 August 2008.

Natural Ingredients Resource Center. *Synthetic Fragrances*. 2006. April 2008 <http://www.naturalingredient.org/syntheticfragrances.htm#toxins>.

NYC Department of Environmental Protection. *Residential Water Use*. 9 August 2007. April 2008 <http://www.nyc.gov/html/dep/html/residents/wateruse.shtml>.

Swan, Shanna H., et al. "Decrease in Anogenital Distance among Male Infants with Prenatal Phthalate Exposure." August 2005. *Environmental Health Perspectives*. 23 July 2008 <http://www.ehponline.org/docs/2005/8100/abstract.html>.

U.S. Department of Agriculture Agricultural Marketing Service. *Cosmetics, Body Care Products, and Personal Care Products*. April 2008. 16 September 2008 <http://www.ams.usda.gov/AMSv1.0/getfile?dDocName=STELPRDC5068442&acct=nopgeninfo>.

U.S. Food and Drug Administration. *FDA Authority over Cosmetics*. 3 March 2005. April 2008 <http://www.cfsan.fda.gov/~dms/cos-206.html>.

In the Bedroom

Georgia Cotton Commission. *Georgia Cotton Commission Facts*. 2007. 11 June 2008 <http://www.georgiacottoncommission.org/index.cfm?show=10&mid=6>.

Gertz, Emily. "Naughty by Nature." 6 December 2005. *Grist*. 15 June 2008 <http://www.grist.org/news/maindish/2005/12/06/gertz/>.

Gordon, Jacob. *How to Green Your Sex Life*. 14 December 2007. 15 June 2008 <http://www.treehugger.com/files/2007/02/how-to-green-your-sex-life.php>.

Greene, Alan, MD. *Raising Baby Green*. San Francisco: Jossey-Bass, 2007.

Minnesota Department of Health. "Formaldehyde in Your Home." 19 March 2008. *Minnesota Department of Health*. 22 September 2008 <http://www.health.state.mn.us/divs/eh/indoorair/voc/formaldehyde.htm>.

Organic Consumers Association. "Clothes for a Change: The Background." *Organic Consumers Association*. 14 June 2008 <http://www.organicconsumers.org/clothes/background.cfm>.

Organic Trade Association. *Cotton and the Environment*. 2008. 11 June 2008 <http://www.ota.com/organic/environment/cotton_environment.html>.

———. *Organic Cotton Facts*. 2006. 11 June 2008 <http://www.ota.com/organic/mt/organic_cotton.html>.

Thomas, Pauline Weston. *Vintage Clothes 3 Tips for Sellers and Buyers of Vintage Textiles via the Internet*. 18 February 2005. 11 June 2008 <http://www.fashion-era.com/Vintage_fashion/3_selling_vintage_fashion_tips.htm>.

Treehugger. "Color Grown Cotton: Fox Fibre." 18 April 2005. *Treehugger.* 21 September 2008 <http://www.treehugger.com/files/2005/04/color_grown_cot.php>.

Under the Canopy. *Frequently Asked Questions.* 11 June 2008 <http://www.underthecanopy.com/faqs.htm>.

Venolia, Carol. "Recommendations for a Healthy Bedroom." 13 June 2005. *Green Home Guide.* 13 June 2008 <http://www.greenhomeguide.com/index.php/knowhow/entry/632/C218/>.

In the Nursery

Batista, Elisa. "The Poop on Eco-Friendly Diapers." *Wired*. 2004.

Bear, Jacci Howard. *Color Meanings: Symbolism of Color and Colors That Go Together.* 11 July 2008 <http://desktoppub.about.com/cs/colorselection/p/white.htm>.

Children's Health Environmental Coalition. *Carpets and Rugs.* October 2003. 11 July 2008 <http://checnet.org/healthehouse/education/articles-detail.asp?Main_ID=334>.

Chua, Jasmin Malik. *Discovery Planet Green: Choose Baby-Safe Bottles, Formula.* 23 March 2008. 18 July 2008 <http://planetgreen.discovery.com/home-garden/choose-safe-baby-bottles.html>.

Environmental Protection Agency. *An Introduction to Indoor Air Quality.* 17 September 2008. 22 September 2008 <http://www.epa.gov/iaq/formalde.html>.

———. *Lead in Paint, Dust and Soil.* 15 April 2008. 11 July 2008 <http://www.epa.gov/lead/pubs/leadinfo.htm#protect>.

Environmental Working Group. "EWG's Guide to Infant Formula and Baby Bottles: Guide to Baby-Safe Bottles and Formula." 2007. *www.ewg.org.* 18 July 2007 <http://www.ewg.org/babysafe>.

———. "Safety Guide to Children's Personal Care Products." *Cosmetics Database.* 19 July 2008 <http://www.cosmeticsdatabase.com/special/parentsguide/EWG_parentsguide.pdf>.

———. "Study Shows Infants Exposed to Reproductive Toxins from Shampoo, Lotion, and Powder." 4 February 2008. *Environmental Working Group.* 19 July 2008 <http://www.ewg.org/node/25964>.

Environmental Working Group's Skin Deep. *Products Targeted to Children Contain Hazardous Chemicals and Ingredients Not Found Safe for Kids.* 19 July 2008 <http://www.cosmeticsdatabase.com/special/parentsguide/>.

Garden-Robinson, Julie. *What Color Is Your Food? Taste a Rainbow of Fruits and Vegetables for Better Health.* August 2003. 11 July 2008 <http://www.ag.ndsu.edu/pubs/yf/foods/fn595w.htm>.

Gavigan, Christopher. *Healthy Child Healthy World: Creating a Cleaner, Greener, Safer Home.* New York: Dutton, 2008.

Greene, Alan, MD. *Raising Baby Green.* San Francisco: Jossey-Bass, 2007.

Lunder, Sonya, and Jane Houlihan. "EWG's Guide to Infant Formula and Baby Bottles." December 2007. *Environmental Working Group.* 24 July 2008 <http://www.ewg.org/node/25570>.

Malkan, Stacy. *Not Just a Pretty Face.* Gabriola Island, British Columbia: New Society Publishers, 2007.

Minnesota Department of Health. "Formaldehyde in Your Home." 19 March 2008. *Minnesota Department of Health.* 22 September 2008 <http://www.health.state.mn.us/divs/eh/indoorair/voc/formaldehyde.htm>.

Mothering. "The Politics of Diapers: A Timeline of Recovered History." *Mothering.* January/February 2003.

National Institute of Environmental Health Sciences, National Institutes of Health. "Draft NTP Brief on Bisphenol A." 14 April 2008. *National Toxicology Program.* 22 September 2008 <http://cerhr.niehs.nih.gov/chemicals/bisphenol/BPADraftBrief VF_04_14_08.pdf>.

Nature Neutral. *What Is Offgassing?* 2005. 24 July 2008 <http://www.natureneutral.com/learnOff.php>.

Pennock, Alex. "Creating a Safe, Healthy Room for Your Child." 11 October 2005. 11 July 2008 <http://www.greenhomeguide.com/index.php/knowhow/entry/795/C223>.

Shapley, Dan. "How to Avoid Phthalates: 3 Steps to Help Avoid a Hormone-Mimicking Chemical." 4 February 2008. *The Daily Green.* 22 September 2008 <http://www.thedailygreen.com/environmental-news/latest/phthalates-47020418>.

Trasande, Leonardo, MD. "Is Your Home Affecting Your Children's Health?" 4 October 2005. 11 July 2008 <http://www.greenhomeguide.com/index.php/knowhow/entry/793/C223>.

In the Living Room

Clean Air Gardening. *Top Houseplants for Improving Indoor Air Quality.* 2008. 18 June 2008 <http://www.cleanairgardening.com/houseplants.html>.

Environmental Protection Agency. *Mercury: Spills, Disposal and Site Cleanup: What to Do If a Fluorescent Light Bulb Breaks.* 24 June 2008. 25 July 2008 <http://www.epa.gov/mercury/spills/index.htm#fluorescent>.

Green Home Guide. *About VOCs.* 2 June 2006. 18 June 2008 <http://www.greenhomeguide.com/index.php/knowhow/entry/920/C224>.

———. *Selecting Healthy and Environmentally Sound Paints.* 9 August 2005. 18 June 2008 <http://www.greenhomeguide.com/index.php/knowhow/entry/750/C224>.

National Geographic. *Product Report: Wood Furniture.* 17 April 2006. 18 June 2008 <http://www.thegreenguide.com/reports/product.mhtml?id=26>.

Vanity Fair. "Fifty Ways to Help Save the Planet." *Vanity Fair.* 17 April 2006: 9.

Wolverton, B.C. "A Study of Interior Landscape Plants for Indoor Air Pollution Abatement." July 1989. *NASA Technical Reports Server.* 18 June 2008 <http://ntrs.nasa.gov/archive/nasa/ssctrs.ssc.nasa.gov/indr_landscape2/indr_landscape2.pdf>.

Wolverton, B.C., Anne Johnson, and Keith Bounds. "Interior Landscape Plants for Indoor Air Pollution Abatement—Final Report." 15 September 1989. *NASA Technical Reports Server.* 18 June 2008 <http://ntrs.nasa.gov/archive/nasa/ssctrs.ssc.nasa.gov/indr_landscape/indr_landscape.pdf>.

Wortman, David. *Wood Furniture: FSC Certified.* November/December 2003. 18 June 2008 <http://www.thegreenguide.com/doc/99/wood>.

In the Laundry Room

Conova, Susan. "The Dirt on Clean Hands." 4 December 2002. *Columbia University Health Scientists.* 27 June 2008 <http://www.cumc.columbia.edu/news/in-vivo/Vol1_Iss20_dec04_02/washing.html>.

Environmental Protection Agency. *An Introduction to Indoor Air Quality: Organic Gases.* 14 November 2007. 25 June 2008 <http://www.epa.gov/iaq/voc.html>.

———. *Clothes Washers.* 24 September 2007. 25 June 2008 <http://www.energystar.gov/index.cfm?c=clotheswash.pr_clothes_washers>.

———. *What Is Energy Star?* 14 December 2007. 25 June 2008 <http://energystar.gov>.

Green Home Guide. *Top Cleaning Product Ingredients to Avoid.* March/April 2006. 25 June 2008 <http://www.thegreenguide.com/doc/113/ingredients>.

Grist. *Good Clean Fun.* 2007. 27 June 2008 <http://www.grist.org/advice/possessions/2003/03/18/possessions-cleaning/index.html>.

Hollender, Jeffrey, and Geoff Davis. *Naturally Clean: The Seventh Generation Guide to Safe and Healthy, Non-Toxic Cleaning.* Gabriola Island, British Columbia: New Society Publishers, 2005.

In the Office

Buechner, Maryanne Murray. *The Global Warming Survival Guide: What You Can Do (Pay Your Bills Online).* 2008. 8 July 2008 <http://www.time.com/time/specials/2007/environment/article/0,28804,1602354_1603074_1603109,00.html>.

Co-op America. "Carbon Offsets Demystified." March/April 2007. *Co-op America: Real Money.* 28 July 2008 <http://www.coopamerica.org/pubs/realmoney/articles/carbonoffsets.cfm>.

Ecology Action. *E-Waste Electronic Recycling Program.* 8 July 2008 <http://www.ecoact.org/Programs/Waste_Reduction/Recycling/ewaste.htm>.

ForestEthics. *Catalogs.* 2008. 8 July 2008 <http://forestethics.org/section.php?id=15>.

———. *ForestEthics Launches "Do Not Mail" Campaign to Stop Junk Mail.* 11 March 2008. 8 July 2008 <http://forestethics.org/article.php?id=2077>.

Good Magazine. "Vampire Energy." January/February 2008. *Good Magazine.* 28 July 2008 <http://awesome.goodmagazine.com/transparency/008/trans008vampireenergy.html>.

Greensprings Natural Cemetery. *Greensprings FAQ.* 9 July 2008 <http://naturalb.server320.com/index.php?Itemid=27&id=25&option=com_content&task=view>.

Richard, Michael Graham. *Treehugger Homework: Unplug Your Charger.* 26 November 2005. 8 July 2008 <http://www.treehugger.com/files/2005/11/treehugger_home_2.php>.

Social Invest. *Socially Responsible Investing Basics for Individuals.* 2006. 8 July 2008 <http://www.socialinvest.org/resources/sriguide/>.

Terra Pass. *Carbon Footprint Calculator.* 2008. 8 July 2008 <http://www.terrapass.com/carbon-footprint-calculator/?selectairport=lax#air>.

Treehugger. *How to Green Your Work.* 10 December 2006. 8 July 2008 <http://www.treehugger.com/files/2006/12/how_to_green_your_work.php>.

Vanity Fair. "Fifty Ways to Help Save the Planet." *Vanity Fair.* 17 April 2006: 9.

Walsh, Bryan. *The Global Warming Survival Handbook: What You Can Do (Ride the Bus)*. 3 May 2007. 8 July 2008 <http://www.time.com/time/specials/2007/article/0,28804,1602354_1603074_1603122,00.html>.

Worldwatch Institute. *Paper.* 2008. 8 July 2008 <http://www.worldwatch.org/node/1497>.

Outdoors

Center for Transportation Excellence. *Factoids.* 2006. 30 June 2008 <http://www.cfte.org/factoids/default.asp>.

Chameldes, Dave. "Help the Planet: Offset Your Car's Emissions." 20 February 2007. *Edmunds.* 30 June 2008 <http://www.edmunds.com/advice/fueleconomy/articles/119580/article.html>.

Chua, Jasmin Malik. "How to Green Your Pet." 5 March 2007. *Treehugger.* 1 July 2008 <http://www.treehugger.com/files/2007/03/how-to-green-your-pet.php>.

Coats, Joel. "Catnip Repels Mosquitoes More Effectively Than DEET." 28 August 2001. *Science Daily.* 1 July 2008 <http://www.sciencedaily.com/releases/2001/08/010828075659.htm>.

Earth 911. *Benefits of Aluminum Can Recycling.* 2008. 30 June 2008 <http://earth911.org/recycling/aluminum-can-recycling/benefits-of-aluminum-can-recycling/>.

———. *Benefits of Glass Recycling.* 2008. 30 June 2008 <http://earth911.org/recycling/glass-recycling/benefits-of-glass-recycling/>.

———. *Facts about Glass Recycling.* 2008. 30 June 2008 <http://earth911.org/recycling/glass-recycling/facts-about-glass-recycling/>.

———. *Facts about Plastic Bottles.* 2008. 30 June 2008 <http://earth911.org/plastics/facts-about-plastic-bottles/>.

———. *Facts about Steel Recycling.* 2008. 30 June 2008 <http://earth911.org/recycling/steel-recycling/facts-about-steel-recycling/>.

———. *The Seven Types of Plastic.* 2008. 30 June 2008 <http://earth911.org/recycling/plastic-bottle-recycling/the-seven-types-of-plastic/>.

———. *Why Is It Important to Recycle Paper?* 2008. 30 June 2008 <http://earth911.org/recycling/paper-recycling/why-is-it-important-to-recycle-paper/>.

Environmental Defense Fund. *Eight Ways to Green Your Road Trip.* 9 June 2008. 30 June 2008 <http://www.edf.org/article.cfm?contentID=7910>.

Environmental Protection Agency. *WaterSense: Use Your Water Wisely.* 26 June 2008. 1 July 2008 <http://www.epa.gov/WaterSense/water/simple.htm>.

Gavigan, Christopher. *Healthy Child Healthy World: Creating a Cleaner, Greener, Safer Home.* New York: Dutton, 2008.

Gilliom, Robert, et al. "The Quality of Our Nation's Waters: Pesticides in the Nation's Streams and Ground Water, 1992–2001." 15 February 2007. *United States Geological Survey.* 1 July 2008 <http://pubs.usgs.gov/circ/2005/1291/>.

Gordon, Jacob. *How to Green Your Car.* 16 November 2006. 30 June 2008 <http://www.treehugger.com/files/2006/11/how_to_green_your_car.php>.

Howard, Brian Clark. *What Do Recycling Symbols Mean?* 30 June 2008. 30 June 2008 <http://www.thedailygreen.com/green-homes/latest/recycling-symbols-plastics-460321>.

Miller, Virginia. "Public Transit Ridership Continues to Grow in the First Quarter of 2008." 2 June 2008. *American Public Transportation Association.* 30 June 2008 <http://www.edf.org/article.cfm?contentID=7910>.

National Coalition for Pesticide-Free Lawns. *Welcome to the National Coalition for Pesticide-Free Lawns.* 1 July 2008 <http://www.beyondpesticides.org/pesticide-freelawns/>.

National Recycling Coalition. *Conversionator Recycling Calculator.* 30 June 2008 <http://www.nrc-recycle.org/recyclingcalculator.aspx#>.

———. *Top Ten Reasons to Recycle.* 30 June 2008 <http://www.nrc-recycle.org/top10reasonstorecycle.aspx>.

Organic Consumers Association. "Clothes for a Change: Background Info." *Organic Consumers Association.* 1 July 2008 <http://www.organicconsumers.org/clothes/background.cfm>.

Osaka, Sherri. *Take Steps Toward A Poison-Free, Sustainable Lawn.* 21 March 2006. 1 July 2008 <http://www.greenhomeguide.com/index.php/knowhow/entry/847/C282/>.

Safe Lawns. *Fertilizers and Pest Control.* 1 July 2008 <http://safelawns.org/tips/pcontrol.cfm>.

Santino, Ian. "What You Should Know to Keep Your Pets Safe." 2007. *Pesticides and You.* 1 July 2008 <http://www.beyondpesticides.org/infoservices/pesticidesandyou/Fall%2007/pets.pdf>.

Sparky Boy Enterprises. *Composting 101: What to Use.* 1 July 2008 <http://www.composting101.com/what-to-use.html>.

University of Southern Mississippi, Department of Polymer Science. *What Do Those Recycling Numbers Mean?* 2005. 30 June 2008 <http://pslc.ws/macrog//work/recycle.htm>.

U.S. Environmental Protection Agency. "Driving More Efficiently." *Fuel Economy.* 30
    June 2008 <http://www.fueleconomy.gov/FEG/driveHabits.shtml>.

————. "Keeping Your Car in Shape." *Fuel Economy.* 30 June 2008 <http://www
    .fueleconomy.gov/FEG/maintain.shtml>.

————. *Municipal Solid Waste: Recycling.* 6 June 2008. 30 June 2008 <http://www
    .epa.gov/msw/recycle.htm>.

————. *WasteWise: Recycling.* 27 December 2007. 30 June 2008 <http://www
    .epa.gov/epaoswer/non-hw/reduce/wstewise/wrr/recycle.htm>.

Vanity Fair. "Fifty Ways to Help Save the Planet." *Vanity Fair.* 17 April 2006: 9.

Walsh, Bryan. *The Global Warming Survival Handbook: What You Can Do (Ride the
    Bus).* 3 May 2007. 8 July 2008 <http://www.time.com/time/specials/2007/
    article/0,28804,1602354_1603074_1603122,00.html>.

Zimmerman, Martin. "Hybrid Sales Are Zooming." 23 May 2008. *Los Angeles Times.*
    30 June 2008 <http://www.latimes.com/news/printedition/front/la-fi-hybrid23-
    2008may23,0,6028313.story>.

Index

A

AGM (absorbent gel material), 121
allergies
  AGM in diapers, 121
  body care products, 132
  food, 130–31
  fragrance additives, 77
  latex, 126–27
  soy, 54
AllergyKids, 131
aluminum, 204–5
ammonia, 164
Ann Arbor, Michigan, 2–4
  Woman in the Shoe, 95
antibiotics in food, 42–43, 44
antioxidants
  foods richest in, 29
  in organic foods, 28
APEs (alkyl phenoxyl ethanols), 164
aquaculture, 14, 45–46
arnica, 14

Aubrey Organics, 76, 129
Avalon Organics, 129

B

baby clothes, 117, 118
baby food and feeding
  bottles, 125–27
  BPA warning, 124–25
  breastfeeding, 123–24
  eating a rainbow, 127–28
  formula, 124–25, 126
  jars, organic, 127–28
  making, 127–28
  baby products, 128–29, 132–34
Back to Eden (Kloss), 35
baking soda, 168, 242–43
bamboo, 89, 99, 100
bathroom, 61–85
  cleaning, 167–72, 242
  cutting purchases for, 84
  nail polish, 78
  multi-tasking in, 61

personal products overhaul, 68–84
showers or baths, 65–66, 155
tip on sunscreens, 83
toilet, 61, 63, 66–67
toilet flushing jingle, 61
toilet paper, 84–85, 95, 139, 178
water conservation, 63, 64–68
WaterSense appliances, 68
window in, 62–63
bedroom, 87–105
bed, 88–90
clothes and shoes, 93–102
light, 92
linens (bedclothes), 90
mattress, 88–89
noise, 93
pillow, 89
sex, going green, 103–5
sleep, 91–93
temperature, 93
benzene gases, 139–40

beverages
  antioxidant-rich, 29
  fruit juice, 10
  fruit smoothie, 239
  ginger orange celery
    tonic, 240
  herbal tea, 10
  organic coffee and
    tea, 18
  "tea 'n' juice mix," 10
BHA, 133
biodiversity, 29
biodynamic agriculture, 49
Blue Horizon Organic, 14
Blumenthal, Mark, 75–76
borax, 170, 241
boric acid, 133
BPA (bisphenol A),
    124–25, 244
Brand, Stewart, 4
breakfast bars, 239
Bronopol, 133
Burt's Bees, 76, 129
butyl cellosolve, 164–65

C

California Baby, 129
candles, 104, 146
carbon footprint, 183, 185
  CO_2 offsets, 198–99
  fuel emissions, 187–88
carcinogens
  in cleaning products,
    163–66
  in cosmetics and
    personal care
    products, 73, 74,
    77–81, 132
  formaldehyde, 81, 139
  hydroquinone, 81–82
  lawn care, 208–9
  lead, 82

petrolatum and
    petroleum distillates,
    80
  phthalates, 77–78, 79
  PVC, 119
  trichloroethylene, 139
carpets and rugs, 112–13
cars
  CO_2 offsets, 198–99
  commuting, 187,
    197–98
  greening your ride,
    194–99
  hybrids, 18, 194–95, 199
  top ten tips, 195
cashmere, 99, 100
Ceteareth, 132, 133
CFLs (compact fluorescent
    bulbs), 18, 149–51
Chadwick, Alan, 217
chamomile, 75
children. See also baby
    clothes; baby food and
    feeding; baby
    products; nursery
  ADHD and, 131
  food allergies, 130–31
  gardening with, 39
  junk food and, 10–11
  lawn chemicals and,
    208–9
  pesticide exposure,
    27–28
  secondhand clothes, 95
chlorine bleach, 165
chocolate, 49–50, 104
cleaning products, 160–73
  antibacterial, 162
  baking soda, 168,
    242–43
  borax, 170, 241
  cutting back on, 161–62
  disposing of, 172
  effects of, 163–66

essential oils, 171–72
  green-cleaning tool kit,
    167
  greener, 166–73
  hydrogen peroxide,
    170–71, 242–43
  ingredients to avoid,
    164–66
  lemon juice, 169, 241,
    243
  natural cleaning recipes,
    240–43
  olive oil, 169–70, 241,
    243
  soap, 169, 241
  spices, 172–73
  tea tree oil, 171, 241
  vinegar, 152, 167–68,
    240–43
  VOCs from, 163
clothes and shoes, 93–102
  baby clothes, 117, 118
  condition descriptions,
    96
  eco-fibers, 99–100
  Fair Trade, 100
  green fashion shows, 19
  handmade, 100
  organic, 94, 98–99
  recycled, 94–97
  T-shirt, cotton, 95
  vegan, 94, 102
Clothing Warehouse,
    96–97
coffee, 18, 19, 49–50
colors (for paint), 109–10
compost, 7–8, 9, 218–22
condoms, 103
cooking techniques, 228
cosmetics, personal care,
    and body care
    products, 68–84
  baby products, 128–29,
    132–34

companies rejecting
    harmful chemicals, 74,
    76, 129
European guidelines,
    74, 80
fragrance in, 76–77, 132
harmful ingredients in,
    73–74, 76–83, 132–34
natural or herbal, 71
organic labeling on, 70
paraben-free label, 80
phthalate labeling, 78
replacing with safe,
    83–84
responsible purchasing,
    71–73
sexual lubricants, oils,
    and rubs, 103
sunscreens, 82–83, 134
cotton
    chemicals in, 97–98,
        101, 117
    color-grown, 99–100,
        117
    "green," 100
    mattresses, 88
    organic, 88, 98–99,
        101–2, 117, 118
    T-shirt, 95
crystalline silica, 165
CSA (community-
    supported
    agriculture), 33–34,
    37

D

DEA (diethanolamine),
    165
Demeter organization, 49
diapers, 121–23
dioxane, 165
Discovery Network, 17, 23

DMC (dichloromethane)
    or methylene chloride,
    165
DMDM Hydantoin, 132,
    133, 134
Dr. Hauschka company, 76
dust mites, 89, 116
dwellings
    author's childhood, 5–7,
        62–63, 175
    discovering your home's
        footprint, 183, 185
    Mark Retzloff's, 184–85
    old homes, 17–18
    solar heat, 6–7

E

Earth 911, 201, 206
Ecco Bella, 76
eco-fibers, 99–100, 117
Eden Foods, 4, 11, 147,
    184
eggs, 47–48
EMFs (electromagnetic
    fields), 113
energy conservation
    CFLs, 18, 149–51
    Energy Star appliances,
        158, 160
    household use, 158
    insulation, 152–53
    laundry, 156–58
    lights and appliances,
        155
    phantom draw, 180–83
    refrigerator, 55
    thermostat, 151–52
    windows, 152
EPA (Environmental
    Protection Agency),
    63–64, 98, 141, 158
essential oils, 171–72

ethylene glycol, 165
EWG (Environmental
    Working Group), 25,
    76, 82, 83, 128

F

Fair Trade products, 19,
    49–50, 51, 100
family and community, 9,
    11–13
farmer's markets, 31–33
    finding by zip code, 37
fats, dietary, 53–54, 55
faucets, 65, 68
FDA (Food and Drug
    Administration), 25,
    73
FINCA (Foundation for
    International
    Community
    Assistance), 186
fish. *See* seafood
FishWise, 46
flax/linen, 99
floors
    bamboo, 116
    carpets, 112–13, 241
    cleaning products, 169,
        241
    wood, 112, 241
fluoride, 134
food
    allergies, 130–31
    American diet, 4
    antioxidant-rich, 29
    author's childhood and,
        9–11
    baby food and feeding,
        123–28
    canning, 38
    children and junk food,
        dealing with, 10–11

food *(continued)*
  "clean foods," 130–31
  cooking for a family, 228–29
  cooking techniques, 228
  "dirty dozen" list, 25–26
  "eating a rainbow," 129
  family meals, 229
  frozen, 7, 38, 48–49
  genetically modified, 51, 54–55
  goat's milk, 159–60
  home grown, 7, 38–39
  how to start lifestyle changes, 24, 27–28
  leftovers, packing, 56
  locally grown, 7, 34, 36–38
  natural foods movement, 2, 4, 147–48, 184
  natural label, 43–44, 50–52
  organic, 18, 19, 25–34
    (see also organic food)
  pesticide-free, 229
  pesticide load, 25–28
  seasonal, 7
  what to avoid, 52–55
food labels
  antibiotic-free, 44
  biodynamic, 49
  cage free, 48
  Fair Trade, 49–50, 51
  free range, 47–48
  frozen, 48–49
  GMOs, 54–55
  greenwashing, 42
  HFCS, 52–53
  hormone free, 44
  "local," 48
  "natural," 43–44, 50–52
  reading, 57–58

saturated or trans fats, 53–54
seafood, 46
USDA organic categories, 31, 32, 42–43
what to avoid, 52–55
food shopping, 40–55
  CSAs, 33–34
  farmer's markets, 31–33
  frequency of, 41–42
  frozen food, 48–49
  hormone free, 44–45
  label reading, 42
  local label, self-stable foods, 48
  natural animal products, 43–44
  "natural" food labeling, 50–52
  organic animal products, 42–43
  produce, conventional or organic, 26
  seafood options, 45–47
  supermarkets, 37–38, 40–41
  what to avoid, 52–55
formaldehyde, 81, 115
  in baby furniture, 107, 115
  in cleaning products, 165
  in the home, 139
  in mattresses, 88, 117
  plants to filter, 139
  in pressed wood, chipboard, plywood, or particleboard, 81, 89–90, 139, 143, 165
  as a VOC, 88, 141
fragrance additives, 76–77

Fresh Living Changes (charts), 246
  for a Much Later Date, 251
  I'll Make Next Month, 248
  I'll Make Next Year, 250
  I'll Make Six Months from Now, 249
  I'll Make Today, 247
Frey, Katrina, 217
Frey Vineyards, 217
fruits
  antioxidant-rich, 29
  buy organic recommendations, 26
  "Cleanest Twelve" (buy conventional), 26
  from CSAs, 33–34
  from farmer's markets, 31–33
  frozen, 48–49
  ginger orange celery tonic, 240
  healthy smoothie, 239
  home grown, 11
  juice, 10
  locally grown, 34, 36–38
  oatmeal fruit bars, 238
  organic, 18, 28
  pesticide load, 25, 26, 27, 230–31
  pumpkin banana bread, 237
FSC (Forest Stewardship Council), 143
funerals/burials, 189–91
furniture and cabinetry
  baby furniture, 114–16
  bamboo, 116, 144
  eco or green makers, 144
  finishes and stains, 107, 144–45

formaldehyde in, 81,
89–90, 107, 115
living room, 143–46
low-toxicity, 116
modular pieces, 116
reclaimed, used, antique,
145–46
of recycled materials,
116, 146
upholstery, 144–45
wood, reclaimed or
sustainably harvested,
89, 115, 143

G

gardens, 215–22
attracting butterflies,
216, 218
composting, 218–22
container or small-patch,
39, 215–16
edible plants, 215–16
global warming,
reversing with, 217
grow a salad bowl, 215
herb, 39
home, organic, 7,
38–39
indoor, as family activity,
139
insect-friendly and
repelling plants, 216,
218
mint patch, 8
organic fertilizers, 211
vegetable harvesting
times, 216
wildflower, 210
Get Fresh with Sara Snow
(TV show), 17, 189
ginger, 75
tonic, 240

glass
baby bottles, 126
for leftovers and, 56
recycling, 199, 205
glycol ethers, 165
GMOs (genetically
modified organisms),
51, 54–55, 218
goldenseal, 14
GOTS (Global Organic
Textile Standards),
99
greenwashing, 42

H

hairspray, 77
heating and cooling
insulation, 139, 152–53
solar, 6–7
thermostat, 151–52
windows, 152
hemp, 99
Herbamare, 5
herbs and spices
alternatives to
pharmaceuticals, 14,
35, 75, 104
antioxidant-rich, 29
deodorizers and
pesticides, 172–73,
243
ginger orange celery
tonic, 240
home grown, 39
Mark Blumenthal and,
75
natural aphrodisiacs,
104–5
responsible business
practices and, 36
HFCS (high-fructose corn
syrup), 52–53

homes. *See* dwellings
Horizon Organic Dairy, 4
Howard, Linda, 159–60
hydrogen peroxide,
170–71, 242–43
hydroquinone, 81–82

I

insulation, 139, 152–53
International Federation of
Organic Agriculture
Movements, 98

J

Jordan, June, 131

K

Kiss My Face, 76
kitchen, 23–59
cleaning products, green,
167–72, 241–42
conservation, 55–57,
155
five tips, 57
food choices, 34–55,
58
Reenie's transformation,
23–24, 58
taking action, 57–59
Kloss, Jethro, 35
Kushi, Michio, 3

L

Laloo's ice cream, 159–60
latex, 88, 104, 116,
126–27

laundry
  cleaning products, green,
    167–72, 243
  cold water for, 157
  detergent, 109
  dryer, 157–58
  Energy Star appliances,
    158, 160
  line-drying, 155–56, 157
  spot-treating and
    brightening whites,
    155
  UF resins, 139
  water conservation,
    156–58, 160
lawn care, 193, 208–12
  carcinogens and, 208–9
  chemicals, avoiding, 211
  clippings, 211
  hand-powered
    equipment, 212
  organic fertilizers, 211
  pesticides and pet
    poisoning, 223
  size of lawn, 209–11
  spiking your grass, 211
  top five tips, 210
  water conservation,
    212–15
lead danger, 82, 111–12,
  118–19
lemon juice, 169, 241, 243
lighting
  CFLs, 18, 148–51
  LEDs, 148
  optimal for sleeping, 92
  turning off, 155
linens (bedclothes), 90, 98
  for baby, 117, 118
lipsticks, lip balms, lip
  gloss, 80, 81, 82
Living Fresh (TV show), 17
living room, 137–53
  candles, 146

conservation, 148–53
furniture, 143–46
heating and cooling,
  151–53
natural decor, 137–38
paint, 141–43
plants, 137, 138–41
Sara Snow's, 137
three most toxic gases
  in, 139
locavores, 38
LOHAS (Lifestyles of
  Health and
  Sustainability), 184

M

macrobiotics, 3–4, 10
mail and junk mail, 176–77
Marine Stewardship
  Council, 46
mattress, 88–89
  crib, 114, 116–17
  flame retardants in, 88,
    116, 117
  formaldehyde in, 88
  no-nos, 117
  pesticides in, 88
  wool, cotton, or latex,
    88, 116
meats
  antibiotic-free label, 44
  antibiotics in, 42–43, 56
  beef production, 56
  cows and methane gas,
    56
  farmer's markets, 31–33
  free range, 47–48
  hormones in, 43, 44
  minimally processed, 24
  natural, 43–44
  USDA organic, 42, 43
mercury, 81

microfinance, 186
milk
  antibiotics in, 42–43
  hormones in, 43, 44–45
  natural, 43–44
  organic, 4, 24, 43, 58
Monterey Bay Aquarium's
  Seafood Watch, 46–47
MSG (monosodium
  glutamate), 53

N

nail polish, 78–79
NASA, 138–40
National Cancer Institute,
  139
"natural" label, 50–52
neurotoxins
  in cleaning products,
    164–66
  fluoride, 134
  in fragrance additives, 77
  mercury and thimerosal,
    81
nitrobenzene, 165
noise, 93
nursery, 107–35
  baby clothes, 117, 118
  baby monitor, 113
  as balanced
    environment, 114,
    134–35
  body care products,
    128–29, 132–34
  breastfeeding, 123–24
  conservation, 134–35
  crib mattress, 114,
    116–17
  diapers, 121–23
  electronics and EMFs,
    113–14
  floors, 112–13

formaldehyde, 107, 115
formula and baby
    bottles, 124–27
furniture, 114–16
infants exposure to
    pollutants and toxins,
    108
linens, 117, 118
paint, 109–12
preparing for a newborn,
    107–8
timing of remodeling,
    107–9
toys, 118–20
what to buy/not to buy
    secondhand, 114

O

oats/oatmeal
    breakfast bars, 239
    fruit bars, 238
O'Brien, Robyn, 130–31
off-gassing, 90, 107, 108–9,
    138
office/home office, 175–91
    cut your commute,
        187–89
    energy conservation,
        180–83
    e-waste, 178–79
    greener supplies, 177–80
    ink cartridges, 178
    mail makeover, 176–77
    socially responsible
        investing, 185–86
Ohsawa, George, 3
olive oil, 169–70, 241, 243
Olowo-n'djo Tchala, 72
100-mile dieters, 38
organic agriculture, 4, 11
    environmental preserva-
        tion and, 29–30

goal of, 30–31
Katrina Frey and,
    217–18
USDA standards for, 30
organic food, 18, 25–34
    benefits, 28–29
    produce to buy, 26
    USDA organic
        categories, 31, 32
    USDA organic label, 29,
        54–55
    for your pet, 223
Organic Food Alliance, 184
Organic Gardening
    magazine, 4
organic nonfood products,
    99–100
    cosmetics, personal care,
        and body care
        products, 69, 74, 76,
        83–84
    cotton, 88, 98–100
    eco-fibers, 99–100
    mattresses, 88–89
    wool, 88–89, 100
organic products industry,
    18–19, 98
Organic Trade Association,
    98
outdoors, 193–225
    gardens (*see* gardens)
    lawn care, 193, 208–12
    recycling, 199–208
    water conservation,
        212–15
oxybenzone, 134

P

paint, 141–43
    color choice, 109–10,
        111, 142
    latex vs. oil-based, 142

lead-based, what to do
    about, 111–12
natural, 142–43
picking, low- or no-
    VOC, 111, 141, 142
paper
    bags, 57
    catalog cutback, 177
    mail recycling, 176–77
    recycled, use of, 177,
        178, 199–200
    recycling, 57, 205–6
    saving, 179–80
    towels, avoiding, 56
    TP, 84–85, 95, 139, 178
paper shredding, 176–77
parabens, 79–80, 103, 132
para-dichlorobenzene, 166
parsley, 75
particulates, 133
PBDE or pentaBDE, 88,
    116, 117
PEG Compounds, 133,
    134
peppermint, 75
pesticides
    children and, 27–28
    in cosmetics, 73
    cotton crops, 97–98, 101
    "dirty dozen" list, 25–26
    lawn care and, 208–9
    in mattresses, 88
    OP insecticides, 27–28
    pet danger, 223
    in produce (full list),
        230–31
    spices as green
        alternative, 172–73
    USDA PDP, 27
pesto, 232
petrochemicals, 132, 133
petrolatum and petroleum
    distillates, 80
pets, 222–25

phthalates, 77–78, 104,
117, 119, 128, 132
pillow, 89
plants. *See also* gardens
filtering toxins, 139–40
in the home, 137, 138–41
pet caution, 140–41
top fifteen to clean your
home's air, 140
plastic
avoiding for leftovers, 56
baby bottles, 125–27
BPA linings in infant
formula containers,
124–25
disposable diapers, 121
labeling of types, 125,
207, 243–44
recycling, 206, 243–44
safer and which to avoid,
125
shopping bags, 56–57
spotting PVC, 119
toys, precautions, 119
waste, 56–57
polenta, 233–34
pollution, environmental
babies' exposure to, 108
children's exposure to,
27–28
condoms and, 104
cosmetics, personal care,
and body care
products, 71
cows and methane
gas, 56
farming and, 29–30, 102,
159–60
fuel emissions, 187–88,
194–95, 198
garbage, 199
gas-powered lawn care
equipment, 212
lead, 82, 111–12, 118–19

mercury and thimerosal,
81
paper production and,
178
plastic bags and, 56–57
reducing by recycling,
199
polystyrene, 244
polyurethane foam, 117
poultry, 47–48
market-fresh stir fry, 236
pregnancy, 108, 112
pumpkin banana bread, 237
PVC (polyvinyl chloride),
104, 117, 119, 244

R

rain barrel, 214–15
recipes, 232–43
breakfast bars, 239
broiled salsa fish, 235
fruit smoothie, 239
ginger orange celery
tonic, 240
market-fresh stir fry, 236
natural cleaning, 240–43
oatmeal fruit bars, 238
pesto, 232
pumpkin banana bread,
237
southwest polenta and
vegetables, 233–34
tofu spaghetti sauce,
234–35
tomato sauce and pasta,
39–40
Recombinant Bovine
Growth Hormone
(rBGH or rBST),
43, 44
recycling, 199–208
aluminum, 204–5

e-waste, 178–79
e-waste recycling
centers, locating, 179
glass, 199, 205
greener office supplies,
178–80
home collection center,
200, 202
materials used in
furniture, 116
methods, 201
old homes and, 17–18
paper, 57, 177–80,
199–200, 205–6
percentage of U.S. waste,
200
plastic, 206, 207,
243–44
plastic bags, 56
progress chart, 204
setting up a center,
201–3
sign on products, 200
steel/tin cans, 206, 208
website for drop-off
centers, 201, 206
what to recycle, 203–8
Redmond, Elizabeth,
6, 14
Redmond, Joe, 6, 14
Redmond, Nate, 5, 14
Redmond, Pattie, 3, 10,
11–12, 189–91
Redmond, Tim, 2–5, 11,
14, 147–48
Retzoff, Mark, 4, 184–85
Rodale, Robert, 4
Rodale Institute, 101

S

Sadler, Drake, 35–36
Sam's Club, 19

seafood
  best/worst choices, 47
  broiled salsa fish, 235
  fresh or frozen label, 46
  Seafood Watch ratings, 46–47
  sustainable and organic, 45–46, 147
  website, 46
Seventh Generation paper products, 85
sex, going green, 103–5
  condoms, 104
  natural aphrodisiacs, 103–4
  oils and rubs, 103
  toys, 103–4
showerhead, 64–65
sick building syndrome, 138
silk, 99
skin whiteners, 81–82
sleep, 91–93
slippery elm, 75
SLS (sodium lauryl/sodium laureth sulfates), 80–81
smoothie, healthy fruit, 239
Snow, Ryan, 16
Snow, Sara
  birth, 2
  childhood chores, 7–8
  childhood food, 9–11
  childhood hand-me-downs, 94–95
  childhood home, 5–7, 62–63, 175
  childhood low-impact living, 8–9
  Emmy Awards, 15
  family and community, 11–13
  grandparents, 5, 12–13
  home with husband, 17–18, 152

living room, 137
plants in home, 137
siblings, 5, 6, 14
sleep deprivation, 91–92
upbringing, 2–5
website, 20, 84, 227
young adulthood, career, and marriage, 13–18
soap, biodegradable, 169
socially responsible investing, 185–86
sodium borate, 133
soy
  allergies, 54
  market-fresh stir fry, 236
  milk (tonyu), 11
  organic fibers available, 99, 100
  tofu spaghetti sauce, 234–35
Starbucks, 19
sunscreens, 82–83, 134
sweeteners, 52–53

T

tea, 10, 18, 49–50
tea tree oil, 171, 241
temperature (room), 93, 151–52
thermostat setting, 151–52
TM (Traditional Medicinals), 35
toilets
  cleaning, 167, 168, 169
  dual-flush, 66–67
  low-flow, 66
  older, reducing water use with, 67
  stopping leaks, 67
TP (toilet paper), 84–85, 95, 139, 178
toothpaste, 80–81, 134

toys, 118–20
  green pet toys, 224
TransFair USA, 50
travel
  cut your commute, 187
  greener stays, 188–89
  green your hotel stay, 189
  planes, trains, or automobiles, 187–88
  public transit, 198
  travel planning, 187–88
trichloroethylene, 139
triclosan, 133, 134
triethalonamine, 134

U

UF (urea-formaldehyde), 139
Under the Canopy clothing catalog, 100–101
USDA, 25
  Food Safety and Inspection Service, 50
  labeling of cosmetics, personal care, and body care products, 70
  NOP (National Organic Program), 30, 70
  organic categories, 32
  organic label, 31
  PDP (Pesticide Data Program), 26
U. S. Department of Energy, 158

V

vegan
  clothing, 94, 102
  -friendly condoms, 103

vegetables
  antioxidant-rich, 29
  buy organic
    recommendations,
    26
  "Cleanest Twelve" (buy
    conventional), 26
  CSAs and, 33–34
  "dirty dozen" list,
    25–26
  farmer's market,
    31–33
  frozen, 48–49
  ginger orange celery
    tonic, 240
  hearty tofu spaghetti
    sauce, 234–35
  home grown, 11
  locally grown, 34,
    36–38
  market-fresh stir fry,
    236
  organic, 18
  pesticide load, 25, 26,
    27, 230–31
  production, vs. beef, 56
  southwest polenta and,
    233–34
vegetarianism, 56
vinegar, 152, 167–68
  cleaning recipes,
    240–43
VOC (volatile organic
  compound)
  cleaning products, 163
  formaldehyde as, 88,
    141, 143
  in furniture finishes,
    144–45
  health effects of, 141
  off-gassing and, 109, 115
  in paint, 111, 141
  remodeling the nursery
    and, 107–8

volunteerism, 187
Vruit, 11

W

Wal-Mart, 37–38
water
  average household
    consumption, 65
  in bathroom, 63, 64–68
  capturing wasted, 213
  dish-washing, 55, 155
  Energy Star appliances,
    158, 160
  factory farming and
    pollution, 159–60
  filtering system, 124
  fluoride, filtering out,
    124
  infants' intake of, 108
  laundry, 158, 160
  lawns and landscaping,
    212–13
  per person, per day, 63
  rainwater harvesting,
    213–15
  shortages predicted, 63
  showers and baths, 63,
    66, 155
  tip for measuring
    outdoor watering
    needs, 213
  toilet use, 66–67
  U.S. daily total
    consumption, 63
  use, and energy
    consumption, 63–64
Waterkeeper Alliance,
  159–60
WaterSense appliances, 68
wax paper, 56
Weleda, 76
Weleda Baby, 129

Whole Earth Catalog
  (Brand), 4
Whole Foods Market, 14,
  83–84, 101
windows
  bathroom, 62–63
  natural cleaning, 241
  weather-stripping or
    replacing, 152
wine, 104
wood
  cleaning products, 168,
    169, 241
  FSC-certified, 143
  healthier finishes for,
    144
  paper production and
    total harvest, 178
  pressed wood,
    chipboard, plywood,
    or particleboard,
    89–90, 139, 143, 144
  reclaimed, 115
  sustainably harvested,
    89, 115, 143
wool
  mattresses, 88, 116
  organic, 88–89, 99, 100
  pillow, 89

X

xenoestrogens, 77–78, 79

Y

Yacht, Vander, 2

Z

Zaroff, Marci, 100–101

About the Author

SARA SNOW is a lifelong advocate of organic, healthy living and travels the country as a green lifestyle expert. She is the popular host of two cable television shows, *Living Fresh* and *Get Fresh with Sara Snow*. In addition to her Discovery Network shows, Sara is advising the network on their newest cable network, PlanetGreen, a channel devoted entirely to green living, writes a column for *treehugger.com*, is host of a regular segment for CNN.com called *Living Green with Sara Snow*, and is on the board of The Organic Center. She lives with her husband Ryan and their dog Makana in Indianapolis.